# WOMEN IN HONG KONG

# WOMEN IN HONG KONG

Edited by
Veronica Pearson
Benjamin K. P. Leung

Contributors
Choi Po-king, Carol Jones, Linda C. L. Koo,
Benjamin K. P. Leung, Terry T. Lui, Ng Chun-hung,
Veronica Pearson, Tsang Gar-yin, Jon Vagg,
Thomas W. P. Wong, Rose Y. M. Yu

HONG KONG
OXFORD UNIVERSITY PRESS
OXFORD  NEW YORK
1995

Oxford University Press
Oxford  New York
Athens  Auckland  Bangkok  Bombay
Calcutta  Cape Town  Dar es Salaam  Delhi
Florence  Hong Kong  Istanbul  Karachi
Kuala Lumpur  Madras  Madrid  Melbourne
Mexico City  Nairobi  Paris  Singapore
Taipei  Tokyo  Toronto
and associated companies in
Berlin  Ibadan

Oxford is a trade mark of Oxford University Press

First published 1995

Published in the United States
by Oxford University Press, New York

© Oxford University Press 1995

All rights reserved. No part of this publicaiton may be reproduced,
stored in a retrieval system, or transmitted, in any form or by any means,
without the prior permission in writing of Oxford University Press (China) Ltd.
Within Hong Kong, exceptions are allowed in respect of any fair dealing for the
purpose of research or private study, or criticism or review, as permitted
under the Copyright Ordinance currently in force. Enquiries concerning reproduction
outside these terms and in other countries should be sent to
Oxford University Press (China) Ltd at the address below

This book is sold subject to the condition that it shall not, by way
of trade or otherwise, be lent, re-sold, hired out or otherwise circulated
without the publisher's prior consent in any form of binding or cover
other than that in which it is published and without a similar condition
including this condition being imposed on the subsequent purchaser

British Library Cataloguing in Publication Data
available

Library of Congress Cataloging-in-Publication Data
Women in Hong Kong / [edited by] Veronica Pearson, Benjamin K. P.
Leung.
p. cm.
Includes bibliographical references and index.
ISBN 0-19-585954-5
1. Sex discrimination against women—Hong Kong. 2. Women—Hong
Kong—Social conditions. I. Pearson, Veronica. II. Leung,
Benjamin K. P., [date].
HQ1237.5.H85W66  1995
305.42'095125—dc20   95-6985
CIP

Printed in Hong Kong
Published by Oxford University Press (China) Ltd
18/F Warwick House, Taikoo Place, 979 King's Road, Quarry Bay, Hong Kong

# Contributors

**Dr Choi Po-king**
Lecturer, Department of Educational Administration and Policy, the Chinese University of Hong Kong

**Dr Carol Jones**
Lecturer, Department of Sociology, the University of Hong Kong

**Dr Linda C. L. Koo**
Lecturer, Department of Community Medicine, the University of Hong Kong

**Dr Benjamin K. P. Leung**
Senior Lecturer, Department of Sociology, the University of Hong Kong

**Ms Terry T. Lui**
Lecturer, Department of Politics and Public Administration, the University of Hong Kong

**Dr Ng Chun-hung**
Lecturer, Department of Sociology, the University of Hong Kong

**Dr Veronica Pearson**
Senior Lecturer, Department of Social Work and Social Administration, the University of Hong Kong

**Ms Tsang Gar-yin**
Executive Secretary, Association for the Advancement of Feminism

**Dr Jon Vagg**
Lecturer, Department of Sociology, the University of Hong Kong

**Dr Thomas W. P. Wong**
Lecturer, Department of Sociology, the University of Hong Kong

**Ms Rose Y. M. Yu**
Research Associate, Department of Social Work and Social Administration, the University of Hong Kong

# Acknowledgements

In the last decade the issues that are so central to this book have become matters of increasing importance to our students and colleagues. As such, we are indebted to many people (in and out of the classroom) with whom we have engaged in debate, and who have been influential in the development and structuring of our thoughts on women's issues in Hong Kong.

More specifically, we would like to acknowledge the invaluable help of Andrew Byrnes (Faculty of Law, the University of Hong Kong) at a difficult moment in the book's gestation. The research on which Chapter 9 is based was supported by a grant from the Hang Seng Bank Golden Jubilee Education Fund for Research, administered by the Centre of Asian Studies at the University of Hong Kong.

# Contents

| | |
|---|---|
| Contributors | v |
| Acknowledgements | vi |
| Preface | ix |
| List of Tables & Figures | xi |
| Chronology of Women's Achievements<br>    Tsang Gar-yin | xiv |
| Introduction: Perspectives on Women's Issues in Hong Kong<br>    Veronica Pearson and Benjamin K. P. Leung | 1 |
| 1  Women and Social Change: The Impact of Industrialization on Women in Hong Kong<br>    Benjamin K. P. Leung | 22 |
| 2  Women and Work: Opportunities and Experiences<br>    Thomas W. P. Wong | 47 |
| 3  Bringing Women Back In: Family Change in Hong Kong<br>    Ng Chun-hung | 74 |
| 4  Women and Education in Hong Kong<br>    Choi Po-king | 101 |
| 5  Political Participation<br>    Terry T. Lui | 133 |
| 6  The New Territories Inheritance Law: Colonization and the Élites<br>    Carol Jones | 167 |
| 7  Women and Crime in Hong Kong<br>    Jon Vagg | 193 |
| 8  Women, Health, and Medicine<br>    Linda C. L. Koo | 215 |
| 9  Business and Pleasure: Aspects of the Commercial Sex Industry<br>    Veronica Pearson and Rose Y. M. Yu | 244 |

10  The Women's Movement at the Crossroads    276
    Tsang Gar-yin

Index    292

# Preface

Back in 1988 the co-editor of this book, Benjamin Leung, invited me to write a chapter on women for a book he was editing called *Social Issues in Hong Kong* (Hong Kong: Oxford University Press, 1990). It was a labour of love to which I turned with enjoyment and enthusiasm; too much enthusiasm as the chapter soon burst through the word limits set by the editor. Every section cried out to be a chapter in its own right, even as Ben and I wrestled to keep it at a manageable length. It was at that point that I determined that one day there would be a book.

What is remarkable to me is how much, in the intervening years, women's issues and concerns have become part of the legitimate agenda. Back in 1988 those of us who showed an interest in the area were treated by many as, at best, obsessed with minority interests for no apparent reason, at worst, a threat to the established order. Now, even the government has grudgingly acknowledged that women's issues are worthy of its attention with the production of a Green Paper and the Legislative Council's espousal of the Convention on the Elimination of All Forms of Discrimination Against Women (CEDAW).

Of course, attention does not equate with action. CEDAW has not been extended to Hong Kong yet, nor has a bill outlawing discrimination on the grounds of sex passed into law. What is different is that both now seem possible; seven years ago that was not the case. There is greater general awareness of sexual harassment, not only women think that the highly sexist XO brandy adverts are distasteful, and many people are aware of the sexist and ageist barriers to employment older and less educated women are facing as manufacturing enterprises increasingly relocate into China. In other words, while problems still exist, it is more widely acknowledged that there are problems: a very necessary precursor to seeking solutions.

Another feature of the intervening years is that the number of academics interested in women's issues in Hong Kong has now reached 'critical mass'. The amount of material on women being produced is greater in quality and quantity than ever before, and I have no doubt at all that this trend will continue. Hong Kong is not a suitable environment for anyone seeking a restful existence. Rapid change characterizes our lives, particularly during the countdown to 1997 and resumption of sovereignty by China. Hong Kong's citizens are adept at adapting to new demands and new developments, if for no other reason than that lack of choice in the matter has given them practice. The impact of change on women's lives is going to be charted by the growing number of researchers who see women's experiences as an important part of Hong Kong's development. This book is both a contribution to that literature and a testament to those who 'hold up half the sky'.

Veronica Pearson
Hong Kong
May, 1995

# List of Tables & Figures

**Tables**

| | | |
|---|---|---|
| 1.1 | Trends in total fertility rate, women's educational attainment, and women's labour force participation rate, 1960–1990 | 27 |
| 1.2 | Percentages of all female and male employees in selected occupations, 1961–1991 | 30 |
| 1.3 | Ratio of median income of female employees to median income of male employees by selected occupations in 1991 | 32 |
| 2.1 | Age, sex, and specific labour-force participation rate, various years (in percentage) | 50 |
| 2.2 | Occupational distribution of women by age groups, 1976 and 1991 (in percentage) | 53 |
| 2.3 | Occupational distribution of working men and women (in percentage) | 55 |
| 2.4 | Proportion of working men and women in different occupational groups (in percentage) | 56 |
| 2.5 | Gender disparity in a few selected occupational groups, 1976 and 1991 | 57 |
| 2.6 | Educational attainment of working population by sex, 1961 and 1991 (in percentage) | 58 |
| 2.7 | Occupational distribution of working women with a university degree, 1991 (in percentage) | 58 |
| 2.8 | Monthly income (in HK dollars) and female–male earnings ratio, 1976, 1981, 1986, 1991 | 61 |
| 2.9 | Income ratios between men and women for selected occupations, 1991 | 62 |
| 2.10 | Educational attainment (aged 20 to 64) by sex, conjugal status and year, 1976 and 1991 (in percentage) | 64 |
| 2.11 | Occupational distribution by sex and conjugal status, 1991 (in percentage) | 65 |
| 3.1 | Clothes washing by household members (in percentage) | 80 |
| 3.2 | Actual and ideal persons responsible for four types of family tasks (in percentage) | 94 |
| 4.1 | Percentage of female students at various education levels, 1961–1990 | 102 |

| | | |
|---|---|---|
| 4.2 | Percentage of women undergraduates in various faculties at the University of Hong Kong, 1971–1990 | 104 |
| 4.3 | Percentage of women undergraduates in various faculties at the Chinese University of Hong Kong, 1971–1990 | 105 |
| 4.4 | Percentage of female students in full-time secondary level technical/vocational (including commercial) education, 1972–1990 | 106 |
| 4.5 | Percentage of female students in full-time post-secondary technical/vocational training, 1972–1990 | 106 |
| 4.6 | Percentage of women students in teacher (primary) training, 1961–1990 | 107 |
| 4.7 | Gender ratios for subjects in the arts, science, and applied vocational streams, Certificate of Educational Examination, 1976–1992 | 110 |
| 4.8 | Age and gender profile of teachers at various levels, 1991 | 115 |
| 4.9 | Percentage of women teachers in secondary schools by rank, 1991 | 116 |
| 4.10 | Gender distribution of full-time teaching staff at the University of Hong Kong and the Chinese University of Hong Kong, 1992–1993 | 118 |
| 4.11 | Gender distribution of full-time teaching staff at the Hong Kong Polytechnic and the City Polytechnic of Hong Kong, 1992–1993 | 119 |
| 4.12 | Gender distribution of full-time teaching staff at colleges of education, 1991 | 120 |
| 4.13 | Gender-role acceptance of adolescents and young people in Hong Kong, 1981 and 1986 | 121 |
| 4.14 | Attitude towards onset of nocturnal emission (boys) and menstruation (girls), 1981 and 1986 | 123 |
| 4.15 | Sexual mores held by university students, 1991 | 125 |
| 5.1 | A typology of political participatory activities | 137 |
| 5.2 | Percentage of female councillors at the three levels of the political system | 138 |
| 5.3 | Percentage of women in the administration | 139 |
| 5.4 | Percentage of women in the judiciary | 141 |
| 5.5 | Percentage of female members in advisory and independent organizations | 142 |

| | | |
|---|---|---|
| 5.6 | Percentage of female candidates running for political office, 1991 | 145 |
| 5.7 | Male/female voters' participation in elections, 1991 | 146 |
| 5.8 | Male/female participation as members of political parties | 148 |
| 5.9 | Female membership in the central executive committees of political parties | 149 |
| 8.1 | Life expectancy at birth from selected countries | 222 |
| 8.2 | Male and female suicide statistics in Hong Kong, 1966–1990 | 233 |
| 9.1 | Enrolment in Vocational Training Council courses, 1993, analysed by gender | 248 |

**Figures**

| | | |
|---|---|---|
| 8.1 | Trends in maternal and infant health in Hong Kong, 1955–1990 | 216 |
| 8.2 | Trends in life expectancy at birth in Hong Kong, 1971–1991 | 221 |
| 8.3 | Trends in female mortality in Hong Kong, 1966–1990 | 224 |
| 8.4 | Trends in female cancer incidence rates for seven sites, Hong Kong 1974–1988 | 226 |
| 8.5 | Trends in mortality from heart disease by age group and gender, Hong Kong | 229 |
| 8.6 | Trends in mortality from cerebrovascular disease by age group and gender, Hong Kong | 230 |
| 8.7 | Trends in death rates from pneumonia among infants by gender, Hong Kong 1966–1990 | 234 |
| 8.8 | Trends in death rates from accidents among infants by gender, Hong Kong 1966–1990 | 235 |

# Chronology of Women's Achievements

*Tsang Gar-yin*

| | |
|---|---|
| 1921 | Hong Kong University (established in 1911) admits its first female student, Miss Rachel Irving, daughter of the then Director of Education, Mr R. E. Irving. Miss Irene Ho Tung (daughter of Sir Robert Ho Tung) is also admitted in the same year. |
| 1926 | Miss Eva Ho Tung (daughter of Sir Robert Ho Tung) becomes the first woman to graduate from the Faculty of Medicine at the University of Hong Kong. |
| 1947 | Establishment of the Hong Kong Council of Women (HKCW). |
| 1961 | Helen A. Lo and Partners, the first law firm in the territory to be established by a woman, is set up in Hong Kong. |
| 1963 | The Joint Committee on Equal Pay for Equal Work comprising various women's and social organizations is formed. |
| 1965 | The government decides to implement, in ten years' time, equal pay in the civil service. However, teachers and nurses are not to be affected by the new scheme. |
| 1966 | Appointment of Hong Kong's first female Legislative Councillor, Dr Ellen Li. |
| 1970 | Launching of the Equal Pay Campaign by female nurses. The government finally agrees to implement equal pay for the nursing profession in 1971. |
| 1971 | Passage of the Marriage Reform and related ordinances, establishing that a marriage should be monogamous, and recognizing a woman's right to inheritance. |
| 1971 | For the first time, six years of schooling becomes free, compulsory, and universal. |
| 1972 | The International Feminist League is established. This organization is dissolved in 1975 and most of its active members join the HKCW. |
| 1973 | Passage of the Offence Against Person (Amendment) Bill, allowing for legal abortions when two doctors agree that continuation of pregnancy would cause greater physical or psychological harm to the woman concerned. |

| | |
|---|---|
| 1976 | Appointment of the first female Executive Councillor, Mrs Joyce Symons. |
| 1977 | Launching of the War on Rape campaign by HKCW. |
| 1978 | Passage of the Crimes (Amendment) Bill. Complainants are given anonymity to protect them from identification in the mass media. The provisions are extended to cases of indecent assault in 1979. |
| 1978 | Three years of secondary education becomes free, compulsory, and universal. |
| 1979 | A coalition including HKCW, the Hong Kong Christian Industrial Committee and twenty other organizations starts a campaign for paid maternity leave. |
| 1981 | Passage of the Employment (Amendment) (No.2) Bill entitling women workers to ten weeks of maternity leave with two-thirds pay. |
| 1982 | The first District Board Election is held. Twenty of the candidates are women, five of whom are eventually elected. |
| 1984 | Setting up of the Association for the Advancement of Feminism (AAF) and launching of AAF's first project, a survey on the social participation of women in Hong Kong. |
| 1984 | Signing of the Joint Declaration by the Chinese and British governments. Appendix 3 to the Joint Declaration states that inheritance rights along the male line for New Territories indigenous residents will be preserved after 1997. This provision is later included in the Basic Law (1990). Since 1984, women's groups had been campaigning for the removal of this discrimination against New Territories women. |
| 1985 | The first shelter for battered women, Harmony House, is set up following a campaign on domestic violence by HKCW. |
| 1985 | A series of exhibitions and drama performances are held by AAF in different local communities to commemorate the United Nations Decade for Women. |
| 1985 | Setting up of the Gender Research Programme at The Chinese University of Hong Kong. |
| 1986 | Passage of the 1986 Domestic Violence Bill which gives the victim the right to apply for an injunction to forbid molestation or to keep the batterer away from the matrimonial home. |
| 1986 | Women's Centre (HKCW), the first service and |

| | |
|---|---|
| | activity centre for women in Hong Kong, comes into operation. |
| 1986 | Joint committees on various issues are set up during the year, including the Concern on Pornography and Violence in the Mass Media Coalition, the Joint Committee on Maternity Rights, and the Joint Alliance on Women's Legal Rights. On the social service front, a Joint Committee of Social Workers Specializing in Women's Work and a Women's Service Development Working Group are also formed. |
| 1986 | Passage of the 1986 Control of Obscene and Indecent Articles Bill and the setting up of the Obscene Articles Tribunal to scrutinize pornographic materials. Materials classified as pornographic are to be banned from distribution. Materials classified as obscene are to carry a warning and cannot be sold to persons under eighteen years of age. |
| 1986 | Over 200 women from various women's and grass-roots groups hold a march in Central District to celebrate International Women's Day. |
| 1986 | Appointment of the first woman District Judge, Ms Helen Ho. |
| 1987 | Appointment of the first woman to Secretary level in the Civil Service as Mrs Anson Chan becomes Secretary of Economic Services. |
| 1988 | Setting up of the Hong Kong Women's Christian Council. |
| 1989 | Passage of the 1989 Inland Revenue (Amendment) (No. 3) Bill introducing separate taxation for married women beginning 1990. The Bill also removes the discriminatory clause which said an '"individual" did not include a wife unless she was living apart from her husband' for the purpose of personal assessment. |
| 1989 | The coalition Women in Support of Democracy in China is formed. |
| 1989 | Setting up of the Hong Kong Women Workers' Association (HKWWA). |
| 1990 | The Women's Campaign for Childcare Services Coalition, set up by women's and grass-roots women's groups, holds a demonstration in Central District on International Women's Day demanding the government recognize women's right to work, and supporting improved child-care provisions. 8,000 signatures are collected on a petition presented to the Governor. |

| | |
|---|---|
| 1990 | Passage of the Bill of Rights. |
| 1991 | Women's groups form a coalition to press the government to set up a working party to develop policies for women. A booklet entitled Broadsheet on Women in Hong Kong is published. |
| September 1991 | The first direct election for Legislative Council is held. Out of the fifty-five candidates, six are women. Ms Emily Lau Wai-hing is the only female candidate elected. |
| 1991 | Several women's groups form the Women Voters Development Programme to encourage women to exercise their political rights. A Joint Women's Platform is published and candidates and political groups are lobbied to include women's concerns in their agendas. |
| November 1991 | The Legislative Council forms the Ad Hoc Group on a Women's Commission to study the setting up of a women's commission. |
| March 1992 | The government sets up the inter-departmental Working Party on Sex Discrimination at Work to study the extent of sex discrimination in employment and the need for legislative reforms. At the same time, an alliance of women and labour groups is formed to campaign for equal employment opportunities for women. |
| May 1992 | The Legislative Council recommends the setting up of a women's commission of advisory status. |
| December 1992 | The Legislative Council passes a motion by Ms Emily Lau, initiated by a women's group, to extend the United Nations Convention on the Elimination of All Forms of Discrimination Against Women (CEDAW) to Hong Kong. The government working party on sex discrimination in employment releases its findings just before the debate, claiming the extent of sex discrimination is not serious and denying the need for legislative and other reforms. The government states that it will issue a green paper for public consultation in 1993. |
| 1993 | Appointment of Mrs Anson Chan as Hong Kong's first female Chief Secretary. |
| 1994 | New Territories Land (Exemption) Ordinance passed, permitting women to inherit land in the New Territories. |
| 1995 | Ms Felicia K. S. Wong becomes the first female Assistant Commissioner in the police force. |

# Introduction: Perspectives on Women's Issues in Hong Kong

*Veronica Pearson and Benjamin K. P. Leung*

On the surface, the women of Hong Kong do not seem particularly disadvantaged, especially when compared with their counterparts in some other South-East Asian countries. The economic and social advances that have marked the development of Hong Kong since the end of the Second World War have benefited both men and women. However, underneath the surface there is a far more complex story to be told. Hong Kong developed as an industrial and financial centre very rapidly; changes that took place over decades elsewhere have been accelerated in Hong Kong. Most people are surprised to discover that polygyny was legal until as late as 1971, and that primary education only became compulsory, and universal in the same year. There are sufficient numbers of high-ranking, successful, and highly visible women in both politics and the commercial world to foster the illusion that gender equality has been achieved, but this is not the case. As Choi (1993) points out, while a small number of women are able to make inroads into formerly all-male territory, the fundamental structures of gender division and hierarchy remain unchanged.

Although there has been an awareness of gender issues in Western countries since the mid-1960s, it has only recently found a place on Hong Kong's agenda. There is no gender or women's studies degree programme in any of the tertiary institutions, and it remains difficult to convince the general public, academics, and officials that a woman's experience of life is not only substantially different from that of a man, but on occasion, rather worse.

Since the mid-1980s, there has been an increasing number of articles, reports, and books written concerning women's issues in Hong Kong, yet there is still no volume in English that offers comprehensive coverage of the major topics with the aim of providing a foundation from which other volumes in the future can extend and develop the debate. The goal of this volume is to examine and explain the various dimensions of gender inequality in contemporary Hong Kong, in the context of the society's socio-economic, political, and cultural systems.

It is an assertion commonly made by social scientists that the passing of traditional societies is accompanied by the eclipse of the ascription orientation, and the increasing dominance of the achievement orientation. Simply put, this assertion holds that within traditional societies, a person's social status is determined very much by her or his ascriptions at birth: aristocrat or plebian, landlord or serf, male or female, and so on. In modern societies, the argument runs, status is conferred on the basis of the individual's own achievements. Yet the international literature attests that even in countries that have been trying to combat gender inequality for decades, women continue to be disadvantaged — in pay, in political participation and representation, and in job segregation — and that they carry in addition the double burden of work and housework. It is hardly surprising that Hong Kong women share these experiences.

Male dominance is an almost universal phenomenon (Giddens, 1989). What accounts for this? Liberal feminists[1] argue that gender socialization and 'sex-role conditioning' within the family, education, and the mass media have the effect of inculcating in people the belief that women and men are equipped by nature to perform different social roles whose value is assessed differently. The ensuing sexist ideology is held to be the main culprit in generating and perpetuating the subjugation of women. In the context of Hong Kong, where the overwhelming majority of the population is Chinese, it is tempting, in the light of this theoretical position, to explain gender inequality in terms of traditional Chinese patriarchy and its continuing impact on socialization in modern Hong Kong.

Alternatively, one can follow the Marxist feminist thesis and attribute women's subordination in Hong Kong to the territory's capitalist economy. According to this view, capitalism gains from sexism, which, in reducing the worth of women, renders them either as unpaid domestic labour or cheaper labour for the capitalist economy. Marxist feminists of course recognize that gender inequality exists, often in even more extreme forms, in non-capitalist societies. Their interest lies mainly in demonstrating how capitalism sustains and fosters sexism.

Most liberal and Marxist feminist theories are not explanations of the origins of gender inequality. They take patriarchy for granted and are only concerned with explaining its persistence. It is the radical feminists who see patriarchy as rooted in women's biology — their reproductive physiology and their associated role in nursing and caring for the infant which lasts for many years before the child is independent. This biological fact has fostered a sexual division of labour tending to confine women to the domestic, private sphere of the family. The biological imperative has subsequently been overlaid by social institutions, in particular the family and the economy, which buttress men's domination over women. The consequence is a male-dominated, patriarchal social system.

The radical feminist thesis thus carries the implication that women's entry into the public domain of work and politics will eventually liberate them from the yoke of patriarchy. This is not to argue that women have not been economically productive in the past. But work tended to be on family-owned land or in family-owned businesses, where their contribution was subsumed by family interests and gave them little or no control over material resources. The significance of modern societies and work in the twentieth century is that increasingly it has been outside the home and away from the family and, as such, has given women a foundation for independence.

It was a deliberate decision by the editors of this volume not to ask the contributors to toe any particular 'party line'. The field of gender studies in Hong Kong is as yet too young to benefit from the imposition of any one paradigm. Consequently, the ensuing chapters represent a variety of different perspectives. On the whole, the authors have tended to accept that a patriarchal framework is of great relevance in Hong Kong. Some, for instance Choi's chapter on education (Chapter 4) and Wong's on work (Chapter 2), adopt a macro, functionalist approach. They look at the collective experience of women, rather than focusing on the individual meaning that women attribute to their experience, as is done in Pearson and Yu's chapter on women working in the commercial sex industry. The editors believe that there is positive value in such diversity.

## Gender Inequality in the Hong Kong Context

In our view, gender inequality in Hong Kong is intricately related to and sustained by several distinct features of the society: it is a predominantly Chinese society; it is a British colony; and it is a capitalist economy whose well-being has been heavily dependent on low labour costs enabling its exports to compete successfully in overseas markets. Thus, the framework in which this book is located is socio-cultural, socio-political, and socio-economic. These three dimensions interrelate in providing the context in which individual women in Hong Kong seek to play out the script of their lives, and in which they search for a meaning to their experience. In order to understand the modern context of Hong Kong, it is necessary to begin with a brief review of patriarchy in traditional Chinese society. This will be followed with a discussion of the extent to which this patriarchal tradition has been retained and modified in colonial, capitalist Hong Kong.

The model of behaviour for women in relation to men in traditional Chinese society was prescribed in the four books of Confucius and his disciples:

> Woman yields obedience to the instructions of man, and helps to carry out his principles.... When young, she must obey her father and elder brother; when married she must obey her husband; when her husband is dead, she must obey her son.... Woman's business is simply the preparation and supplying of drink and food. (cited in Koo, 1985: 64)

The precarious status of woman as wife is evident from the Confucian teaching that a man could secure divorce from a wife on grounds of her jealousy, talking excessively, failing to serve parents-in-law appropriately, contraction of a malignant or repulsive disease, or failure to produce a male child. The predicament of woman as daughter was no better; the much-reported practices of female infanticide and the selling of daughters into prostitution, domestic service, or concubinage testify to their ill fate in traditional Chinese society (Croll, 1978; Hershatter, 1991; Jaschok, 1988). Women's significance was defined mainly by their role in reproduction; as one writer observes, 'Chinese traditionally have relegated women to the home, emphasizing their duty to produce male descendants. Women's productivity was measured in terms of their fecundity' (Jackson, 1980: 48). One can multiply the illustrations, (Lebra and Paulson, 1980; Stockard, 1989; Watson, 1991) but the above suffice for the purpose of throwing light on the patriarchal tradition in Chinese culture.

It is tempting to see the prejudice and discrimination against women in modern Hong Kong as remnants of traditional patriarchal Chinese culture. The central explanation here is 'gender socialization' — within the family, in formal education, and in the mass media — supporting traditional images of women as the weaker, subordinate sex, but such an explanation has its problems. In the first place, patriarchy as a system of dominance of men over women based essentially on a sexual division of labour, assigning women a domestic and hence economically dependent role, does not seem to be viable in modern industrial Hong Kong, where women make up a significant portion of the extra-domestic labour force.

Secondly, capitalism is a class system, not a system founded on men's domination and exploitation of women, and as such the interests of capitalism and those of patriarchy do not necessarily coincide. One can conceivably see working-class women and men as the underprivileged in capitalism, but to assert that women remain the dominated gender in capitalism is to usher in an explanatory variable alien to the orthodox critique of capitalism. While the Marxist feminists rely on the thesis of 'female domestic labour' and 'lower-paid female labour' to explain the persistence of patriarchy in modern capitalism, one can also argue that with its ideology of individualism, achievement orientation, and equality of opportunity, industrial capitalism works to reduce rather than reinforce gender inequality.

The point is that any explanation of gender inequality in Hong Kong in terms of traditional Chinese patriarchy has to address the issue of how patriarchy complements, or has been modified by, Hong Kong's brand of industrial capitalism. Furthermore, gender inequality has to be carefully delineated from class inequality to show that the explanation of the former cannot be subsumed under that of the latter. The third argument against the culturalist, and the attendant 'gender socialization' explanation, is that as a British colony and a highly Westernized society, Hong Kong can be expected to have departed substantially from the patriarchal values and practices of traditional Chinese society. In short, although an explanation of gender inequality in contemporary Hong Kong must include an awareness of the influence of traditional Chinese patriarchy, more significant is the context of Hong Kong's current socio-economic and political circumstances.

Part of the explanation lies in the nature of British colonial rule in Hong Kong. As several writers have noted (Scott, 1989; Lau, 1982; King, 1981), a central and perennial concern of the colonial government has been that of legitimating British rule in a society where the overwhelming majority of the population are Chinese. The main political strategies of legitimation in this context have been the co-option of the Chinese élites into the government's administrative structure (King, 1981), coupled with the government's calculated non-interference in the way of life of the Chinese community (Lau, 1982). The relevance of these colonial political strategies to women's oppression and subjugation is poignantly evident in the persistence into the twentieth century of the *mui tsai* system and of concubinage (Jaschok, 1988; Watson, 1991), both of which were steadfastly defended by the Chinese élites as rightful and legitimate customs within the Chinese cultural context.

Another example is the inheritance system in the New Territories which deprived female residents of the right to inherit their family property (Jones, Chapter 6). What is often overlooked is that when Hong Kong was ceded to Britain in 1842, attitudes of the male, British colonial administrators towards women would not have been wholly dissimilar to those of Chinese males. Patriarchal attitudes were something that the two groups had in common. Furthermore, such attitudes of patriarchy and British colonialism spilled over into the general administration of the territory, evidenced by the lack of direct political representation until close to the end of colonial rule. Because of the lack of accountability, government paternalism enjoyed an unexpectedly long life. It is not surprising that a paternalistic government did not recognize the special needs of women, seeing their troubles as belonging to the private sphere of the Chinese family and most suitably handled by the paterfamilias.

Indeed it was, and is, a deliberate ploy of the government to utilize the tradition of economic and material support within families that typified life in China to minimize the necessity for the government to become actively involved in the provision of welfare (Tam and Yeung, 1994). This was especially true in the 1950s and 1960s when a substantial portion of the Chinese community were living close to subsistence level. Traditional Chinese familism, characterized by the family's claim on its members' loyalty and subordination of individual members' interests in reciprocation for the assistance it affords, thus survives into modern industrial Hong Kong.

The inherent subordination of women within the traditional Chinese family is in this way sustained, though in a less stringent form, in the Chinese family system in modern Hong Kong. This is one of the main arguments in the chapters of Leung (Chapter 1) and Ng (Chapter 3) in this volume. Due to the centrality of the family in the individual's life, women's subordinate familial role has ramifications in other domains of their life. The prevalence of family-owned industrial firms in Hong Kong, an off-shoot of familism in the economic domain, is a fine example of how the patriarchal values of the family can have a pervasive influence in the workplace in a local context (Lau, 1981; Wong, 1988; England, 1989). No wonder, as Thomas Wong's discussion of women and work (Chapter 2) demonstrates, women are often given the lowest-status and lowest-paid jobs in Hong Kong's industrial enterprises, family-owned or not.

Hong Kong's capitalist economy also benefits from patriarchal familism and, because of this, has been a willing partner in the exploitation of women. Hong Kong's capitalist employers, participating in the highly competitive and volatile overseas markets, have to secure for themselves a labour force that is cheap and flexible. Female labour meets these requirements. With the social expectation, nurtured and sustained by patriarchal familism, that women's primary role in life is housework and child care, and that their paid employment is but auxiliary, employers conveniently take advantage of women workers by paying them less, by putting them on piece rates, or sacking them in slump periods. However, it cannot be said that Hong Kong is unique in the region in its use of women in this way. Many have argued that the rise of South-East Asia as an economic growth area since 1980 has been assisted by the reputation of its women for fast and nimble fingers (useful in manufacturing work) and a willingness to work for low wages (Heyzer, 1986; Foo and Lim, 1989; Junsay and Heaton, 1989). Hong Kong's economic success has been achieved at the price of such hidden injuries of gender.

Some may also believe that what is here identified as gender discrimination is, in fact, the result of poverty and may more properly be seen as class discrimination, disadvantaging working-class men and women equally. The editors do not consider this to be the case. Although women have been 'allowed' to enter the world of work, very little has been done to structure that world according to women's particular needs. Nor has very much changed in relieving women of their domestic duties, caring for children, husband, and other family members. Thus the work environment is accepting of women, as long as they can be treated like men. With the exception of paid maternity leave, there are few concessions; crèche facilities at work are almost unheard of and bosses often see women as unreliable as it is the duty of the wife or mother to take the child to the doctor, to stay at home when a family member needs to be cared for, and so on.

In its turn, the family is accepting of a wife and mother working as long as she continues to maintain her domestic responsibilities. Neither the institutions of work nor the family wish to make changes to accommodate these dual demands. Thus, even working-class men, however much they are exploited at work, can look forward to coming home as a cessation of work. For a woman, coming home is exchanging one kind of work for another: cooking, cleaning, washing, and supervision of homework.

Women in Hong Kong, according to the level of resources they have at their disposal, cope with this in different ways. Some rely on mothers or mothers-in-law for child care or use child minders. Overwhelmingly, since the beginning of the 1980s, the middle class and above have coped by employing a domestic helper, usually from the Philippines. But this has not changed the expectation that it is a woman's responsibility to take care of domestic matters. Rather, women have contracted out their responsibilities in this sphere to another woman, whom they are then expected to supervise. Ultimately, the household and its smooth running are still the responsibility of the mistress of the house, even if the daily labour is performed by another's hands. The availability of Filipina domestic workers has freed middle-class women for the labour market, but it has done little to change the traditional structure of the family or workplace.

An important theme that runs through this book is the question of the government's response to gender issues. On the whole, it is typified by two guiding principles. The first is that its official policy on all matters is to adopt a stance of non-interventionism whenever possible. The second is that matters to do with women are largely family concerns and thus should be seen as essentially private.

The government published in 1993 a Green Paper called *Equal Opportunities for Women and Men*. Compared with the energy, enthusiasm, and consultation spent on other Green Papers, such as the 1992 paper on rehabilitation, the effort displayed in the equal opportunities paper was poor indeed, presumably reflecting the lack of priority the government was prepared to give to this topic. Even the name obfuscates the issue, disguising as it does the pre-existing structures (particularly in family and education) that disadvantage women and reduce the concept of 'equal opportunity' to a cynical ploy. Indeed many women's groups and commentators believe the Green Paper was intended as a stalling technique, consultation rather than action. Certainly, it is difficult for women to take seriously the contention in paragraph 7 that the purpose of the Green Paper is 'to establish whether, in view of the opportunities available, women and men participate equally in all fields'. It has been clear for many years that they do not. The issue is not whether gender inequality exists, but what is to be done about it. One of the most contentious areas is equal pay for equal work. The Green Paper has this to say regarding taking a pro-active stance: 'Equal pay legislation and its associated framework would entail a certain degree of government intervention in the operation of individual employers and the labour market. This could induce rigidities into what has been a highly competitive and self-adjusting market' (para. 53: 19). This hardly constitutes a clarion call to action.

Another, and related, area of contention between the government and women's groups is the extension of the international agreement known as the United Nations Convention on the Elimination of All Forms of Discrimination Against Women (CEDAW), which both the United Kingdom and the People's Republic of China have ratified, but which has not been extended to Hong Kong. To do so would commit the government to address seriously such issues as equal pay and anti-discrimination legislation for which it shows little enthusiasm. As Lui points out in Chapter 5, in December 1992 Hong Kong's Legislative Council passed a motion urging the British and Hong Kong governments to extend CEDAW to Hong Kong. While the administration announced its intention to seek the extension of CEDAW in March 1994, little progress on this front has been made. The matter has, apparently, not yet been placed on the agenda of the Joint Liaison Group, and no firm indication has been given of when the Convention will be extended to Hong Kong. The government seems content to take credit for this victory while showing no determination at all to turn words into actions.

The Bill of Rights, enacted in June 1991, only covers government and public authorities — private employers, for example, are not covered. Presumably this is seen as a triumph by the business lobby who worked hard against the bill, the initial draft of which did cover private parties (Choi, 1993). The notion of producing an anti-discrimination law was distasteful to the government as it would interfere with market mechanisms, treated with particular reverence in Hong Kong. To remedy this situation, Legislative Councillor Anna Wu introduced an equal opportunities bill into the Legislative Council in 1994. Her bill would make it unlawful for public authorities and individuals to discriminate on the grounds of sex, race, age, marital status, physical or mental disability, political opinion or religious belief, spent conviction, union membership, or sexuality.

Goaded into action, the government then produced its own Sex Discrimination Bill in October of the same year. It is not our intention here to examine in detail the differences in the two bills. Suffice it to say that the government's bill is much more limited, addressing discrimination on the grounds of sex, marital status, and pregnancy (the latter two only in terms of employment). Ms Wu was prevented by the government from introducing a companion bill to establish a Human Rights and Equal Opportunities Commission to ensure the implementation of her Equal Opportunities Bill. Instead, the government proposed the establishment of an Equal Opportunities Commission in its Sex Discrimination Bill. This Commission is intended to have many of the same functions and powers as Wu's proposed commission, although Wu's commission would have had significant additional ones. From the point of view of those concerned about gender discrimination, there are grounds for optimism. From the point of view of those concerned with the wider issues of discrimination and human rights, there are grounds for concern. At the time of writing (February 1995) the final outcome is by no means clear. The best compromise outcome would be to have Anna Wu's broad anti-discrimination bill passed into law, accompanied by the government's Equal Opportunities Commission as the agency of its implementation.

It would be nonsense to deny that since the Second World War very significant gains for Hong Kong women — and men — have been obtained. Universal, free education and improvements in health care, while probably aimed at producing a healthier workforce generally, have nonetheless swept women along on a progressive tide. As the ensuing chapters will show, such an optimistic view disguises the difficulties that remain entrenched in social, political, and economic institutions and, perhaps, in women's view and understanding of their world.

## The Chapters

In contemporary Hong Kong, as in other modern industrial societies, large numbers of women have taken up paid employment outside the home and are making an important contribution to their family's income. To the extent that women's subordination in traditional societies is closely related to their confinement to the home, and hence to their financial dependence on the male breadwinner, their liberation from the domestic domain and entry into the world of work should have brought them social status and material rewards similar to those of their male counterparts. That this has not been the case in Hong Kong is the subject of inquiry in Benjamin Leung's opening chapter on women and social change. Through a survey of women's experiences at work and in the family, Leung observes that while working-class women have newly won resources, their income is often subsumed under the purview of the patriarchal family. Even women at the top find their authority and behaviour at work still very much circumscribed by traditional stereotypical images. Leung finds the explanation for this in Hong Kong's socio-economic and political context which renders the family, with its patriarchal values, the centre of commitment and reference in the social and working lives of the majority of Hong Kong Chinese.

Next to family life, the workplace is usually the most dominant feature in most people's existence. As Leung has shown, the structures that characterize the family are also imported into the world of work. Therefore, it should not surprise us that quantifiable gender inequalities are to be found. In his chapter on work, Wong presents data that, to some extent, question the commonly held belief that education will eventually iron out the uneven distribution of employment achievement between the two sexes. Wong shows that women with the same educational levels as men do not earn as much and rise to less senior positions. Although they seem to have made some progress in entering the professions, when the teaching profession is removed from the equation it is found that men outnumber women by 2.5:1. In administrative and managerial positions the ratio is 10:1. The areas in which women have enjoyed most success are those in which their roles within the home are replicated within the workplace: the 'caring' professions, clerical work and service industries.

Political issues in Hong Kong have taken on increasing

importance since the signing in 1984 by China and the United Kingdom of the Joint Declaration on the future of Hong Kong. Political participation is seen to be a way of assuring Hong Kong people an acceptable degree of both freedom and control over their own future. If this holds good for all people, then it should certainly apply to women. As Lui argues in Chapter 5, it is logical that the more women there are participating in politics the more likely it is that there will be real progress towards eliminating discrimination. She examines the various avenues to political influence in Hong Kong — through appointment and direct election, through voting behaviour, and through political parties and pressure groups. Hong Kong society does not deny women the right to political expression. Indeed, there are a number of high-profile women involved in politics. But their high profile obscures the fact that women's participation in the political process is lower than that of men. As Lui points out, women are most active in pressure groups centred around women's issues, rather than in the mainline political parties, which has a tendency to marginalize their political activity. The likely political turbulence that will ensue as 1997 approaches will mean that women's issues will probably be buried under other concerns. At the same time, notions about equality, fairness, and non-discrimination are unlikely to have any real impact in a society which does not uphold the philosophy of equal respect for all people. Thus the issue of women's rights is intimately linked with the issue of human rights.

Both Lui and Jones point out the potential significance to Hong Kong's women of CEDAW. The Hong Kong government's *Report of an Inter-Departmental Working Group on Sex Discrimination* concluded that workplace discrimination is not serious in Hong Kong — a view not held by the authors of this book. The working group also recommended against introducing anti-sex discrimination laws on the basis of the adverse effect they anticipated this would have on the economy. As Jones suggests, a government that is unwilling to admit to the prevalence of discrimination against women in Hong Kong is hardly likely to pursue the implementation of CEDAW with any vigour.

The main thrust of Jones's chapter is to show how the socio-economic and political structure of the colony has affected the writing of laws, or the absence of laws, protecting women's interests. She examines the issue of the New Territories inheritance law, the remit of which, according to Jones, extended far beyond the indigenous villages of common supposition. She identifies a commonly used government strategy that justifies a lack of intervention by arguing that it is undesirable to interfere in Chinese custom and culture. The underlying motivation is not fear of alienating local people but of upsetting the male Chinese élite, whose interests are threatened by change. The acceptance and continuation of the colonial administration rested on the support of this élite. The result of this, far from preserving indigenous tradition, has been that the government has artificially constructed an 'authentic' tradition that always happens to be in support of the status quo and entrenched interests. The effect has been ultimately to preserve patriarchal and discriminatory values enshrined in both the law and the absence of law prohibiting sexual discrimination.

Vagg's work in Chapter 7 examines women's position *vis-à-vis* crime. As is the case elsewhere, women comprise a small proportion of detected offenders and generally commit the more minor crimes. Men outnumber women arrested for every kind of offence, including shoplifting, generally considered to be the archetypal 'female' crime. Much of Vagg's chapter focuses on the issue of young women and their involvement with crime and social control. He identifies three issues he considers to be of significance. Firstly, between 1982 and 1992 juvenile delinquency among women rose faster than that among men. Secondly, female juveniles are subjected to patriarchal forms of welfare protectionism which judges them in terms of their sexual behaviour. Thirdly, the bias towards the protection of young women, however well-intentioned, blurs the boundaries between the treatment of young offenders and young women who have not been detected in the commission of delinquent acts, but who are considered to be 'at risk'. This in turn means that some young women enter the system as victims, for instance those in need of a 'care and protection' order; what happens to them thereafter (detention in a remand home or other institution) is perceived as undeserved punishment. Sexual activity by a young woman that would routinely be overlooked in a young man of the same age is seen as evidence of her being out of control. Various other acts of non-conformity (infringing dress and hair-style rules at school) frequently seem to escalate into full-fledged delinquency as a result of the punitive use of authority in an attempt to induce compliance.

Commercial sex workers (discussed by Pearson and Yu in Chapter 9) also suffer for their unwillingness to comply with the ideal standards of sexual behaviour for women in Hong Kong society. As in most places, there is a double standard for men and women. A desire for sexual variety is accepted as legitimate for men but not for women. Thus, if men's 'legitimate' needs are to be met, sexual continence for some women can only be achieved at the expense of others who are willing to risk opprobrium for monetary reward. The chapter is based on lengthy interviews with eight streetwalkers in Shamshuipo. The aim is to offer a view of the job that is primarily developed from the women's own experience and words, without the intrusion of the interviewers' value judgements or priorities. Commercial sex does offer a reasonably lucrative alternative for women whose probable alternatives would be the manufacturing or service industries. Among the topics covered are their daily working routines, why they enter the trade and what keeps them in it, their attitudes towards themselves and their job, their relationships with customers, customer requirements, and how the women balance their work identity with their domestic identities as wives and mothers. The commercial sex industry in Hong Kong has so far largely managed to escape empirical academic attention, and this is the first time that an attempt has been made to portray the experience of one facet of its many forms of operation.

More than anything else, women are defined by their roles within the family. If women's lot in life is to be improved, then the familiar litany of their oppression within the familial structure has to be rendered out of date. Ng (in Chapter 3) criticizes the functionalist analysis of family change, which is usually based on the effects of industrialization and Westernization as though a universal world pattern is driven by a single engine. The assumption of this form of analysis seems to be that women's lot within the family will inexorably improve. While there are measurable changes in family size, composition, and household form, these changes are not necessarily beneficial for women. Ng suggests through an analysis of the division of household labour and conjugal power that families are still essentially male dominated.

Ng's thesis is too sophisticated to be easily distilled. He challenges commonly accepted wisdom about women's economic inertia before industrialization and suggests that it is modern domestic ideology that has emphasized women's place in the home, fixing them firmly into their domestic roles. Women are now affected both by traditional and modern definitions of their behaviour in the socialization process. He suggests that both ideals of the female role may be exerting their powerful influence, with results seen differently in different sections of the female population depending on class. He concludes that ultimately there must be a systematic explanation that takes account of societal factors impinging on the family, takes note of the genuine advances that women have made, and still offers an explanation for the persistence and regeneration of gender inequalities in Hong Kong society.

Education is generally seen as a means of improving social mobility and socializing young people into the desired conventions of society. Those wishing to improve the lot of women have thought that this is the route through which most may be achieved. Choi shows in Chapter 4 that, although there is no formal discrimination against women in education (with all children entitled to nine years of free compulsory schooling), the experience and opportunities offered by the education system may be profoundly different for young men and women.

She discusses the 'genderization' of the curriculum, particularly the way in which science subjects are more greatly valued and are defined as 'male', while arts subjects are seen as soft options, suitable largely for young women and those young men who have failed to make the grade in sciences. Choices made at an early age are significant because they affect career opportunities. The traditional and more prestigious professional and academic areas continue to remain male dominated. It is only in business administration that women have made significant gains, but this does not take account of their less favourable career experience after graduation.

Within the schools themselves, traditional gender patterns are replicated both within the text books used and in male-dominated authority hierarchies. Women cluster at the bottom of the various teaching grades, particularly as primary school teachers. Sadly, this pattern of males dominating more senior positions continues up to the university level, where 85 per cent of teaching staff are male. Thus, while no one doubts that the education system is a powerful medium, the messages conveyed there are by no means of a kind that will change accepted attitudes about gender or support anti-discrimination measures.

In any volume of this nature, the emphasis is almost bound to lie with the need for improvement. However, we should not be blind to those areas in which notable successes have been achieved. Hong Kong has some of the lowest maternal and child mortality figures in the world. Life expectancy for women here is also very high. The major causes of death are cancer, heart disease, and cerebrovascular disease, patterns typically found in wealthy developed societies. But as Koo points out in Chapter 8, women's health is inextricably intertwined in the social and economic context. She finds that Hong Kong women may still suffer from gender discrimination in health status in two particular respects.

First, the mortality rates from accidents among baby girls are higher than for boys, and the decline in deaths from pneumonia has been less pronounced for girls than for boys. Both these trends are contrary to what one would expect from the international data. Both involve maternal care and may suggest that female babies are being given less care than males. Second, among older age groups, the decline in cardiovascular mortality was more marked for men than for women. One explanation for this is that women are subject to less aggressive screening and treatment than men, partly because they may not have the same access to quality health care as men and partly because physicians believe that women are less susceptible to heart disease and therefore do not make the correct diagnosis. Lack of screening for breast and cervical cancer, especially among older, poorer women also contributes to preventable deaths.

The book ends with Tsang's review of the history, development and future direction of the women's movement in

Hong Kong (Chapter 10). Tsang argues forcibly that women's groups should move away from the stance of portraying women as victims and combating oppression as a matter of individual empowerment, to an analysis of discrimination that locates it firmly within the economic, political, and social structures that pertain today. This in turn will mean a strategy that addresses the concerns of the 'grass roots', that will develop and empower women who bear the brunt of the oppression by patriarchal customs and practices in their everyday life — which is to say the poor and ill-educated. Tsang sees hope in the willingness of various women's groups to combine resources over matters of common interest, for instance lobbying the Legislative Council over the extension of CEDAW to Hong Kong. But like other authors in the book, she expresses concern that women's issues will be ignored as political matters take on even greater urgency in the years before 1997.

## Conclusions

The world of women is a diverse one and the topic as a subject of academic study has only recently gained credence in Hong Kong. This present volume is a contribution to what is anticipated will be a long and fruitful debate. As such, it contains a wide range of issues chosen because they are of fundamental importance. Inevitably this has meant that other topics have been omitted (for example, migrant workers and expatriate women). Doubtless other scholars will soon fill these gaps as well as entering into a dialogue with the opinions stated here.

That a woman's experience of the world should be substantively different from that of a man is still something of a novel idea in Hong Kong. Indeed, judging from the government's unwillingness to concede that there is significant gender discrimination in Hong Kong, it would be possible to argue that there is a general attitude of cosy complacency about the position of women in Hong Kong society. It is true that in comparison with some of our Asian neighbours (or European countries, Switzerland, for instance), Hong Kong women are substantially better off. This knowledge may provoke the reaction of wondering what Hong Kong women have to be concerned about. Anyone reading the contributions to this volume should have no difficulty in answering that question.

## Notes

1. In the following discussion, we broadly classify feminist theories into liberal feminism, Marxist feminism, and radical feminism. We would like to point out that this is a heuristic device to facilitate explanation and analysis, and that many feminist studies cannot be encompassed within any one particular theory. The following studies in our view provide good illustrations of the major feminist theories. Liberal feminism: Michelle Rosaldo (1974), 'Woman, Culture, and Society: A Theoretical Overview' in Michelle Rosaldo and Louise Lamphere, eds., *Women, Culture, and Society* (Stanford: Stanford University Press), pp. 17–41. Marxist feminism: Michelle Barrett (1980), *Women's Oppression Today* (London: Verso). Radical feminism: Shulamith Firestone (1974), *The Dialectic of Sex: The Case for Feminist Revolution* (New York: Morrow).

## References

Barrett, Michelle (1980), *Women's Oppression Today*, London: Verso.
Choi, Po-king (1993), 'Women', in P. K. Choi and L. S. Ho (eds.), *The Other Hong Kong Report*, Hong Kong: The Chinese University Press, pp. 369–400.
Croll, Elisabeth (1978), *Feminism and Socialism in China*, London: Routledge and Kegan Paul.
England, Joe (1989), *Industrial Relations and Law in Hong Kong*, Hong Kong: Oxford University Press.
Firestone, Shulamith (1974), *The Dialectic of Sex: The Case for Feminist Revolution*, New York: Morrow.
Foo, Gillian H. C. and Lim, Linda Y. C. (1989), 'Poverty, Ideology and Women Export Factory Workers in South East Asia', in Haleh Afshar and Bina Agarwal (eds.), *Women, Poverty and Ideology in Asia*, London: MacMillan, pp. 212–34.
Hershatter, Gail (1991) 'Prostitution and the Market in Women in Early Shanghai', in Rubie S. Watson and Patricia Buckley Ebrey (eds.), *Marriage and Inequality In Chinese Society*, California: University of California Press, pp. 256–85.

Heyzer, Noeleen (1986), *Working Women In South East Asia; Development, Subordination, Exploitation*, Milton Keynes: Open University Press.

Hong Kong Government (1993), *Green Paper on Equal Opportunities for Women and Men*, Hong Kong: Hong Kong Government Printer.

Giddens, Anthony (1989), *Sociology*, Cambridge: Blackwell/Polity Press.

Jackson, L. (1980), 'Prostitution', J. Lebra and J. Paulson (eds.), *Chinese Women in Southeast Asia*, Singapore: Times Books International, pp. 32–65.

Jaschok, Maria (1988), *Concubines and Bondservants*, Hong Kong: Oxford University Press.

Junsay, Alma T. and Heaton, Tim B. (1989), *Working Women: Comparative Perspectives in Developing Areas*, New York: Greenwood Press.

King, Ambrose Y. C. (1981), 'The Administrative Absorption of Politics in Hong Kong: Emphasis on the Grass Roots Level', Ambrose Y. C. King and Rance P. L. Lee (eds.), *Social Life and Development in Hong Kong*, Hong Kong: The Chinese University Press, pp. 127–46.

Koo, Linda (1985), 'The (Non) Status of Women in Traditional Chinese Society', *The Bulletin of the Hong Kong Psychological Society*, 14: 64–70.

Lau, S. K. (1981), 'Utilitarianistic Familism: The Basis of Political Stability', Ambrose Y. C. King and Rance P. L. Lee (eds.), *Social Life and Development in Hong Kong*, Hong Kong: The Chinese University Press, pp. 195–216.

Lau, S. K. (1982), *Society and Politics in Hong Kong*, Hong Kong: The Chinese University Press.

Lebra, Joyce and Paulson, Joy (1980), *Chinese Women in South East Asia*, Singapore: Times Books International.

Rosaldo, Michelle (1974), 'Women, Culture, and Society: A Theoretical Overview', in Michelle Rosaldo and Louise Lamphere (eds.), *Women, Culture, and Society*, Stanford: Stanford University Press, pp. 17–41.

Scott, Ian (1989), *Political Change and the Crisis of Legitimacy in Hong Kong*, Hong Kong: Oxford University Press.

Stockard, Janice (1989), *Daughters of the Canton Delta*, Hong Kong: Hong Kong University Press.

Tam, Tony S. K. and Yeung, Sum (1994), 'Community Perception of Social Welfare and Its Relations to Familism, Political Alienation and Individual Rights: The Case of Hong Kong', *International Social Work*, 37: 47–60.

Watson, Rubie S. (1991), 'Wives, Concubines, and Maids: Servitude and Kinship in the Hong Kong Region, 1900–1940', in Rubie S. Watson and Patricia Buckley Ebrey (eds.), *Marriage and Inequality in Chinese Society*, California: University of California Press, pp. 231–55.

Wong, Siu-lun (1988), *Emigrant Entrepreneurs*, Hong Kong: Oxford University Press.

# 1 Women and Social Change: The Impact of Industrialization on Women in Hong Kong

*Benjamin K. P. Leung*

Few people would dispute that the welfare and social status of women has improved significantly in the modern and modernizing societies of today. This paper examines the impact of industrialization and modernization on women in Hong Kong. It outlines the main contours of Hong Kong's development since the early 1950s, when the society's industrialization took off. Its aim is to provide some general evidence and an explanation of what women have and have not yet achieved in industrial Hong Kong. As such, this chapter provides the background for the more detailed treatment of specific topics in later chapters. To gauge the change in status of Hong Kong women since industrialization, we begin with a cursory examination of their lot in pre-industrial Hong Kong.

## Women in Pre-industrial Hong Kong

Hong Kong before the 1950s was predominantly an entrepôt economy. Britain's main purpose in acquiring Hong Kong as a colony was to use it as a trading station between Britain and China. Because of this, until at least the end of the nineteenth century, the colonial government saw its role as primarily that of protecting and advancing the interests of the merchants, particularly the British and European merchants. It was, as one writer puts it, a minimal government,[1] and as such it left the Chinese population to their own way of life and to look after their own needs. The British also had neither the incentive nor the intention to mix socially with the Chinese. With the British viewing themselves as a superior race, and the overwhelming majority of the Chinese working as labourers, there existed huge racial and class barriers between the two groups.[2] Consequently, Hong Kong was socially and culturally segregated into the European and the Chinese communities. It was such segregation that enabled the Hong Kong Chinese to retain the cultural values and practices which they brought with them from their homeland to the colony. The predicament of Chinese women in pre-industrial Hong Kong thus, by and large, resembled that in traditional Chinese society.

There is a paucity of studies on the plight of women in pre-industrial Hong Kong, but the deprivations and discrimination they experienced can be inferred from the few studies of special categories of women in early twentieth-century Hong Kong. The *mui tsai* (Cantonese term for 'little maids') and the concubine are good illustrations. The official definition given in a Hong Kong Census Report of 1921 described *mui tsai* as 'young girls whose parents have assigned their rights of guardianship to other families for a monetary consideration, and whose labour is at the free disposal of the new guardian till the age for marriage'.[3] But the official definition glosses over the degradation and ill fate in store for the *mui tsai*, as Maria Jaschok observes on the basis of her field studies:

> Often exploited for domestic purposes, she could also be transferred into brothels of the large cities, sold for a number of years into contract labour . . . or she could be trained by her owner for prostitution. Her servitude might be temporary; it could, however, also culminate in prolonged and at times indefinite states of slavery (1988: 8).

The prevalence of the *mui tsai* practice, and by implication, the widespread exploitation of women, was noted by Andrea Sankar, who points out that in the early 1900s *mui tsai* constituted the majority of nonfamily labour in households in Hong Kong (1978: 53). Rubie Watson similarly estimates Hong Kong's servile population around the end of the last century to consist mainly of girls and women (1991: 235).

Like the *mui tsai*, the concubine was acquired through purchase, from a brothel, from dealers in concubines and maids, or from her parents, ideally for the purposes of reproduction but often also for her consort's pleasure and status enhancement (Watson, 1991: 239–40). Her position in her consort's family depended largely on her ability to produce male heirs, failing which she might be forced to leave. The wife, in comparison with the *mui tsai* and the concubine, had a more established and secure position within the household, but even she could be used as an exchange object: 'The literature suggests that a man could "sell" both his wife and his concubines.... For example, he could pawn his wife or give her away in payment for a debt' (Watson, 1991: 242). The above cursory accounts cannot capture the full dimension of women's oppression and misery in traditional Hong Kong, but they provide poignant illustrations of the abuse of women in a society where the patriarchal family and its values prevailed.[4]

## The Winds of Change: Industrial Development in Hong Kong

Hong Kong society underwent a drastic change in the early 1950s. The impetus for this change came from developments in China and in international politics. The civil war in China and the subsequent establishment of the People's Republic of China in 1949 led to a large influx of refugees from the Mainland. The territory's population stood at around 840,000 in 1931; it grew to over two million in 1951 and roughly three million in 1961.[5] In addition, China's military confrontation with the United States in the Korean War of 1950–3 resulted in the United Nations' imposition of a trade embargo on China. Hong Kong's entrepôt economy was severely crippled, and the society was forced to overcome this crisis by producing its own industrial products for export to overseas markets. It was against this background that Hong Kong entered into a phase of industrialization. In this, the economy benefited substantially from the 'refugee' injection of capital, entrepreneurship, and technical know-how from Shanghai. The fast-growing refugee population also provided a cheap and docile labour force for the burgeoning manufacturing economy. The first industries to emerge and flourish were textiles and garment-making, followed later by the electronics and plastic goods industries. By the end of the 1960s, Hong Kong had successfully established itself as an export-oriented industrial economy.

Yet despite the fundamental transformation in the territory's economy, the change in its political system was negligible.

The government continued to be run, as in pre-industrial Hong Kong, by a small closed circle of top government bureaucrats and appointed Chinese élites consisting mainly of wealthy businessmen. Still subscribing to the *laissez-faire* policy of a minimal government, it did little to improve the livelihood of the population. Ian Scott thus describes the consequences: 'Social services were either minimal in quality and quantity or non-existent. By the 1960s, there was an enormous, accumulated, century-old, social debt' (Scott, 1989: 51).

Hong Kong society went through another major change from the mid-1970s. The expansion of the financial and service sectors, and the revival of the entrepôt trade consequent upon China's open-door policy from the late 1970s, culminated in the increasing importance of the tertiary sector and the relative decline of the secondary manufacturing sector in the local economy. This led to the creation of more white-collar, better-paid middle-class jobs and significantly increased the opportunities for upward mobility. At the same time, in response to the social disturbances of the mid-1960s, and fuelled by Hong Kong's phenomenal economic growth, the government vastly expanded its provision of social services, notably in housing, education, social welfare, and medical and health services.

A new era in Hong Kong's political development began in 1982, when as an initial step towards the development of a more representative administration, the Hong Kong government implemented the District Administration Scheme. Under this scheme, a district board was formed in each of 18 districts (19 after 1985) in the urban area and the New Territories. The district board initially comprised both officials (government representatives), as well as unofficials (government-appointed members and publicly elected members); from 1985 to early 1994, the district board was composed of unofficials only.

After the signing of the Sino-British Joint Declaration in 1984, in a move to prepare the society for self-government after the transfer of sovereignty in 1997, the Hong Kong government in 1985 introduced an elected element into the Legislative Council. Twenty-four of the fifty-seven seats of the 1985 Legislative Council were filled by members elected indirectly through the district boards and the functional constituencies. The other seats comprised 11 government representatives and 22 appointed members. A further advancement towards representative government was made in 1991, when 18 of the 60 Legislative Council members were returned through direct election based on geographical constituencies. Indirectly elected members, now numbering 21, were returned solely through functional constituencies. Civil servants and appointed members were reduced to 4 and 17 seats respectively. The Executive Council remains an entirely appointed body. While still far from enjoying a democratic constitution, the Hong Kong government has evidently advanced a long way from the closed exclusive political system of the past.

## Women's Increased Participation in the Labour Force

One would expect that the demand for labour, and hence the expansion of job opportunities, concomitant with Hong Kong's phenomenal economic development would be conducive to women's greater participation in the labour force. This, indeed, is borne out by the statistics on rates of women's labour force participation since 1960 in Table 1.1.

Job opportunities, as Ho (1984) points out, are but one of the variables affecting women's labour force participation. Two other important variables mentioned by Ho are, first, availability — this refers to the degree to which women are freed from the burdens associated with marriage and childbearing and so are able to participate in the workforce. Thus, a lower fertility rate is held to increase women's labour force participation. Secondly, marketability, which is concerned with women's ability in respect of skills and educational qualifications to compete successfully in the job market; higher educational attainment thus enhances women's marketability. Table 1.1 indicates that a decline in the fertility rate and women's rising educational attainment have indeed been concomitant features of Hong Kong's socio-economic development. The data thus suggest an encouraging trend for women within and outside the family. Increased participation in the labour force presumably enhances financial

Table 1.1 Trends in total fertility rate, women's educational attainment, and women's labour force participation rate, 1960–1990

| Year | Total fertility rate** | Women's educational attainment*: Secondary | University undergraduate | Labour force participation rate*** |
|---|---|---|---|---|
| 1960 | 5.0 | 39.2 | 24.3 | 36.8 |
| 1965 | 4.5 | 42.1 | 35.8 | n.a.*** |
| 1970 | 3.41 | 42.9 | 33.3 | 42.8 |
| 1975 | 2.70 | 46.1 | 29.6 | 43.6 |
| 1980 | 2.05 | 50.3 | 34.6 | 45.3 |
| 1985 | 1.46 | 50.4 | 37.8 | 48.5 |
| 1990 | 1.19 | 50.0 | 37.2 | 46.8 |

* The figures below pertain to women as a percentage of those enrolled in the respective levels of education. Data before 1990 based on Mak (1992: 172) table 7.3. The 1990 data are based on Hong Kong Annual Digest of Statistics, 1991, tables 15.2 and 15.8.
** The total fertility rate is a measure used by demographers to estimate the average number of children that each woman can be expected to bear during her lifetime. Data based on Ronald Skeldon (1991: 254), table 9.
*** Women's labour force participation rate refers to women in the labour force as a percentage of women aged 15 and over. Data based on various census reports. n.a. = Not available.

independence and contribution to the family income, and hence women's status within the family. The dropping fertility rate should reduce their burden in childcare, and their higher educational attainment ought to lift them to higher occupational positions and incomes. One would therefore expect a greater parity between women and men in modern industrial Hong Kong.

F. M. Wong (1984) subscribes to this view in his study of the impact of industrialization upon the pattern of family role and power differentiation in Hong Kong. He takes the mother's paid employment as an indicator of the influence of industrialization on the family, and examines the effect of maternal employment, and hence of industrialization, on the mother's role and power in the marital relationship. He concludes, on the basis of his empirical study of 637 Chinese families in Kwun Tong, Hong Kong:

> A mother's employment leads to her decrease in household task performance and decision-making and a corresponding increase in her husband assuming some of the routine household duties and making decisions about them. Her employment also enables her to enjoy a relatively more equal status with her husband and maintain a collaborative type of relationship with him . . . (1984: 231).

More specifically, Wong's findings show that the employed mother in comparison with the full-time housewife played a greater role in the household's 'instrumental' tasks, such as budgeting and purchase of household items, and a lesser role in 'expressive' tasks like childcare and control. The study maintains that industrialization by way of providing paid employment for women enhances their bargaining power and status. It also suggests that through altering women's role within the family, women's employment may eventually bring about a change in the traditional social image of women. But other studies,[6] as Ng's chapter on women and the family in this book also points out, give us a less rosy picture of women's status advancement in industrial Hong Kong. P. K. Chan's research provides a fine example of this.

Through a judicious analysis of the data on women and work, Chan (1986) cautions against uncritically attributing to industrialization a beneficial impact on women. Her research has led her to the view that 'women in Hong Kong over the last ten years were conditioned by their role in reproduction' (1986: 40). She demonstrates powerfully that women's childbearing role and the associated childcare and domestic duties are still a formidable barrier and discriminatory factor in respect of their employment outside the home. Surveying the age-specific labour force participation rates in 1971 and 1981, she notes that the female participation rate dropped substantially after women reached the age of 25, whereas the male rate increased between the ages 25 to 54. The female participation rate for the age bracket 20 to 24 was 69.5 per cent in 1971; it dropped to below 40 per cent after the age of 25. In 1981, the corresponding drop was from 79.7 per cent to below 57 per cent. In contrast, the male participation rate remained in both years above 96 per cent for the age brackets 25 to 54. Since women's mean age of marriage was around 24 in that decade, Chan deduces that a large number of women had to retreat from the labour market after marriage or the birth of their first child. Men were unencumbered in this respect. In fact, as Chan observes, their freedom to work after marriage was based on the non-freedom of their wives. Direct support for Chan's contention can be drawn from Choi and Chan's research findings (1973) which show that 45.1 per cent of the wives in their study who did not work after marriage felt that their work in the home kept them fully occupied.

In addition, the statistics and research findings on outwork (work done outside the shop or factory that arranges it) give us a grim picture of women struggling to carry child care and their household burdens on the one hand, and their financial responsibilities to the family on the other. In 1981 and 1991, around 80 per cent of Hong Kong's outworkers were women, most of whom belonged to the age bracket 25 to 49 (Hong Kong Census and Statistics Department, 1982; General Household Survey, 1991). Citing evidence from *The Report on Working Mothers in Family Functioning*, Chan observes: 'A considerable number of respondents were found to be engaged in "bring-home-crafts" distributed by factories so that they could undertake wage labour, childcare and household chores simultaneously' (1986: 41).

T. L. Lui's recent study of married women's participation in industrial outwork in Hong Kong (1991) offers a clue to their adoption of this strategy of coping. Most of his respondents (78 per cent) stated that their husbands wanted them to stay home to look after their children (Lui, 1991: 12). The constraint felt by the wives is captured succinctly in one of the respondents' accounts:

> Even if I go out to work again, I still need to take care of my housework.... I won't earn much. So I work to pay the nursery fee. And then I have to worry about the quality of nursery.... Why not I stay at home to look after my kids and earn some extra money by doing outwork? (Lui, 1991: 14).

## Table 1.2 Percentages of all female and male employees in selected occupations, 1961–1991*

| Occupation | | Managers and administrators | Professional, technical and related workers | Clerical and related workers | Production and related workers |
|---|---|---|---|---|---|
| 1961 | F | 0.7 | 6.3 | 3.3 | 47.2 |
| | M | 4.0 | 4.6 | 6.9 | 49.4 |
| 1971 | F | 0.6 | 7.0 | 8.1 | 54.8 |
| | M | 3.3 | 4.3 | 8.4 | 51.0 |
| 1981 | F | 1.0 | 6.3 | 18.0 | 49.3 |
| | M | 3.5 | 5.6 | 8.8 | 51.7 |
| 1991 | F | 4.9 | 14.3 | 28.8 | 17.1 |
| | M | 11.8 | 13.8 | 8.0 | 33.9 |

*As there was a change in the classification of occupations between the 1981 and 1991 Population Censuses, the figures for 1991 provide only a broad comparison with those for previous years.
Source: 1961–1981 data based on *Hong Kong Statistics*, 1981. 1991 data based on *Hong Kong 1991 Population Census*.

This account is illuminating not only in showing that women's employment outside the home is likely to place an extra burden on them besides household chores, but also in suggesting that women's low pay in the labour market discourages them from seeking full-time employment outside the home. It seems that even in industrial Hong Kong, there are forces from within and outside the family that obstruct women's liberation from the domestic role and hamper their participation in income-earning work as men's equivalent.

### Women's Work Roles

Table 1.2 shows that the development of Hong Kong's economy in the past three decades has brought about a change in the occupational structure. The change is particularly obvious in the decade between 1981 and 1991, and is characterized by a shift from occupational roles in the secondary manufacturing sector (production and related workers) to those in the tertiary sector (the other three occupational categories in the table). In the case of women, the percentage drop during the 1980s in production and related work (from 49.3 to 17.1) is dramatic, and this is accompanied by a corresponding percentage increase in the managerial/administrative (from 1.0 to 4.9), professional (from 6.3 to 14.3), and clerical (from 18.0 to 28.8) categories.

This pattern of change suggests that there has been a significant improvement in the occupational status of women, and of men, in at least the past fifteen years of Hong Kong economic development. But it should be noted that the disparity between the sexes remains in the highest-ranking 'managers and administrators' category, though over the years the gap has been proportionally narrowed in women's favour. At the lower end, women's drop in the 'production' category is replaced to some extent by an increase in the 'clerical' category, suggesting that the improvement in women's occupational status has been limited and restricted mainly within the lower-ranking jobs. Finally the strong representation of women in the 'professional' category must, as Wong points out (Chapter 2), be interpreted in light of the fact that this category includes occupations such as teaching and nursing in which women predominate numerically. The overall picture suggests that over the past three decades the inequality gap in occupational distribution between men and women has narrowed, but the difference remains significant. The same pattern occurs in the income differentials between the sexes. In 1976 and 1981, women's median income was 65 per cent that of men's; the ratio improved to 70 per cent and 77 per cent in 1986 and 1991 respectively (*Hong Kong Statistics* 1986, and *Hong Kong 1991 Population Census*). But the above analysis masks the gender inequality within occupations. The following discussion throws light on this.

Table 1.3 shows that in 1991, within each of the major occupational categories, women's income is below that of men. It is further worth noting that even in occupations that have conventionally been considered to be primarily women's, the senior positions are predominantly filled by men, and the lower ones by women. Choi's chapter in this book, for instance, shows that most of the senior positions in Hong Kong's educational system are occupied by men. Grace Mak similarly observes that 'taken as whole, women serve mainly

*Table 1.3  Ratio of median income of female employees to median income of male employees by selected occupations in 1991*

| Occupation | Ratio of median income |
| --- | --- |
| Managers and Administrators | 0:83 |
| Professionals | 0:83 |
| Associate professionals | 0:94 |
| Clerks | 0:91 |
| Craft and related workers | 0:65 |
| Plant and Machine operators, and Assemblers | 0:58 |

Source: Hong Kong Government 1993, *Green Paper on Equal Opportunities for Women and Men*, p. 14.

at the base of the teaching force. In 1987, 99 per cent of the kindergarten teachers, 75 per cent of the primary school teachers, 51 per cent of the secondary school teachers, and 28 per cent of teachers at the post-secondary level were female' (1992: 175). A similar pattern of disparity exists in the 'feminized' electronics and plastics industries, as P. K. Chan's study (1986) of employment figures demonstrates. The higher technologist and technician positions were occupied mostly by men. For instance, at the technologist level, in 1974, the ratio of female to male employees was 1 to 377.5. The ratios in 1976 and 1980 were 1 to 74.5 and 1 to 36.3 respectively. At the lower operative level, however, women outnumbered men in a ratio of 9 to 1 in 1974, and 5.9 to 1 and 4.8 to 1 in 1976 and 1980, respectively. The situation in the plastics industry was similar. In 1975, male workers had a complete monopoly of the technologist level. Women entered this level in later years, but in 1981 they were still in the minority of one female to every 32.9 males. In contrast, at the lower, unskilled level, women workers were in the majority. Here for every male worker, there were 5.2 female workers in 1975, and 2.6 female workers in 1981. While Chan's study shows that women's entry into the senior positions in the two industries was very much restricted, one can perhaps take comfort in the fact that their situation improved over the years.

We noted earlier the income differential between men and women. We wish to point out here that the disparity exists even in cases where women's educational attainments are the same as men's. In 1976, 23 per cent of female, but 37 per cent of male university graduates, earned a monthly income of HK$3,000 and above. The disparity persisted over the years, with 27 per cent of the females and 43 per cent of the males earning a monthly income of HK$5,000 and above in 1981 (*Hong Kong 1981 Population Census*). Recent available data also show that with similar levels of educational attainment, men have been far more likely to enter the upper occupational categories than women.[7]

So what does the above account tell us about the status of the working women in modern industrial Hong Kong? The evidence shows that women have been over-represented in the low-status, poorly paid occupational categories and positions. The persistence of sexual discrimination is most poignantly demonstrated by the fact that for similar work, women are often paid less than men, and that with equivalent educational attainment, women often occupy positions and receive remunerations lower than those of men. What sustains this discrimination? P. K. Chan gets to the heart of the matter when she contends: 'The subsidiary position of Hong Kong women in the labour market cannot be explained without regard to their role as the chief caretaker of children and the family. Their participation in wage labour is seen to be a supplementary activity' (1986: 41).

In attributing the subordinate position of women in the labour market, and by implication in the larger society, to their child-caring and familial role, Chan is contending that industrialization and social change in Hong Kong have by no means eliminated the 'domestic' stumbling blocks that handicap and hold back women in their 'public' endeavours. We now look at the evidence in this respect, beginning with a study of successful career women in Hong Kong who should presumably be among those most liberated from the constraints of family and childcare.

## Women at the Top

There are few studies of middle- and upper-class Chinese working women in Hong Kong, but a glimpse of their experiences at work and in the family can be obtained from Cashmore's study (1989) of 35 women occupying senior positions in commerce/industry, the professions, and government. The accounts they provided in interviews with the researcher often reflect family influences which they had to overcome to reach their present positions of eminence. Cashmore observed summarily: 'Every woman in the project had grown up in a family with at least traces of a mentality supporting male dominance' (1989: 11). A respondent's report shows how she had to free herself from such influence:

> My father never encouraged me educationally, or in any other sense. Nor did my mother. She never worked. My mother couldn't do a thing. ... So I had to think of myself as something different from her. ... My own mother and father influenced me, but I suppose it was in showing me what not to do or be. ... I can look back on my family background and ... say to myself, 'Look, you are not going to be a matron, or worse, a slave' (Cashmore, 1989: 11).

Another respondent observed, referring to her own and many of her senior female colleagues' experiences, that with few exceptions women achieved seniority typically in 'the serving business' where human-relations skills are important, and were largely excluded from the more vital centres of high finance, industry, and trade. Other respondents' reports show that even these supposedly powerful women could not bargain with men on equal terms. 'Most men don't want a woman boss. ... Men look down on women in high positions. ... A man has expectations of a woman, and if you don't measure up to them, then life is going to be very tough' (Cashmore, 1989: 24). These women were thus forced to play and reconcile contradictory roles. On the one hand, they had to prove themselves worthy of the position of authority; on the other, to make life easy for themselves, they were obliged to live up to men's expectations that women are soft, gentle, and vulnerable. To resolve the dilemma, many chose to rely on feminine charm. Cashmore thus describes these women's situation: 'Faced with the possibility of being totally excluded or using whatever resources they might have to engineer situations to their advantage, they resort to using feminine characteristics' (1989: 24).

The patriarchal tradition dampens young, aspirant women's career opportunities as well. In this, ironically the women at the top play a part. Most of Cashmore's respondents expressed a preference for appointing men rather than women to positions of power and heavy responsibility: 'I have to be wary about women; they might get married someday. Then their ambitions get changed to having children.... So I've got more confidence in men. This doesn't mean I don't like to use women, but the reality doesn't allow me to do so' (Cashmore, 1989: 34).

From Cashmore's study, we have an empirical confirmation of P. K. Chan's contention on which the discussion in this section is based. Industrialization in Hong Kong has not obliterated traditional conceptions of woman as mother and homemaker. Because of these conceptions, women at work, including those at the top, encounter prejudices and discriminatory treatment which hamper their career development. Liberated and enlightened though they may be, successful career women often have to subscribe to patriarchal values and practices, and in so doing, partake in the perpetuation of a system that obstructs their kind from attaining equality with men. In so far as women are employed on men's terms, their procreative functions remain stumbling blocks in their career advancement. Cashmore's study of women at the top has been dwelt on at some length because their experiences are perhaps the most poignant demonstration of the pervasiveness and dominance of patriarchy in modern industrial Hong Kong. One can expect the less successful and less fortunate members of their sex to face more blatant prejudices and greater hardships.

## The Women of Low-income Families

Salaff's highly acclaimed book, *Working Daughters of Hong Kong* (1981), and Ng's recent research (1991b) on women from low-income families bear centrally on our discussion of women and social change. Their work not only advances our knowledge of the lives of women from Hong Kong's low-income groups, but also offer explanations of their predicament in the light of the social–structural changes in Hong Kong since the start of industrialization. Their studies are separated by a decade, but their conclusions are similar, suggesting that little has changed in the intervening years.

Salaff's study of 28 working daughters shows that their fate was intimately bound up with the fate of their families; they still lived very much under the shadow of the patriarchal family. When the need arose, they were usually the ones to quit schooling, to work to supplement the family's income and enable their brothers to continue with their education. Elder daughters also shouldered the responsibility of looking after younger siblings. They handed over three-quarters of their income to their families, but their gain in status within the family was by no means commensurate with their contribution. They were allowed greater freedom in making friends and in the choice of marital partners, but were barred from important family decision-making. 'Daughters were permitted to make decisions concerning matters that heralded little for the family future. My respondents could often decide the quality and type of household purchase but never the level and duration of sibling education or the scale of extravagant family banquets.... Daughters' contributions to the family budget in no case merited a permanent seat on family councils...' (Salaff, 1981: 270–1). Working daughters' family burdens only lightened with improvement in the family's financial position, but they were still 'expected at all times to keep family prerogatives in full view' (Salaff, 1981: 270–1).

Ng's study (1991b) of the lives of married women from low-income families in Tuen Mun shows that their state was no better than that of Salaff's working daughters. Most of these women had held full-time employment in the past, but over half had left their jobs at the time of the study mainly because of their marriage, pregnancy, and childcare responsibilities. Some planned to seek paid employment again as their family's income was inadequate. Others would remain full-time housewives to look after their children. The task of attending to the children's general well-being, schoolwork, and leisure activities was undertaken almost exclusively by the respondents, be they full-time employees or housewives. Over 80 per cent described themselves as the main bearer of household responsibilities. Most respondents did not belong to any voluntary association and seldom took part in activities organized by public bodies. Most of them also knew nothing about the social welfare services in their community, and few ever made use of these services. In short, these women seemed to be living their lives in the service of their families and children. Ng comments on their predicament:

> Obviously, family prerogatives are still impeding women's ability to direct their own lives.... Whether women can make use of the opportunities that come with industrialization depends on the resources under their control — whether they can free themselves from the bondage of the family, whether men would make corresponding changes, and whether government and social institutions would whole-heartedly forsake and combat stereotypical images of men and women (Ng, 1991b: 179; original text in Chinese).

One may add that recent economic changes do not seem to have improved the lot of the working-class woman. Hong Kong's industrial restructuring since the early 1980s — the relocation of industrial production to south China and the contraction of the manufacturing sector — has in fact widened the gender inequality within manufacturing industries and generated a host of problems for many female manufacturing workers. A combination of factors have contributed to this. Firstly, as it is mainly those productive processes requiring little technical skill that have been relocated, and as women have been employed predominantly in these lower-level jobs, the female worker far more than the male has suffered from the ensuing consequences of job displacement and unemployment.

Secondly, the abundant availability of cheap labour in China has had the effect of depressing the wage of the manufacturing worker, especially the unskilled and semi-skilled worker, in Hong Kong. For the reason just mentioned, female workers have been hit particularly hard by this. On the other hand, middle-level employees, such as clerical workers and skilled technicians, who are overwhelmingly male, have received substantial wage increases.[8] The overall consequence has been a growing wage differential between male and female workers within the manufacturing sector. In the garment-making industry, for instance, the ratio of female to male wages has declined from 0.92 in 1979 to 0.84 in 1990, while that in the spinning and weaving industry has dropped from 0.92 in 1982 to 0.88 in 1990 (Commissioner of Labour, various years). In addition, female workers displaced from the manufacturing industries have fared worse than their male counterparts in seeking employment in the service sector, where employers are often reluctant to appoint women over the age of 35.[9]

## Obstacles to Change

It is unrealistically optimistic to argue that industrialization would bring about gender equality by way of freeing women from their domestic role. This is one central message in Salaff's (1981) and Ng's (1991b) work. Both writers contend that in Hong Kong industrialization has not significantly altered the patriarchal family and its values; it has only led the family to work out a new strategy to adapt to the changing society. They point out that in Hong Kong, where the government has played only a limited role in the provision of social welfare, the family has to rely mainly on itself in responding to the challenges and opportunities generated by industrialization. The family has thus emerged as the centre of the individual's loyalty and concern. Salaff calls this the centripetal family and says:

> In the centripetal form, the family becomes a power base to manipulate other institutions. . . . A centripetal family gathers in its forces by demanding the primary loyalty of its members and mobilizing their labor power, political, and psychological allegiances on behalf of kinsmen. . . . I contend that . . . the life courses of Hong Kong working women were formed by time-honoured centripetal family norms (1981: 8–9).

It is from such a perspective that Salaff depicts Hong Kong working women's vicious cycle of subjugation: factory management's and government officials' presumption that women's main concerns in life are in the home leads to low wages and lack of training and promotion opportunities for women;

such conditions of employment are not conducive to allegiance and commitment to the job, so the family roles of women remain the most salient. In a similar vein, C. H. Ng contends in his chapter in this book that the prerogatives of the patriarchal family still circumscribe the lives of Hong Kong women, especially those from low-income families. Their prescribed domestic role hinders their participation in the labour force, and where they do participate, its mode, timing, and duration are often determined by their families' needs rather than their own preferences.

The centripetal family with its patriarchal values also obstructs the advancement of the women's cause in that it fosters a perception of married women's participation in the labour force as a threat to the family's solidarity and a burden to society. This prejudiced attitude gains respectability and credibility when it is disseminated by some government institutions and academics. The following statements from a prominent Hong Kong newspaper and from a sociologist are good illustrations.

> The number of divorces in Hong Kong could reach a record high of about 3,000 this year — and working wives may be partly to blame, according to the Social Welfare Department.... For after a hard day's work, working wives are less inclined to devote as much attention and energy to their children and housework as full-time housewives (*South China Morning Post*, 25 August 1982).[10]

And sociologist Robert Mitchell in his work on the family in urban Hong Kong writes:

> Let us look closer at the working mother. Her work presumably is a potential source of many social needs and problems. For example, if her children are young, then day nurseries and schools may be required to care for them; if she is unable to supervise her older children, they may become behaviourial problems; and if she works outside the home, then labour laws may be needed to provide her with special protection (1969: 37).

An important clue can be derived from the above remarks to the obstacles that stand in the way of women's liberation. Women have carried the burden of childcare and household chores, and acquiesced in playing subordinate roles in the family and society for so long that people, particularly men, have taken these for granted, as if these were part of nature. Any change in women's status that challenges the status quo or that calls for adjustments in society is therefore often perceived as a violation of the natural order of things rather than a redressing of old imbalances and inequalities. The statements quoted above are only illustrations of a sexist ideology that pervades every walk of life in Hong Kong society — in the mass media, formal education, and social encounters between men and women.[11]

There is also a practical side to this prejudice. Women's liberation implies a displacement of the burdens women have long borne at little or no cost to the public purse. While men in general are unwilling to take over these burdens the way women have done, the government and established interests find the prospective displacement an unwelcome additional drain on their resources. The Hong Kong government's social policy, for instance, has long been characterized by its conspicuous reluctance to allocate resources assisting the family's childcare. Commenting on the development of welfare services in the decade 1971 to 1981, P. K. Chan writes: 'By disclaiming Government's chief responsibility for the social cost of reproduction and childcare, the social policy in this period did not act in the direction of relieving women's role in reproduction' (1986: 47).

In 1990, the government adopted a similar orientation in its proposal[12] to punish parents who leave their children under a certain age alone at home. Indeed, as this book's chapter on the women's movement suggests, the obstacles to women's liberation have been so deeply and extensively lodged in Hong Kong society that their removal is tantamount to a social revolution. Neither the government nor the public at large have had the commitment to such a revolution.

## Conclusions

The aim of this paper has been to examine, with explanations, the extent to which the social changes in Hong Kong resulting from industrialization have freed women from their traditional bondage and subjugation. Industrialization has unquestionably contributed to the advancement of Hong

Kong women's status and welfare in the past few decades. Employed women, in particular, have gained some autonomy and influence within the family, and a few have even reached top positions at work. But the overall picture is still one of pejorative treatment of women. They are generally paid less and occupy lower job positions than men, even when their qualifications are equivalent to those of their male counterparts. Their role in the workplace is still very much constrained and handicapped by their familial role. In particular, working-class women are still largely subservient to the prerogatives of the patriarchal family. In focusing on the relationship between women's familial roles and work roles, and analysing women's subordination in the light of this relationship, this chapter prepares the context for the discussion in the following two chapters.

The explanation of women's continuing subordination lies in the persistence of the centripetal family system in industrial Hong Kong. The cut-throat competition in Hong Kong's industrial capitalism, coupled with the government's *laissez-faire* policy, has forced the family to rely mainly on its own resources in its struggle for survival and social advancement. In other words, the economic and political circumstances of Hong Kong are such that the family's claim on its members' loyalty and commitment is reinforced by industrialization. The consequence is that industrialization's potentially emancipating effect on women is significantly reduced in the Hong Kong context. In light of this analysis, the Chinese family with its patriarchal values remains, even in contemporary Hong Kong, the main impediment to women's liberation. Other social institutions and the public at large, in subscribing to entrenched prejudices and discriminatory practices against women, create additional obstacles. The later chapters examine these obstacles in the areas of law, criminal justice, education, politics, health and medicine, and the commercial sex industry. As the chapter on the women's movement maintains, the battle for Hong Kong women's emancipation has to be fought on many fronts. Their advances in the past few decades have by no means guaranteed them a victory.

## Notes

1. See Ian Scott (1989), *Political Change and the Crisis of Legitimacy in Hong Kong*, chapter 2. Describing the policy of the colonial government in early Hong Kong, Scott writes: 'In line with colonial policy elsewhere, the British government believed that a very limited administration — a minimal state backed by imperial forces — would meet the needs of the inhabitants. Public expenditure was confined to the bare essentials' (Scott, 1989: 39).
2. For a detailed and well-documented account of the racial segregation between the British and Chinese in early Hong Kong, see W. K. Chan (1991), *The Making of Hong Kong Society*, particularly chapter 2.
3. Cited in Maria Jaschok (1988), *Concubines and Bondservants*, p. 8.
4. An Anti *Mui Tsai* Society was established in Hong Kong in 1921. The *mui tsai* practice finally disappeared in the 1950s. For a detailed discussion of the attempts to abolish the *mui tsai* system, see Norman Miners (1990), *The Attempts to Abolish the* Mui Tsai *System in Hong Kong 1917–1941*.
5. Statistics based on David Podmore (1971), 'The Population of Hong Kong', and Mok Hoi (1993), *The Development and Structural Transformation of the Hong Kong Economy*, p. 110 [in Chinese].
6. Data from the 1986 social indicators project undertaken by S. K. Lau and his associates show that 60 per cent of their sampled respondents reported that household duties such as cooking, cleaning, ironing, and the purchase of daily necessities were the main responsibility of the female household head. Only around 6 per cent of the sample reported that such duties were primarily the responsibility of the male household head. In the case of childcare, the corresponding 'female' and 'male' figures were 30 per cent and 10 per cent (Detailed data reproduced in Association for the Advancement of Feminism 1993, *The Hong Kong Woman File*, p. 71, table 8). Another study found that childcare and household duties were the main responsibility of the female household head in slightly over 80 per cent of the sampled households (Tuen Mun District Board 1990, *Report of the Needs of Married Women in Tuen Mun*, pp. 18 and 19).
7. See Thomas Wong (1991), 'Inequality, Stratification and Mobility', in *Indicators of Social Development*, p. 154, table 7.9.
8. Using the garment-making and the textile industries as illustrations, Chiu and Levin (1993: 23) observe that the real wage of lower-level workers dropped by 9.1 per cent from 1982 to 1990, while that of middle-level workers increased by 19.5 per cent.

9. Most employers in the service sector, particularly in sales, restaurants, and tourism, prefer to employ young women to enhance the appeal or 'look' of their business. This is a further demonstration that women's physical appearance is accorded more importance than their other personal assets. Other problems faced by displaced workers, both female and male, include their poor education (employers in the service sector usually would offer appointment only to candidates with Form 3 or above education) and the inadequate preparatory retraining they receive from the Labour Department. The above information was based on the author's recent interview with five retrenched female manufacturing workers and on preliminary interview data from ongoing research on women workers conducted by C. H. Ng and his associates.
10. Cited in Chan, Po-King (1986), 'Industrialization and Sexual Equality — The Case of Hong Kong', *Asian Exchange*, Vol. 4, no. 4 and Vol. 5, no. 1, double issue, p. 28.
11. For studies of sexism in these areas, see Ho Suk-ching (1983), 'Sex Role Portrayals in Print Advertisements: The Case of Hong Kong'; Grace C. L. Mak (1992), The Schooling of Girls in Hong Kong: Progress and Contradictions in the Transition; and Veronica Pearson (1990), Women in Hong Kong. Pearson's article provides one of the best accounts of sexism in various domains of life in Hong Kong.
12. For a brief discussion of this proposal, see Nelson Chow (1990), 'Social Welfare', in, *The Other Hong Kong Report*, pp. 442–3. The proposal was later dropped.

# References

Association for the Advancement of Feminism (1993), *The Hong Kong Women's File*, Hong Kong: Association for the Advancement of Feminism [in Chinese].
Cashmore, E. Ellis (1989), 'The Experience of Successful Career Women in Hong Kong', Hong Kong: Department of Sociology, University of Hong Kong, unpublished manuscript.
Census and Statistics Department (various years), *Census Reports*, Hong Kong: Hong Kong Government Printer.
────── (1991), *Hong Kong Annual Digest of Statistics*, Hong Kong: Hong Kong Government Printer.
────── (1991), *Hong Kong Statistics 1991*, Hong Kong: Hong Kong Government Printer.

────── (1993), *Hong Kong 1991 Population Census*, Hong Kong: Hong Kong Government Printer.
Chan, Po-king (1986), 'Industrialization and Sexual Equality — The Case of Hong Kong', *Asian Exchange* 4 (4, 5): 27–62.
Chan, W. K. (1991), *The Making of Hong Kong Society*, New York: Oxford University Press.
Chiu, Stephen and David Levin (1993), 'Labour under Industrial Restructuring in Hong Kong', *Occasional Paper, no. 21*, Hong Kong: Hong Kong Institute of Asia-Pacific Studies, The Chinese University of Hong Kong.
Choi, C. Y. and K. C. Chan (1973), *The Impact of Industrialization on Fertility in Hong Kong*, Hong Kong: The Chinese University and the Familiy Planning Association of Hong Kong.
Chow, Nelson (1990), 'Social Welfare', in Richard Y. C. Wong and Joseph Y. S. Cheng (eds.), *The Other Hong Kong Report 1990*, Hong Kong: The Chinese University Press.
Commissioner of Labour (various years), *Annual Report*, Hong Kong: Hong Kong Government Printer.
Ho, S. C. (1983), 'Sex Role Portrayals in Print Advertisements: The Case of Hong Kong', *Equal Opportunities International* 2(4): 1–4.
────── (1984), 'Women's Labour-force Participation in Hong Kong, 1971–81', *Journal of Marriage and the Family* 46(4): 947–56.
Hong Kong Government (1993), *Green Paper on Equal Opportunities for Women and Men*, Hong Kong: Hong Kong Government Printer.
Jaschok, Maria (1988), *Concubines and Bondservants*, Hong Kong: Oxford University Press.
Lau, S. K. (1981), 'Utilitarianistic Familism: The Basis of Political Stability', in Ambrose Y. C. King and Rance P. L. Lee (eds.), *Social Life and Development in Hong Kong*, Hong Kong: The Chinese University Press, pp. 195–216.
Lui, Tai-lok (1991), 'Waged Work at Home: Married Women's Participation in Industrial Outwork in Hong Kong', in Fanny M. Cheung et al. (eds.), *Selected Papers of Conference on Gender Studies in Chinese Societies*, Hong Kong: Hong Kong Institute of Asia-Pacific Studies, The Chinese University of Hong Kong, pp. 1–42.
Mak, Grace C. L. (1992), 'The Schooling of Girls in Hong Kong: Progress and Contradictions in the Transition', in Gerard A. Postiglione (ed.) *Education and Society in Hong Kong: Towards One Country and Two Systems*, Hong Kong: Hong Kong University Press, pp. 167–80.
Miners, Norman (1990), 'The Attempts to Abolish the *Mui Tsai* System in Hong Kong, 1917–1941', in Elizabeth Sinn (ed.), *Between East and West: Aspects of Social and Political Development*

*in Hong Kong*, Hong Kong: Centre of Asian Studies, University of Hong Kong.

Mitchell, Robert (1969), *Family Life in Urban Hong Kong*, Taipei: The Orient Cultural Service.

Mok Hoi (1993), *The Development and Structural Transformation of the Hong Kong Economy*, Hong Kong: Joint Publishing Co. [in Chinese].

Ng, C. H. (1991a), 'Familial Change and Women's Employment in Hong Kong', in Fanny M. Cheung et al. (eds.), *Selected Papers of Conference on Gender Studies in Chinese Societies*, Hong Kong: Hong Kong Institute of Asia-Pacific Studies, The Chinese University of Hong Kong, pp. 43–54 [in Chinese].

―――― (1991b), 'Women's Employment and Family Change', in Joseph Y. S. Cheng (ed.), *Building a New Era in Hong Kong*, Hong Kong: Breakthrough Press, pp. 54–68 [in Chinese].

Pearson, Veronica (1990), 'Women in Hong Kong', in Benjamin K. P. Leung (ed.), *Social Issues in Hong Kong*, Hong Kong: Oxford University Press, pp. 114–39.

Podmore, David (1971), 'The Population of Hong Kong', in Keith Hopkins (ed.), *Hong Kong: The Industrial Colony*, Hong Kong: Oxford University Press, pp. 21–54.

Salaff, Janet W. (1981), *Working Daughters of Hong Kong*, Cambridge: Cambridge University Press.

Sankar, Andrea (1978), 'Female Domestic Service in Hong Kong', in Louise Tilly et al. (eds.), *Female Servants and Economic Development*, Ann Arbor: Michigan Occasional Papers in Women's Studies, No.1.

Scott, Ian (1989), *Political Change and the Crisis of Legitimacy in Hong Kong*, Hong Kong: Oxford University Press.

Skeldon, Ronald (1991), 'Emigration, Immigration and Fertility Decline: Demographic Integration or Disintegration?', in Sung Yun-wing and Lee Ming-kwan (eds.), *The Other Hong Kong Report 1991*, Hong Kong: The Chinese University Press, pp. 233–58.

Tuen Mun District Board (1990), *Report of the Needs of Married Women in Tuen Mun*, Hong Kong: Tuen Mun District Board.

Watson, Rubie S. (1991), 'Wives, Concubines, and Maids: Servitude and Kinship in the Hong Kong Region, 1900–1940', in Rubie S. Watson and Patricia Buckley Ebrey (eds.), *Marriage and Inequality in Chinese Society*, California: University of California Press, pp. 231–55.

Wong, F. M. (1984), 'Effects of the Employment of Mothers on Marital Role and Power Differentiation in Hong Kong', in Ambrose Y. C. King and Rance P. L. Lee (eds.), *Social Life and Development in Hong Kong*, Hong Kong: The Chinese University Press, pp. 217–34.

Wong, Thomas W. P. (1991), 'Inequality, Stratification and Mobility', in Lau Siu-kai et al. (eds.), *Indicators of Social Development*, Hong Kong: Hong Kong Institute of Asia-Pacific Studies, The Chinese University of Hong Kong, pp. 145–72.

# 2 Women and Work: Opportunities and Experiences

*Thomas W. P. Wong*

A survey taken in 1990, put this question to a randomly selected sample of Hong Kong residents: 'Could you accept women working long hours for their careers?' While the proportion of respondents that could accept women working long hours was about the same as those who said they could not, more than 40 per cent of the men answered: 'It depends'; more than one-third of the women expressed the same ambivalence or uncertainty. Answers were more certain when respondents were asked if women should put their family before everything else, and give up their work if necessary: a clear majority, both men and women, disagreed.

The same survey also asked if they agreed with the following statement: 'Husbands are masters of the household and wives should submit to their authority.' Slightly more men agreed (one could interpret them as wanting that to be the case) than disagreed, while the reverse was the case for the women. Not surprisingly, it was the younger, more educated men and women who expressed opposition towards the 'patriarchal' regime. But regardless of sex, age, or education, the ambivalence of the respondents was quite evident and marked. In all cases, the answer 'it depends', a 'convenient', but not necessarily 'safe' or 'positive' option, ranged from one-quarter to more than one-third (Lee, 1992).

To an extent such findings highlight the reactions of the general public to the issue of women's commitment to the world of paid employment and their role in the family, but we must now ask: What is the meaning and the reality of, 'it depends'? The disapproval of placing family needs over women's participation in the labour market (we will not go into how much this disapproval is influenced by the utilitarian thought of having an extra pay-packet) has seemingly not translated into a greater willingness to support the development of careers for women: 'Of course, women should work, but do they really need a career?' Nor has the general support for gainful female employment contributed to a more positive espousal of an egalitarian family situation where 'family needs' are not necessarily determined by the masters of the household.

The degree of ambivalence or uncertainty in the responses suggests many problems, of choice and commitment, dilemma and indecision, faced by Hong Kong people, particularly women. With regard to opportunities and work experiences — what kind of jobs are open, are they worth taking, how long should one stay on, and so on — the considerations and circumstances involved in choice and commitment reflect constraints and resources, as they are in turn affected by class and family life-stages. This reality, beginning with individual responses, encompasses the family and institutional practices in the labour market, which should put quantitative findings on gender inequalities or discrimination in perspective.

The issues of choice and commitment, as they are confronted, negotiated, adjusted, and played out in women's lives, thereby influencing the position of women in the family as well as work, are still largely unresearched in Hong Kong. This is not an attempt to fill the lacuna; rather the concern is with the broad issue of gender differences in employment and remuneration. This attempt captures only part, and perhaps not the most important part, of the reality of women and work. The following findings are offered in the belief that the understanding of choice and commitment, and of all the concomitant strategies, is not just a necessary counterpart to overall indicators of gender inequalities; it is also a sociological understanding of important facets of, for want of a better term, the human condition.

The following is thus concerned with some of the gender differences in gainful employment: specifically, the features of the opportunities and experiences, of commitment and remuneration are laid out. Census data have been used: specific disaggregations and useful summary indices or pointers are provided.[1] It is clear that while there are instances where the inequalities and the inequities in women's work are amply supported by the available evidence, there are also issues on which available knowledge is insubstantial, tentative, or, in some cases, altogether lacking.

First the overall labour participation and occupation distribution of working women over the years is examined, assisted by a detailed occupational breakdown, gauging the degree of vertical and horizontal occupational segregation experienced by women. The position of single women is then considered. It is not unreasonable to assume that single women have a greater commitment to the labour market than do married women, and that their commitment is at least as great as that of men. It is thus useful to compare single women with single men for a better understanding of gender inequalities in the world of work: at least it is comparing like with like. Next some of the conceptual issues arising from women's employment are discussed; in particular, the implications of women's role in both work and the family, crucial for providing a necessary vantage point for understanding and judging the inequalities and invidiousness of the workplace. In conclusion there are some ruminations on choice and commitment — on the reasons for choice and the source of strength in commitment — and the way in which women relate to the public world of work and inequality.

## Labour Force Participation

It has been noted that the labour force participation rate for women in Hong Kong has increased over the years, a trend shared with many Western societies (Martin and Roberts, 1980; Arber and Gilbert, 1992). In 1961, the participation rate was 37 per cent; by 1991, it was about 50 per cent. Table 2.1 shows the age–sex-specific labour force participation rate for men and women from 1961 to 1991.[2] For the youngest age group, for both men and women, there has been a decline in the rate, due in part to the increased duration of full-time education. For the other age groups, there has been an increase in the participation rate over time, regardless of sex. Two other features are noteworthy; first, the oldest male age group still retains a fairly high rate, which is quite persistent over time. In contrast, about three out of four women have dropped out of the labour market by the time they reached 55 years or older. Secondly, there is little indication of a bimodal or two-phase work profile for the women, where middle-aged married women returned to work (in particular, part-time employment) after a temporary cessation of their participation following marriage or childbirth. While this work profile

## Table 2.1 Age, sex, and specific labour-force participation rate, various years (in percentage)

| Age | Sex | 1961 | 1971 | 1976 | 1981 | 1986 | 1991 |
|---|---|---|---|---|---|---|---|
| 15–19 | M | 54.3 | 50.4 | 43.0 | 45.2 | 37.9 | 35.2 |
|  | F | 47.9 | 56.4 | 47.2 | 42.6 | 33.6 | 28.6 |
| 20–24 | M | 89.2 | 90.2 | 87.8 | 90.9 | 88.3 | 84.8 |
|  | F | 51.1 | 69.5 | 71.8 | 79.7 | 83.7 | 82.9 |
| 25–34 | M | 97.8 | 98.4 | 97.7 | 98.3 | 97.6 | 96.5 |
|  | F | 33.9 | 39.6 | 47.7 | 56.8 | 64.8 | 68.4 |
| 35–44 | M | 98.3 | 98.6 | 98.4 | 98.6 | 97.7 | 96.9 |
|  | F | 38.0 | 38.7 | 42.9 | 53.4 | 57.9 | 57.0 |
| 45–54 | M | 96.9 | 96.6 | 95.0 | 96.0 | 94.1 | 92.9 |
|  | F | 42.1 | 38.9 | 36.9 | 46.7 | 49.1 | 49.1 |
| 55 & over | M | 73.6 | 70.1 | 61.1 | 60.3 | 71.4 (55–64) | 68.0 |
|  | F | 20.7 | 24.2 | 22.4 | 24.9 | 28.6 (55–64) | 24.4 (64 and above) 22.6 7.5 |
| Overall | M | 90.4 | 84.7 | 80.4 | 82.5 | 80.9 | 78.7 |
|  | F | 36.8 | 42.8 | 43.6 | 49.5 | 51.2 | 49.5 |

Note: The figures in this and other tables have been rounded and may not add up to 100.
Source: *Hong Kong 1976, By-Census, Main Report*; *Hong Kong 1981 Population Census*, Main Report; *1991 Population Census*, Main Report, Table 5.4.

has been a common feature in most Western industrialized societies (irrespective of whether the work is full-time or part-time), in Hong Kong, there is a downhill trend once the rate has peaked in the 20 to 24 age group. In the 1960s and 1970s, nearly two out of three women opted out of paid employment once they reached the age of 35. In the 1980s, it was one out of two.

The participation rate differential between men and women raises a more fundamental problem. For the great majority of adult men, long-term full-time employment is not questioned. The problem of choosing whether to stay in or opt out of the work-force seems only perplexing to women.[3] A recent study used logistic regression to examine the probability of married women working (the dummy variable being: to work or not). The study showed that, as expected, the age of a woman is negatively related to the probability of her working (Pong, 1992). Education is positively related to this probability, and its importance has increased over time: from 1976 to 1986, the positive effect (a partial derivative in terms of increasing the probability of married women working) of each additional year of education increased from 0.7 per cent to 1.5 per cent. This also demonstrates that the female labour force on the whole has become more educated.

Conversely, the positive effect of education has been largely offset by the number of children. A child at the stage of entering primary school reduced the probability of the mother working by 8 per cent in 1976. By 1986, this had increased very significantly to 24 per cent. Children aged 12 years and above still exerted a negative effect on the probability of working. The burden of child-rearing has, of course, long been recognized as a major factor in accounting for women's lower participation rate and their intermittent pattern of participation. What is noteworthy in Pong's analysis is that the benefits of the increase in women's educational level over the years (see Chapter 4), which presumably must have led to a decline in fertility rates as well as greater motivation for career-building, are still much counteracted by the reality of child-rearing. Indeed, with the educational system placing even more emphasis on the primary school performance, this reality has become even more onerous for married women.

It would seem a logical step to refine Pong's analysis by taking into account other variables, such as the socio-economic status and mobility experience of wives and families, and the difference between families at different stages of their lifecycle. Such findings would take us one step closer to the reality of constraints and resources, of choice and commitment. Pending such a study, it would still be helpful to offer a few observations. First, at the micro-level, the extent to which women have made use of the opportunities in the world of paid work is poised between the interplay of individual attributes (such as education) and structural parameters (such as size and complexity of family, the stage of family life-cycle, and the openness of the labour market, amongst others). At this level, every decision is a recognition of these two sets of considerations; every decision is a choice fraught with uncertainty. It is part of that 'it depends' reality, where women, but also their spouses, have to 'negotiate' more or less constantly with their family and with their work, between choice and commitment, picking their way, as it were, through the part-conducive, part-deterring ground of personal aspirations and collective constraints.

Secondly, on a more general level, the issue 'to work or not' is often posed in terms of two major factors determining the choice. The considerations involved include, on the one hand, the unequal and unfair gender division of labour in the world of paid employment, and, on the other, the inculcation of gender-role values leading to an acceptance of marriage and family as women's lot.[4] If the first set of considerations acts as a push factor, pushing away or deterring women from paid employment, the second set serves to pull women into what they perceive as a more attractive alternative.

The full nature of these forces, as played out in different periods of history, in different social classes or types of family, and the relative weight of the two sets of factors, remain to be studied. The data presented here look mainly at the objective conditions of the gender-based division of labour. The reality of the opportunities and segregation involved remains statistical and anonymous. The full meaning of women and work can only be elucidated when one knows both the objective conditions of constraints and opportunities, and the more personal conditions affecting women's choice and commitment in the face of work and family.

Table 2.2 shows how age and sex are related to occupational distributions over the years. It shows that between 1976 and 1991 there have been some interesting shifts in the proportion of women of different age groups in various occupations. Leaving production workers aside, it could be noted that the occupational 'spread' of younger women tends to be more even than that of older age groups, although a concentration of nearly one-quarter of the 20 to 24 age group in the clerical occupations in 1976 hardly contributes to that evenness! There is a notable drop in the number of older women in clerical occupations in both years; from 25 per cent in 1976 for the 20 to 24 age group, to 4 per cent for the 35 to 44 age group; in 1991, from 50 per cent to 17 per

## Table 2.2 Occupational distribution of women by age groups, 1976 and 1991 (in percentage)

| Age group | Year | Prof/Tech | Admin/Managerial | Clerical | Sales | Services | Prod |
|---|---|---|---|---|---|---|---|
| 20–24 | 1976 | 7.9 | 0.6 | 24.3 | 3.0 | 5.0 | 59.2 |
|  | 1991 | 16.6 | 1.4 | 49.7 | 16.7* |  | 15.5** |
| 25–34 | 1976 | 14.7 | 2.2 | 22.8 | 3.1 | 7.8 | 49.3 |
|  | 1991 | 18.0 | 5.3 | 35.4 | 10.6 |  | 30.6 |
| 35–44 | 1976 | 7.3 | 3.1 | 4.3 | 2.0 | 27.8 | 55.4 |
|  | 1991 | 12.3 | 7.7 | 16.8 | 11.7 |  | 51.4 |
| 45–54 | 1976 | 3.7 | 3.7 | 3.5 | 2.5 | 45.2 | 41.4 |
|  | 1991 | 10.8 | 5.9 | 8.3 | 9.6 |  | 65.2 |
| 55–64 | 1976 | 2.4 | 1.9 | 0.5 | 2.2 | 57.4 | 35.5 |
|  | 1991 | 5.6 | 4.4 | 3.5 | 8.1 |  | 78.4 |

\* The 1991 occupational classification scheme uses the category 'Service workers and shop sales workers' to include personal and protective service workers and salespersons, transport and other service workers. It excludes sales and service managers (subsumed respectively under sales and services occupations in the earlier census schemes) as well as street vendors and hawkers who are now grouped under elementary occupations in the 1991 classification.
\*\* For the 1991 classification scheme, 'production workers' includes the 'craft and related workers', 'plant and machine operators and assemblers', and 'elementary occupations'.
*Source*: One per cent sample tape of 1976; *Hong Kong 1991 Population Census, Main Tables*, Table C5.

cent, respectively.[5] In 1976, only 5 per cent of the youngest women were in the services occupations. For women in the 35 to 44 age group, there is a nearly six-fold increase in the proportion in these occupations.

A detailed breakdown of the service jobs shows that the majority are menial jobs such as cooking and cleaning. It is difficult to say if the older women represented an age cohort that had missed out on education, thus explaining the clustering in the lower service occupations, or whether it is a case of the combination of age and family life-cycle effects, where older women had a period of domestic absence, and returned to the labour market only to find job opportunities more limited. In contrast, working men have a more consistent (and, compared with working women, more 'even') occupational 'spread', suggesting that their greater attachment to the labour market has pay-offs in career-building and job security.

However, there have been some important changes for women in the professional group. After recoding the 1961 occupational categories to approximate the 1976 occupational scheme, one finds that the proportion of the 35 to 44-year-old women in professional occupations is only half of that in the 20 to 24 age group. By 1976, there was an increase in the proportion for the older age group, suggesting that more women were staying on in their jobs for a longer time.

## Gender Differences in Occupational Distribution

It is often noted that the gender-based division of labour has resulted in women being concentrated (or entrapped) in so-called women's jobs, and that those particularly disadvantaged are those who are married, relatively poorly educated, and older. The concentration of women into a few specific industries, and within those industries into a few specific occupations, and, further, into the lower-ranking, lower-status levels of those occupations, is borne out by the following tables. Table 2.3 shows the occupational distribution of working men and working women for the years 1961, 1976, 1986, and 1991. The proportion of women in the better occupations has risen: in 1961, 6 per cent of the women were in the professional grouping; in 1986, it had gone up to 10 per cent, and by 1991, to 15 per cent. In the 1980s, while the proportion of working men in the administrative/managerial category was largely unchanged, that of working women doubled. The proportion of women in clerical occupations increased most dramatically in the 1970s, with the result that more than one in four working women are now in 'white blouse' jobs.

It seems plausible to say that compared to working men, women tend to be clustered into a few occupations, something that has hardly changed since the 1960s. In the 1960s, working women were largely concentrated in the service and

Table 2.3 *Occupational distribution of working men and women (in percentage)*

| Occupation | 1961 M | 1961 F | 1976 M | 1976 F | 1986 M | 1986 F | 1991 M | 1991 F |
|---|---|---|---|---|---|---|---|---|
| Professional/Technical* | 4.6 | 6.3 | 5.0 | 7.0 | 7.6 | 9.6 | 14.1 | 15.1 |
| Admin/Managerial | 4.3 | 0.8 | 3.0 | 0.6 | 4.8 | 1.6 | 11.8 | 4.9 |
| Clerical | 6.9 | 3.3 | 8.6 | 11.8 | 9.7 | 22.7 | 8.2 | 28.5 |
| Sales** | 15.7 | 8.6 | 13.6 | 7.8 | 13.0 | 9.6 | 3.7 | 6.0 |
| Services*** | 11.4 | 24.3 | 15.1 | 14.5 | 16.3 | 16.1 | 22.4 | 23.3 |
| Agricultural | 6.6 | 9.2 | 2.8 | 2.4 | 2.0 | 1.8 | 0.6 | 0.4 |
| Production | 49.4 | 47.2 | 50.5 | 55.2 | 46.2 | 38.4 | 38.2 | 21.8 |
| Unclassified | 1.4 | 0.4 | 1.4 | 1.1 | 0.5 | 0.1 | 1.0 | 0 |

* This includes both the 'professional' and the 'associate professional' groups in the 1991 scheme.
** Salespersons and models in the 1991 scheme.
*** Personal and protective services workers, transport and other services workers in the 1991 scheme.

Note: The new occupational classification used in the 1991 census obviously creates many problems of comparability with earlier census data. The lack of guidelines for conversion, and the non-availability of detailed occupational sub-groups descriptions — not to mention the restriction on publishing recoded data based on the one per cent sample — have only complicated the problems.

Source: *Census Report 1961*, vol. III; *Hong Kong 1981 Population Census*, Main Report; *1991 Population Census*, Main Report.

sales occupations; in the 1980s, in the clerical and the service occupations. It is also possible to conjecture that the 'white blouse' jobs, especially those with a lower status, constituted a mobility ladder for the large number of women joining the labour market since the 1970s. These women, because of education or other factors, have a greater (but not necessarily more protracted) commitment to a career. Perhaps more than men, they were able to avoid manual work.[6] This seems to be particularly the case with single women, whose position is discussed in greater depth later.

If we turn to the gender distribution in the various occupational groupings, we find that the trend is towards a more balanced sexual mix in all occupations. From Table 2.4, it

*Table 2.4  Proportion of working men and women in different occupational groups (in percentage)*

|  | 1961 | | 1976 | | 1986 | | 1991 | |
|---|---|---|---|---|---|---|---|---|
| Occupation | M | F | M | F | M | F | M | F |
| Professional/Technical | 62.4 | 37.6 | 60.3 | 39.7 | 56.7 | 43.3 | 60.6 | 39.4 |
| Admin/Managerial | 93.0 | 7.0 | 89.8 | 10.2 | 83.1 | 16.9 | 79.8 | 20.2 |
| Clerical | 83.7 | 16.3 | 58.0 | 42.0 | 41.4 | 58.6 | 32.0 | 68.0 |
| Sales | 82.0 | 12.0 | 80.4 | 19.6 | 69.0 | 31.0 | 49.9 | 50.1 |
| Services | 54.0 | 46.0 | 63.2 | 36.8 | 63.0 | 37.0 | 61.1 | 38.9 |
| Production | 70.0 | 30.0 | 68.6 | 31.4 | 67.0 | 33.0 | 74.1 | 25.9 |

Source: Census Report 1961, vol. III; The Hong Kong Women's File, 1993.

can be seen that in the 1980s, not surprisingly, many more women than men were found in clerical occupations. There are still more male professionals than female; the improvement from the 1970s has not been impressive. However, the greatest disparity remains in the administrative/managerial jobs, the ratio between men and women in 1991 being 4 to 1.

It has been noted that such distribution based on broad occupational groupings may mask more serious gender disparities within individual occupations (Lui and Suen, 1991; AAF, 1993). More specifically, it has been argued that women's concentration in the 'helping occupations' such as nurses and teachers could have inflated the proportion of females in the professional occupations. Table 2.5 shows the gender disparity in a few selected occupational groupings, after taking out the primary/secondary school teacher from the professional category. In 1976, the ratio between women and men in the teacher occupation was 1.7; for the clerical workers, 0.7. The greatest disparities remained in the professional and the administrative/managerial jobs; for every ten professional males, there were four females; and for every ten male administrators/managers, there was only one female (See Lui and Suen, 1991: Table 3 for the 1976 comparison).

## Table 2.5  Gender disparity in a few selected occupational groups, 1976 and 1991

|  | Female:Male ratio 1976 | 1991 |
|---|---|---|
| Professional/Technical | 0:4 | 0:5 |
| Admin/Managerial | 0:1 | 0:2 |
| Teachers (primary & secondary school) | 1:7 | 2:7* |
| Clerical workers | 0:7 | 1:5 |

* The 1991 classification does not include secondary teachers, but does include primary school principals.
*Source*: One per cent sample of 1976 and 1991 *Hong Kong Population Census*.

For 1991, the findings are similar, except that now there are far more female clerical workers than male.[7] It thus seems that gender disparity is indeed greater when a more detailed occupational comparison is undertaken.

Does education make a difference to such disparities? Table 2.6 shows the differences between the female and male working population, with regard to levels of educational attainment, for the period from 1961 to 1991. Women's levels of education were significantly lower than those of men in the early years; the number of uneducated working women exceeded that of working men by 35 per cent in the early 1960s. By 1991, the situation had improved, especially with regard to the attainment of primary and secondary education. The number of women with no schooling dropped from 44 per cent in 1961 to 12 per cent in 1991. But the positive effect of better education on entry into the higher-status jobs was still limited. Table 2.7 shows the occupational distribution of working women with a university education. In 1991, nearly 50 per cent of them were in professional occupations, and 16 per cent in the administrative/managerial occupation. For men with the same educational level, the respective percentages were 50 per cent and 34 per cent. Having accounted for the level of education (and very high educational attainment

Table 2.6  Educational attainment of working population by sex, 1961 and 1991 (in percentage)

| Educational attainment | | 1961* | 1991 |
|---|---|---|---|
| No schooling | M | 7.6 | 6.0 |
| | F | 44.0 | 12.0 |
| Primary | M | 56.2 | 34.2 |
| | F | 37.9 | 30.7 |
| Lower secondary | M | 18.4 | 33.7 |
| | F | 7.4 | 24.0 |
| Matriculation | M | 12.0 | 6.8 |
| | F | 7.5 | 10.7 |
| Tertiary (non-degree) | M | 1.6 | 8.3 |
| | F | 1.5 | 12.2 |
| University | M | 3.8 | 11.0 |
| | F | 1.9 | 10.4 |

* The category 'private tutor' is not taken into account.
Source: *Census Report 1961*, vol. III; *Hong Kong 1991 Population Census*, Main Tables, Table C10.

Table 2.7  Occupational distribution of working women with a university degree, 1991 (in percentage)

| Occupational group | 1991 |
|---|---|
| Professional/Associate Professional | 48.0 |
| | (52.6)* |
| Admin/Managerial | 16.3 |
| | (33.6) |
| Clerks | 9.8 |
| | (4.3) |
| Others | 25.9 |
| | (9.5) |

* Figures for males in parentheses.
Source: *Hong Kong 1991 Population Census*, Main Tables, Table C10.

in this case), the disparity between male and female managers remains quite marked. Yet compared to the 1970s, there are now many more women with a university education in the professional group. Whether this means a larger pay-off for higher education levels remains to be studied with greater rigour.

The kind of education women receive tends to predispose them to certain occupations. In 1976, about 7 per cent of working females had some kind of vocational/technical training, compared to less than 4 per cent among their male counterparts. One-quarter of these women studied for teacher certificates, a figure twice that of men; another 60 per cent of the women enrolled in 'other vocational courses', such as stenography and bookkeeping. (By contrast, the majority of the men took technical and craft vocational training.) Such 'supplementary' education may or may not be undertaken with the purpose of compensating for the inadequacy of formal education, yet the taking of these courses predisposes women to specific occupational positions. In particular, the expansion of the junior white-collar jobs (the routine non-manual work) in the 1970s, of which some ethnographic information has been given by Salaff (1981), was met by a concentrated effort by young women to acquire the necessary skills.

## Occupational Segregation and Remuneration

Do the data examined so far indicate serious occupational segregation along gender lines? In particular, how serious is vertical segregation? Occupational segregation could be approached in two ways: at the level of aggregate data covering the society as a whole, based on census and labour-force survey data, or, at the company or establishment level (Martin and Roberts, 1980: 28). At the level of aggregate data, as noted earlier, indeed, in the professional and managerial occupations, the relative proportion of men and women is highly unequal. For the routine non-manual clerical work and the 'helping professions', there are more women than men, while for the sales, services, and production work, men had a slightly greater predominance. As for vertical segregation, it is easier to find data on segregation within an industry.

Data from the Vocational Training Council provided some evidence for such vertical segregation. In quite a large number of industries, including manufacturing (garments and electronics), commercial (wholesale and retail), and service (hotel) industries, more men than women were found in the more skilled, more responsible, and better-paid occupational positions (AAF, 1993: 19–23).

For vertical segregation within occupational groupings, we need information about the distribution of men and women in different skills and status (and other important aspects of job contentment) at company or establishment level. The census does not have such aggregate data, and no amount of recoding could produce the requisite data set. Levin (1991) made use of manpower surveys and examined the gender distribution among four skill/occupational levels in production-related jobs. In the case of the spinning industry, in 1967, the vast majority of both men and women were in the operative and unskilled category. By 1987, a sizeable percentage of the male workers were in the higher-skilled level of technicians and craftsmen, while the majority of women were still in the operative category. Two decades of industrial change, specific or general, seem to have widened the degree of vertical segregation for this industry.

Generalizations, however, are not easy, according to Levin (1991). The degree of vertical segregation in the clothing industry seems to have narrowed over the years, with women now accounting for over 40 per cent of the higher-skilled levels; in the electronics industry, there has been a sharp decline of women's participation at the technician/craftsman level. Much depends, among other things, on the original degree of women's concentration at the lower levels, and on the peculiar productive/technological characteristics of individual industries. If generalizations are difficult for production-related jobs, then it is nearly impossible for the non-manual occupations, where there is a paucity of information at the workplace level, and where the important differentials are not skills, but more slippery variables such as managerial or supervisory authority, and job status.

So far we have noted some of the features of women's participation in the world of paid work. These features pertain to objective conditions and reflect women's experience with

*Table 2.8   Monthly income (in HK dollars) and female–male earnings ratio, 1976, 1981, 1986, 1991*

| Year | Mean monthly earnings Male | Female | Female-Male earnings ratio |
|---|---|---|---|
| 1976 | 1,046 | 654 | 0:63 |
| 1981 | 2,091 | 1,504 | 0:72 |
| 1986 | 3,784 | 2,750 | 0:73 |
|  | Median monthly income* |  |  |
| 1991 | 6,100 | 4,600 | 0:75 |

* Constructed from 1991 Population Census, Main Tables, Table C18. The figures from the Main Report, Table 5.15 (by sex and age) are 6,000 and 4,250 respectively.
*Source*: Lui and Suen (1991); one per cent tape of 1991 census data.

commitment. What are the returns on job commitment in Hong Kong? In terms of general trends, it has been argued that the gender income gap has been narrowing since the mid-1970s. Table 2.8 gives the mean earnings and the earnings ratio between men and women for the years 1976, 1981, 1986, and the median earnings for 1991. The gap (in terms of mean earnings) has been reduced by about 10 per cent from 1976 to 1986. The difference in mean log earnings is –0.41 (1976), –0.35 (1981), –0.30 (1986), and –0.36 (1991). The narrowing of the gap is undoubtedly important, and more studies, following in the footsteps of the human capital tradition (e.g. studies on the effects of education and training on status — and income — attainment), are needed on the factors responsible for the narrowing. At the same time, after 25 years of better education and greater labour participation rates for women, the gap itself persists and the reduction of the gap is relatively small (although it is true that we have few useful yardsticks for such evaluations).

In considering the relative proportions of men and women in occupational groupings, Lui and Suen (1991) found that

## Table 2.9 Income ratios between men and women for selected occupations, 1991

| Occupational group | Median income ratio 1991 |
|---|---|
| Professional/Associate Professional | 0:87 |
| Admin/Managerial | 0:85 |
| Clerks | 0:92 |
| Service and sales workers | 0:73 |
| Craft and related | 0:65 |
| Plant operators, assemblers and elementary occupations | 0:64 |

*Source*: One per cent tape of 1976 and 1991 *Hong Kong Population Census* data.

the simple correlation coefficient between average male earnings for a specific occupation and the percentage of females in that occupation in 1976 was −0.09, suggesting that the better-paid jobs were more likely to have fewer women. However, the correlation weakened over the years: from −0.04 in 1981 to −0.02 in 1986. It should also be noted that these are overall indicators using broad occupational groupings. As Lui and Suen admitted: 'Finer occupational categories may reveal substantial differences between the sexes' (1991: 5).

Looking at more specific occupations, Table 2.9 shows the median income ratios for selected occupations in 1991. The clerical occupations represent the case closest to parity (0.92). However, inequality is very marked among the craft workers, the generally unskilled occupations of plant operators and assemblers, and the elementary occupations of street vendors and labourers. Overall, this pattern is similar to that in Western societies, where it is found that for the majority of occupations, the within-occupation wage (often hourly rate) ratio between women and men averages two-thirds; only in a few occupations were women paid four-fifths of the men's wages (Reskin and Roos, 1990).

If the variable of education is controlled, it is found that among the professional occupations, the mean income ratio between men and women, both with education up to the matriculation level, was 0.74 in 1976, and 0.82 in 1991. At the university education level, the ratios were 0.82 and 0.85, respectively.[8] The disparities seem to persist even after age difference (as a proxy for work experience) is controlled. Further, for every woman who had an income level more than the mean level in the professional occupations, three men had the same level of remuneration, after educational level had been taken into account. It is not unreasonable to assume that a woman with higher education working in the career-oriented professions represents the farthest a working woman could go, given the opportunity structure of the world of paid work. Then the evidence cited above suggests that her efforts and commitment have been unequally remunerated. This inequality is bound to influence her choice and commitment, and the implications in turn will capture something of the relationship between efforts and returns, between personal resources and social iniquities.

## The Case of the Single Woman

So far the discussion has surrounded the actual experience of women in paid employment, and their proportional over- or under-representation in different occupations. The differential returns on their 'commitment' are the result of actual experience, but this raises a more general issue about opportunity: do men and women have equal opportunities in paid employment? This comparison of men and women without regard to their marital status has been somewhat misleading because it disregards the influence of marriage on women's work opportunities. As Heath puts it, 'to talk of an opportunity is to assume that people can refuse it if they wish' (1981: 276). If a sizeable proportion of women had been socialized into gender-role stereotypes and either see marriage and family as a more attractive, or even natural, alternative, or see part-time, routine non-manual work as the normal pattern for working women, then the issue of refusal (or indeed, acceptance) does not arise for these women. The inequalities of opportunity between men and women cannot be tackled fully if this problem is not resolved. As a first

## Table 2.10 Educational attainment (aged 20 to 64) by sex, conjugal status and year, 1976 and 1991 (in percentage)

| Education | Year | Single women | Married women | Single men | Married men |
|---|---|---|---|---|---|
| Primary | 1976 | 28.1 | 74.3 | 41.0 | 58.9 |
|  | 1991 | 9.2 | 40.2 | 15.6 | 37.2 |
| Lower secondary | 1976 | 13.1 | 8.8 | 19.5 | 13.0 |
|  | 1991 | 12.0 | 21.1 | 24.4 | 23.3 |
| Matriculation | 1976 | 50.3 | 14.5 | 34.8 | 20.8 |
|  | 1991 | 55.9 | 30.2 | 40.2 | 26.5 |
| Tertiary | 1976 | 8.5 | 2.4 | 4.7 | 7.2 |
|  | 1991 | 23.1 | 8.4 | 19.7 | 12.9 |

Source: One per cent sample of 1976; 1991 data provided by the Census and Statistics Department (acknowledged with gratitude).

step the situation of single women must be looked at more specifically, comparing their occupational fortunes with those of single men. The assumption is that a single woman has at least as great a commitment to paid employment as does a man.

Tables 2.10 and 2.11 show, respectively, the educational and occupational profile of single women (aged 20 to 64), compared with that of single men, married men, and married women. Two points are obvious. First, the educational qualifications of single women are undoubtedly better than those of married women; more importantly, they are also better than those of single men. Secondly, as regards occupational fortunes, Table 2.11 shows that these women (presumably many of them upwardly mobile young women) were much more able than married women to avoid the unskilled manual jobs (12.4 per cent for single women, and 26.4 per cent for married women). They were also able to get into the helping professions such as teaching, social work, nursing, etc. (detailed breakdown not shown in the table), and, of course, clerical work.

Table 2.11  Occupational distribution by sex and conjugal status, 1991 (in percentage)

| Education | Single women | Married women | Single men | Married men |
|---|---|---|---|---|
| Professional/ Associate Professional | 18.0 | 12.4 | 18.1 | 11.9 |
| Managers | 2.9 | 6.4 | 5.3 | 15.5 |
| Clerical | 41.3 | 21.4 | 12.3 | 6.0 |
| Services and Sales | 13.7 | 11.8 | 17.1 | 12.1 |
| Craft and related | 3.0 | 5.5 | 22.2 | 20.7 |
| Machine operators and assemblers | 8.7 | 16.1 | 10.9 | 15.8 |
| Elementary occupations | 12.4 | 26.4 | 13.9 | 17.9 |

Source: Data provided by the Census and Statistics Department (acknowledged with gratitude).

Even though it is true that there is a concentration of these single women in junior white-collar work, it is undeniable that they have a greater ability to enter the lower-level professions. This, coupled with their better educational qualifications (compared to single men), again raises the issue of inequality of opportunity. If single women, and not employed women, are the more meaningful group to consider in tackling gender inequality of opportunity, and if these women must have had (though this is going to be somewhat controversial) a greater commitment to work than the single or married man (if only for the reason that they have made an important decision on the dilemma — work or family — faced by all women, but not men), then the achievements of these women would suggest that the inequality of opportunity is after all not that serious. Indeed one may be tempted to say that women actually have better chances.

But the matter does not rest there, for there is a catch. That there are opportunities for single women does not mean that once more women decide to pursue full-time work, even if mostly in 'women's work', the opportunities would still be there. Most probably, as Heath observed, these opportunities would vanish, given the current supply of such jobs (Heath,

1981). In other words, the opportunities will be significantly reduced for women, if more women decide to escape from the private regime of unpaid work and join the public world of paid work. The relatively better chances for the single women are thus, in this sense, 'subsidized' by those who either by choice or by circumstance are kept away from full-time employment. Further, the fact that the managerial occupations and the technician/supervisor positions are still the monopoly of males, suggests that there will be few higher-status and better-paid jobs, in addition to those 'helping professions', open to women.[9] Thus, as long as there is a notable number of women opting out of the labour market, and as long as most women (including the single) are 'debarred' from the managerial and skilled jobs, the full scale of sexual inequality will not be revealed. A further pointer to the actual degree of inequality is that the mean income ratio for single female and male professionals in 1991 is 0.8, after the level of educational attainment has been accounted for. It seems inequality or discrimination persists, even for single women.

The above has been a quantitative sketch of the experiences and opportunities in women's work. While there is improvement in women's education, and in their proportional representation in some occupations, inequalities are still very robust, and the gender income gap is still significant. It is further argued that such manifest inequalities may only be the tip of the iceberg, as the most committed and 'successful' career-oriented women have been, in a sense, subsidized by those who opted out. The real extent of discrimination can only be revealed if and when the latter group join full-time employment. While there are areas where arguments could be put forth with some certainty, there are also areas where data are lacking or inconclusive. In the latter case, the arguments presented here are best seen as tentative pointers and agenda-setters.

## The Cultural and Moral Side of Work

The above has attempted to establish two major points. In terms of experience, working women in Hong Kong are still disproportionately under-represented in the higher-status occupations (especially the managerial/administrative occupations). Despite general improvement in their educational attainment, in many kinds of occupations they are still unequally paid. Also, the occupational opportunities available to working women have increased greatly, especially for single women. However, such expansion has to be considered in the context that single women have benefited at the expense of married women.

We conclude by returning to the ambivalence and uncertainty which are evinced in women's (and men's) response to the questions about women's participation in, and commitment to work. In a way, the reality of 'it depends' claims women as its sole inhabitants. The choice (or dilemma) of 'work or family' is the starting point for all the inequalities and inequities that objective data portray with a greater or lesser exactitude or certainty. There are no subjective, ethnographic data on the considerations involved in the choice and commitment. It would be platitudinous to say that most women are denied choice and that this is so because of gender socialization or other similarly commonplace arguments. The diversities brought about by class, life-stage, cohort, vicissitudes of family, even marital status, are yet to be tackled systematically and rigorously. Moreover, there is little information about the ways women negotiate and build up their identity through family and work. It would be a travesty of what is intended in this chapter if the reader were to conclude from our findings that choice is a foregone conclusion. This is a view the data do not support.

There is a further dimension to the issue of choice and commitment. In the face of inequalities and segregation, one general view is to say that every effort should be dispensed in assisting women in succeeding in the world of paid work, for the latter is also the world of knowledge, and in modern society, possibly the only way to have an identity. Thus, it is frequently said, no effort should be spared to change the gender typing of jobs, the gender rankings of employers, and so on. And if the working woman happens also to be a wife, then her subjugation to the private world of unpaid work makes for a double exploitation. Thus in order to become a free and independent agent, to be sold to the highest bidder in the labour market, she has to rethink completely the domestic division of labour.

Such a view makes sense in so far as it correctly identifies the source of inequality and discrimination. Yet at the same time, it seems to be a poor prognosis of the response. As Gellner said, people feel happier when they are able to endorse the order they have to endure. People prefer to be loyal rather than merely cowed. Pointing out to women that they suffer from double exploitation will not make them happier, and it will not undermine both their and men's loyalties to the family. Moreover, whether and how women's participation in paid work will make them more ready to change the domestic division of labour depends on a number of things: on the kind of occupation they have (are they dead-end jobs anyway?), the values and attitudes instilled in their work life, and their general social experience. It will depend, above all, on whether the wife's socio-political identity is still largely derived from that of her husband.

The woman's choice is thus also a family choice, behind which there will be negotiation, adjustment, and domination. The 'it depends' reality, and the concomitant ambivalence, is only intelligible when this is understood. Too often, the double exploitation view neglects one of the important tenets of Marxism (which remains fundamental, however defective it is in other matters): that inequality and conflict are neither inherent in one's nature nor one's general situation, but in an historically and sociologically specific situation, engendered by the divison of labour and differential control over the means of production (Gellner, 1988: 241). Too often, the issue of double exploitation glosses over the struggles, as well as the stolid nature, of that specific situation.

## 'What do we do and how shall we live?': Ruminations on Work

One important point the above view often misses, is the fact that the choice involved in the 'work or family' dilemma itself could be a source of strength; as the choice is perhaps unique to women, whatever strength contained therein will be theirs only. To 'point the moral and adorn the tale', it is worthwhile to ponder again over the problem that Virginia Woolf mused upon more than fifty years ago. In *Three Guineas*, she asked: should women (or 'daughters of all educated men') join that procession 'of the sons of educated men, ascending those pulpits, mounting those steps, passing in and out of those doors, preaching, teaching, administering justice, practising medicine, making money?' If so, then on what terms? Her answer to the first question, as it appeared slowly but strongly from her insinuating, deceptively hesitant, style, is affirmative. But the choice is not easy, for

> Behind us lies the patriarchal system; the private house, with its nullity, its immorality, its hypocrisy, its servility. Before us lies the public world, the professional system, with its possessiveness, its jealousy, its pugnacity, its greed. The one shuts us up like slaves in a harem; the other forces us to circle, like caterpillars head to tail, round and round the mulberry tree, the sacred tree, of property (Woolf, 1938).

Woman needs to join the procession, so as to have 'a room of her own', to form her independent and intelligent opinion. The most important question is: on what terms? The strength of woman, and the strength that she could muster in making the choice and setting the terms, lies, according to Woolf (1938), in four qualities of women's unpaid-for education. These four qualities are to become the terms on which women join the professional world. First, poverty: by that is meant only enough money to live upon, a modicum of health, leisure, and knowledge for development of body and mind, but not a penny more. Second, chastity: when a woman wishes to live by her work, she must refuse to sell her brain for the sake of money; she must break away from that mulberry tree. Then, derision: abstain from advertising merit, holding ridicule, obscurity, and censure as preferable to fame and praise; if 'badges, orders or degrees are offered you, fling them back in the giver's face'. Lastly, freedom from unreal loyalties: from the 'old school tie', from family pride, gender pride. Women after all have fewer such bondages than men.

No doubt Woolf's 'daughters of educated men' are a little remote from our present compulsory mass education. No doubt, her views are gently advisory, and her exhortations moral in nature. But to the extent that they have a universal purview and contemporary relevance, they also suggest that the choice between family and work is a battle, where women are — if we are not to treat those four qualities flippantly — better empowered than men. It is a battle as critical as that fought at the public legislation front, and too often, the minor issues of the latter cloud the major ones closer to home.

Women's long and continuing dispossessed claim to the top positions in the professional world could be turned into a source of strength, a basis of an identity which is distinct from that conferred by work and the public world of citizenship or civil society. (This is sometimes called the Wollstonecraft dilemma, in contrast to the Hegelian dilemma; see Pateman, 1992a.[10]) This strength means that women, in choosing whether to work and in laying down the terms, could better reveal the invidiousness and iniquities of the male world, and the debilitating effects of endless work. What women could contribute is thus far more important, in a generally cultural and moral way. In a sense, they contribute to a socialist cause, if by socialism we agree with Orwell that, shorn of its intellectual garbage, it is basically common decency and justice. The four qualities of women's unpaid-for education could serve to highlight the need for common decency and justice in both the public world of employment and the domestic one of family labour. They bring fundamental values to centre stage, and there, on that stage, if *The Road to Wigan Pier* script is to be enacted, sexist or misogynist charges and counter-charges would give way to a common desire and common efforts for a rightful and civilized place in work as in family, and for a personal life that is more than recovering from work.

## Notes

1. The recent publication by the Association for the Advancement of Feminism (AAF) of the *Hong Kong Women's File*, in particular, the chapters on employment and family, has collated most of the existing quantitative data on our topic. The book has almost single-handedly placed the study of Hong Kong women on a secure and irrevocable — both empirical and theoretical — footing. If that book has not obviated the need for yet another attempt to broach a similar topic, or more generally, the problem of women in Hong Kong, it is not for the reason that we have

better data or better vision. The justification lies more in attending in a more detailed manner to issues raised in the book, and in suggesting alternative or additional knowledge building blocks for the field as a whole.
2. There are two points concerning the use of census materials for this and other tables. First, in order to have common classification categories for faciliating comparison of the different censuses (thus making it possible to ascertain the pattern or direction of changes), it is sometimes necessary to resort to 1 per cent sample data as well as from the findings published in main reports or main tables. Obviously the coexistence of figures drawn from the 1 per cent data sets and figures constructed from the full samples is not wholly satisfactory. The findings presented must then be interpreted with this caveat in mind. Secondly, as statistics from the 1 per cent data of the 1991 census could not be published, the continuity in longitudinal comparison becomes impossible. The published tables on age–sex-specific labour force participation rates for 1961, 1971 and 1976 have a different age group classfication from the later censuses. The access to the 1 per cent data sets makes it possible for the researcher to overcome these comparison problems, as well as facilitating the formulation of new hypotheses and pointers. To take another example, one could not derive the mean incomes for the 1991 census (for a different, but perhaps equally justified, research or analytical purpose), other than constructing the figures from the full sample. (Published data are on the median incomes only.) Some of the 'anomalies' in the tables of this chapter, different values of the variables or different classification schemes, thus result from the difficulties in making public the findings from the 1991 of data set 1 per cent.
3. Lest it be thought that such a choice necessarily implies dilemmas and hardships, it is ruminating on the possible strength in making that choice, which is done in a later section.
4. In 1991, the labour participation rate of married women was about half that of unmarried women.
5. Due to the use of different occupational classification schemes in the various censuses, the comparability of occupational groupings is always ambiguous. In cases where the differences are not critical, the original categories will be retained. In other cases, the more recent census schemes are recoded to the earlier schemes in order to make comparisons possible.
6. A breakdown of the professional grouping (based on either the two-digit or three-digit group in the census) for the census years shows that half of the women 'professionals' were teachers, roughly double that of the men.

7. The position of women manual workers has not been dealt with in detail partly due to the fact that the census schemes are not quite amenable to meaningful disaggregation in terms of skill and occupation level, and partly because Levin (1991) has given a succinct description of women workers in a few selected manufacturing industries.
8. Lui and Suen (1991) gave the income gap between male and female employees having university level education as 35 per cent. Having accounted for the type of education, it does seem that the gap is narrowed somewhat.
9. The idea of 'job queue, gender queue' proposed by some scholars is useful to capture the changing occupational offerings that become available to women, as men in these occupations go to greener pastures. The extent that women make inroads into these traditionally male-dominated occupations (as real estate agents, reporters, or even bus drivers, to take the American case in the 1970s), to queue up to enter better jobs as they come along will depend on occupational growth, employers' re-ranking of the sexes, men's re-ranking of occupations, not to mention the efforts by women to change employers' preferences and general gender stereotyping in occupations (see Reskin and Roos, 1990).
10. This is a variant of the debate between 'equality' and 'difference'. The gist of the matter, according to feminist theorists like Pateman and Flax, is this: how does one struggle for a different conception and reality of women's citizenship, while taking into account the rights, capabilities, and, above all, distinctiveness of women and motherhood, under the conditions of a patriarchal state or public sphere? Feminists in the 1980s were trying to get to grips with Wollstonecraft's ideas, to see how far one could go in following her argument. Mary Wollstonecraft argued simultaneously for equality and the recognition of difference. She called for equal civil and political rights for women and their economic independence from their husbands — stating, 'Let woman share the rights and she will emulate the virtues of man' — and, at the same time, for women's citizenship to be expressed differently from men's (Pateman, 1992b).

## References

Arber, Sara and Gilbert, Nigel (1992), *Women and Working Lives*, London: Macmillan.

Association for the Advancement of Feminism (1993), The *Hong Kong Women's File*, Hong Kong: Hong Kong Association for the Advancement of Feminism [in Chinese].
Census and Statistics Department (various years), *Census Reports*, Hong Kong: Hong Kong Government Printer.
Census and Statistics Department (various years), *Hong Kong Population Census*, Hong Kong: Hong Kong Government Printer.
Charles, Maria (1992), 'Cross-National Variation in Occupational Sex Segregation', *American Sociological Review*, 57(4): 483–502.
Heath, Anthony (1981), 'Women who Get on in the World — Up to a Point', *New Society*, 12 February, pp. 275–8.
Larkin, Philip (1983), *Required Writing*, London: Faber and Faber.
Lee, M. K. (1992), 'Family and Gender Issues', in S. K. Lau et al. (eds.), *Indicators of Social Development 1990*, Hong Kong: Institute of Asia-Pacific Studies, The Chinese University of Hong Kong, pp. 1–32.
Levin, David (1991), 'Women and the Industrial Labour Market in Hong Kong: Participation and Perceptions', in S. G. Scoville (ed.), *State Influences in Third World Labour Markets*, New York: de Gruyter.
Lui, H. W. and Suen, W. (1991), *'The Narrowing Gender Gap in Hong Kong: 1976–1986'*, mimeographed paper.
Martin, Jean and Roberts, Ceridwen (1980), *Women and Employment: A Life-Time Perspective*, London: Her Majesty's Stationery Office.
Pateman, Carole (1992a), 'The Patriarchal Welfare State', in Linda McDowell and Rosemary Pringle (eds.), *Defining Women*, London: Polity Press, pp. 223–45.
Pateman, Carole (1992b), 'Equality, Difference and Subordination: The Politics of Motherhood and Women's Citizenship', in G. Bock and S. James (eds.), *Beyond Equality and Difference*, London: Routledge, pp. 17–31.
Pong, Suet-ling (1992), 'Education, Women's Work and Family Income Inequality', in Y. P. Chung and Richard Y. C. Wong (eds.), *The Economics and Financing of Hong Kong Education*, Hong Kong: The Chinese University Press, pp. 141–74.
Reskin, Barbara and Roos, Patricia (1990), *Job Queues, Gender Queues: Explaining Women's Inroads into Male Occupations*, Philadelphia: Temple University Press.
Salaff, Janet W. (1981), *Working Daughters of Hong Kong*, Cambridge: Cambridge University Press.
Wainright, Hilary (1980), 'Women and the Division of Labour', in P. Abrams and R. Brown (eds.), *UK Society: Work, Urbanism and Inequality*, London: Weidenfeld and Nicolson, pp. 198–245.
Woolf, Virginia (1938), *Three Guineas*, London: The Hogarth Press.

# 3 Bringing Women Back In: Family Change in Hong Kong

## Ng Chun-hung

We often hear the complaint that the study of Hong Kong society is handicapped by the absence of requisite data on crucial aspects of social life. Until we get the facts right, the complaint goes, all debates remain purely speculative. While it is possible to feel sympathy for such a call for systematic fact finding for Hong Kong studies, a caveat must be registered.

Facts do not speak for themselves. The questions posed determine much of what is found. On the subject of women and the family, a sizeable pool of pertinent 'facts' have accumulated over the years. However this has brought us no closer to a consensus on what has happened, and how things will change.

This chapter is an attempt to construct a pointed narrative that will flesh out the major lines of dissension in the existing studies, highlight some important but neglected findings about women and the family, and show why it is time to ask a different set of questions. The key spirit of the argument, as the title of the paper states, is to bring women themselves back into studies about family change. That is, to recognize the active role that women play both inside and outside their families. In this respect, this chapter complements the broad, structural approach adopted in Benjamin Leung's chapter on women and social change, where the predicament of Hong Kong women is analysed essentially in terms of the large-scale changes that have occurred in the society. The purpose of the following discussion is to add 'flesh and blood' to the 'skeletal framework' of the earlier chapter.

Two poles of thought have emerged over the last ten years in studies of women and families in Hong Kong: the dominant, functionalist tradition, and the 'new orthodoxy' on gender inequality. The recent spate of empirical findings seriously questions the optimistic, functionalist view concerning women and the family. It is found that women continue to be socially and economically disadvantaged, and that this is intimately connected to their subservient position within the family. This 'new orthodoxy', however, has failed to trigger significant innovative studies, and the functionalist paradigm continues to hold sway in more practice-oriented fields like social work and social administration.

This stalemate stems from the absence of a deeper theoretical examination of the dominant functionalist framework. In fact, in asking simple, factual questions intended to reveal the 'true' patterns of division of labour and power in families, the 'new orthodoxy' shares many of the same problems of the functionalist position. Its reliance on a crude 'gender role socialization' theory also fails to pinpoint the reasons for women's contradictory experience and response. Leung's discussion in Chapter 1 begins with the functionalist perspective on the relationship between industrialization and the alleged concomitant changes in women's status, and then continues with a critique of this perspective with recourse to the thesis of the persistence of traditional Chinese patriarchy and gender socialization. As such it dwells mainly on the functionalist and the 'new orthodoxy' paradigms. In the following discussion, I shall argue for the importance of understanding women's contribution to the household economy, and the ambivalent identity and resultant choice of action on women's part as the basis to break the current deadlock.

## The Functionalist Paradigm

A retrospective look at the study of women and families in Hong Kong highlights a dividing line beginning in the 1980s (Ng, 1994). Studies prior to that period tended to follow the footsteps of Wong Fai Ming's pioneering work on the relations between industrialization and family change. The primary impetus came from a fascination with the impact of post-war Westernization and modernization on local social institutions and practices. The theoretical underpinning was unmistakably functionalist. Functionalism in social studies represents a school of thinking that stresses the universal impact of industrialization on societies. It is said that industrialization everywhere has brought about a drastic transformation of society, Hong Kong being no exception. Institutions respond to the calls and demands of industrialization by changing their outlook, rules and practices (Yang, 1981). Thus the new guiding value of the market emphasizes achievement over ascription, merits over social origins. The search for efficiency and professionalism triumphs over customs and traditions. The widespread social and geographical mobility necessitated by industrialization breaks down age-old ties and establishes novel allegiance and networks. The unwieldy, conservative, extended families that allegedly predominated in the pre-industrial era were the first casualties in this incessant march towards modernization. The nuclear family, with a more open outlook and streamlined composition, provided the 'best fit' for the demands of the new era (Wong, 1975: 985–7).

It is further reasoned that this change in prevalent family size, composition, and form must have major repercussions on intra-familial relationships and ideals. Devoid of the cushion of the extended family, members of modern nuclear families now turn to each other for emotional support. Care and communication take the place of order and discipline. The 'structurally isolated nuclear family' is at the same time a more democratic, egalitarian family (Wong, 1975: 1981).

The impact of such changes on women's lives in and outside the family is obvious. Industrialization provides increased education and employment opportunities which are open to women. The movement to the nuclear form of family is said to have eradicated many of the former obstacles that inhibit women's gainful activities. It, for instance, encourages a lower birth rate and later marriage, which together means lighter and shorter duration of family and child-care burdens. Such impact of industrialization on the lot of Hong Kong women has been amply illustrated in Leung's chapter on women and social change. Further, the emphasis on conjugal support brings a new level of egalitarian relationship in terms of sharing household tasks and decision-making. The net outcome of all this is for women in Hong Kong to break decisively with the stranglehold of the oppressive, patriarchal families of the past, if not precisely now, then surely in the not so far future (AAF, 1993: 57–8). The whole process of change, as befitting the ambitious, confident tone of functionalism in the 1960s, has been posited not only as a likely empirical trend, but also as part of the unfolding of a universal, inevitable world pattern.

This version of women and family change has become the dominant, even exclusive paradigm in the twenty years since Wong's first publication (Ng, 1994). This is not difficult to understand. For one thing, it captures many of the relevant empirical trends of the period. Studies up to this day continue to confirm the by-now indisputable trends towards lower birth, later marriage, predominance of the nuclear family form, and some of the associated changes in gender relations and female economic participation.[1] Perhaps more significantly, the functionalist version was taken to heart because the analysis is neat, robust, and comes with seemingly unimpeachable intellectual credentials. Its influence cuts across the disciplinary boundaries of sociology, social work and social administration, not least for its ability to provide a useful map for identifying adaptive and maladaptive tendencies in Hong Kong families. Small wonder it caught the imagination of policy makers, and became the informing spirit behind policies on youth and family life education which sprang up in the 1970s (Ng, 1989).

## The Rise of the 'New Orthodoxy'

There were contradictory studies even in the heyday of functionalist dominance, but a concerted attempt to construct an alternative version of women and family change only materialized in the last ten years.

Slowly it became clear that most of the solid, empirical observations made concerning women and family change in the functionalist paradigm in fact pertain only to family form and structure, such as family size, composition and household forms. In contrast confident assertions were often made concerning the future of gender relationships and power on the basis of flimsy, anecdotal evidence. This leap of argument reveals the achilles heel of the functionalist paradigm. Functionalism is at root a theory of systems. Its concern is essentially how society, as a complex system, responds to the need for change by initiating a series of adaptive adjustments on the part of its constituent subsystems. In this view, modern society is propelled by the imperatives of industrialization to modify its subsystems, such as the work system, the education system, the political system and, of course, the family system. The causation flows from larger systemic needs to subsystem adaptation (Smith, 1973).

The strength of functionalism lies in spelling out broad stimuli and constraints. Its weakness lies correspondingly in reducing the importance of the actual mechanisms, relationships and experience inside the constituent subsystems. If the larger script is already written, why bother with the detailed, 'nitty gritty' response? Women's fate is submerged within the family system, which is in turn a relatively passive onlooker in historical change. The easy and crude extrapolations from family form and structure to relationships and ideals, can be made so confidently because women's improved situation is seen as a necessary by-product of this long march of human progress (Ng, 1991a: 45–6).

As a result, despite the constant references to changing trends in family form and structure, relatively little evidence has been produced concerning family relationships and power up to the 1980s. Such a glaring gap defines the character of the subsequent critique, and later, the 'new orthodoxy' in women and family studies. The spectre of the patriarchal Chinese family is simply too fresh in our memory and too tenacious in practice for us to accept the verdict on 'symmetrical family' and gender equality. The recent spate of studies under this banner thus concentrated on discovering the 'truth' about family relations and domestic ideals and assessed the 'genuine' extent of gender inequality. The general picture to emerge from these studies seriously questions the validity of the functionalist paradigm. In fact, they cumulatively demonstrate beyond reasonable doubt the contrasting role and power of the sexes inside families in Hong Kong.[2]

## Household Division of Labour

Beginning in the early 1980s, a number of social service agencies carried out surveys to ascertain the 'needs' of women in Hong Kong, with emphasis on their domestic responsibilities (AAF, 1993: 149–53). The studies differ in subjects (married and unmarried, working and non-working, working and middle-class women), sampling method (random and non-random), sample size (from six to over three thousand), format of questionnaire, scope and territorial coverage. However, they concur on the verdict that it is the woman (typically the female household head) who still performs the lion's share of the childcare and everyday household tasks. This picture is confirmed by the three recent social indicators surveys carried out by teams of sociologists from three tertiary institutions in Hong Kong (Lau and Wan, 1987; Lau et al, 1991; Lau et al, 1992). For instance, in the survey of 1986, it was found that in over 60 per cent of cases, it was the female household head who was chiefly in charge of the daily household tasks like cooking, washing dishes, cleaning and ironing. As little as 8 per cent of the cases have a male household head in charge of the same duties (Lau and Wan, 1987). In a survey the author conducted among a sample of largely working-class households in Tuen Mun, the pattern of child-rearing shows an even more skewed picture, with a female head in charge in 82.5 per cent of the cases, and a male head in a paltry 0.6 per cent (Tuen Mun District Board, 1991: 18).

A study carried out by the Hong Kong Young Women's Christian Association and Shue Yan College in 1981 shows a more balanced pattern existing for the professional group of respondents, whether in terms of daily household tasks or childcare (Hong Kong Young Women's Christian Association and Hong Kong Shue Yau College, 1982). However, the lesser burden of the women in this respect had been brought about not by husbands' increasing their share of responsibility, but by delegating such a burden to their parents and employed helpers. In any case, a disproportionate number of female household heads still had to take such matters into their own hands, irrespective of which class they belonged to (Table 3.1).

Moreover, most female respondents in the above-mentioned surveys expressed that their household responsibilities had adversely influenced their employment and work decisions. The study in Tuen Mun shows that prior to marriage or giving birth to the first child, over 90 per cent of the respondents (married females between the ages of 20 and 55) had continuous experience of full-time employment. At the time

## Table 3.1 Clothes washing by household members (in percentage)

|  | Professional | Clerical | Manual | Sample |
|---|---|---|---|---|
| Mother | 40.0 | 47.7 | 52.1 | 48.5 |
| Father | 1.3 | 2.3 | 1.3 | 1.5 |
| Grandparents | 6.3 | 15.1 | 13.7 | 13.5 |
| Parents | 6.3 | 4.1 | 4.2 | 4.5 |
| Siblings | 0.0 | 1.2 | 1.0 | 1.3 |
| Servants | 12.5 | 10.5 | 0.6 | 5.0 |
| Him/herself | 15.0 | 8.7 | 13.7 | 12.2 |
| Others | 2.5 | 0.6 | 1.0 | 1.0 |
| Everybody | 8.8 | 3.5 | 3.5 | 4.5 |
| n.a. | 7.5 | 6.4 | 8.9 | 8.1 |
|  | (n=80) | (n=172) | (n=313) | (n=606) |

*Source*: Hong Kong Young Women's Christian Association and Shue Yan College 1982: 17.
*Note*: Some of the above figures have been rounded off for this table and thus do not add up to 100 per cent.

of interview, 54 per cent did not have any form of gainful activities, 25 per cent were in part-time jobs, and 15 per cent were employed as outworkers. In none of the cases did this pattern of job interruption apply to their spouses (Tuen Mun District Board, 1991: 11–18). Wong (Chapter 2) examines the other side of this coin in his chapter on women and work.

## Conjugal Power

This is one area where firm evidence is understandably hard to come by. Wong (1981) argues, on the basis of his survey evidence, that women who did not work were having more say in decision-making inside the household than those in gainful employment. However the same set of data revealed the increase in female power to be mostly in the areas of child care and control of household duties. Even working women did not make significant gains in the areas of economic and social decisions (Wong, 1981: 228). There were instances of reported 'sharing of decision-making', but the actual nature of such sharing is far from clear. In the Social Indicators Survey of 1990, 32 per cent of the households indicated the male head as the chief decision-maker in family matters, whereas only 13.7 per cent of the female heads were thus indicated (Lee, 1992). In view of the overwhelming predominance of the latter in performing the actual household tasks, this cannot, by any stretch of the imagination, be called an egalitarian pattern. Furthermore, studies in the West have demonstrated the close link between controlling the family purse and a dominant voice in important areas of family decision-making such as timing and pattern of employment for household members, investment, and residential movement (Leonard and Speakman, 1986). In the Social Indicators Survey of 1986, 50.2 per cent of the male heads were reported to be the one chiefly responsible for supplying family expenditure, in contrast to 4.9 per cent of the female heads (Lau and Wan, 1987: 37). There are indeed good reasons to believe that the male household heads are still in a dominant position within the average family in Hong Kong.

It is safe to say that if the status of women inside the families of Hong Kong today is improving, the extent of change is certainly less than dramatic. For women in working-class households, as the plethora of studies referred to demonstrates, the promise of an egalitarian conjugal pattern is obviously premature. Many of them truncated their employment on marriage or on the birth of their children, only to re-enter as part-timers or outworkers, or to languish in dead-end jobs (AAF, 1993: 11–12). They openly deplored their situation in and outside the families, reported instances of depression and low self-esteem, and opted to stay out of the role of full-time housewife if they were to be allowed the choice (AAF, 1993: 77). The resulting message is loud and clear. The dominant interpretation of women and family change is shown to have ignored the continued plight of many women. The situation of women is not part of the unfolding plan of social progress. Seen in conjunction with the systematic disadvantages that women experience in the world of employment, education, social service provision and political participation — the subjects of discussion in several of this book's other chapters — one can say gender inequalities still pervade Hong Kong society on every level (AAF, 1993).

Given such an overwhelming convergence of evidence, it is not difficult to see why a 'new orthodoxy' in family studies has been erected in a relatively short period of time, and why a new political agenda clamouring for the eradication of gender discrimination could take institutional root (Hong Kong Legislative Council, 1992).[3]

However the starkness of the 'facts', and the rapidity with which this new version has been taken on board may have seriously hampered the subsequent vitality of such an intervention. It seems the answers have come before the questions have had time to be formulated properly. As the facts of lingering gender inequalities are so obvious and pervasive, it is easy to count on existing, relatively simple concepts for explanation. Hence gender role theory, postulating the tenacity of culture and the inertia of past socialization practices, becomes the cornerstone of the new paradigm. The persistence of women's plight can then be neatly explained in terms of the survival of obviously powerful traditional Chinese culture, stereotypical socialization practices in child training and schooling, and portrayals in the mass media. After all, in many respects, Hong Kong remains a very traditional, Chinese society despite its cosmopolitan veneer. Industrialization does not guarantee the goods; culture and socialization have to be transformed to enable women to be brought back in.

## Beyond the Stalemate

The new orthodoxy does serve to reopen the case for considering women's continued subordination in society. However, amidst the crescendo of research activities, one can sense that the impetus is petering out, almost as rapidly. This is unfortunate, for there are indeed a host of interesting and difficult questions to be asked. Questions like: if gender role socialization is responsible for women's subordination, then who and what are the agents participating in such socialization? Why do they keep on churning out monolithic messages downgrading the contribution of women? How do parents benefit by constructing an inferior path for their beloved daughters? Why do the mass media continue to typecast women when manifestly women today are diversifying their roles in real life? Have these agents always been successful in perpetuating such 'traditional' gender stereotypes? How do women, who are alleged to be at the receiving end of all this, experience and evaluate their own situation? Why do women continue to give consent to a regime that systematically downgrades their interests?

These questions are about contradictory trends, detailed mechanisms and multiple experiences. They are seldom asked because the gender role socialization framework is a very broad brush not adept at handling such nuanced, troublesome questions. The world of all-conquering, pervasive gender role socialization does not admit contradictions, except as *ad hoc* maladaptations. We can keep on generating facts about unequal sexual division of labour, but the explanation in terms of a vague but overarching pattern of sex role socialization is ultimately unconvincing, because it provides no means to assess the origins of such converging socialization practices, to account for their ambivalent existence, and point to concrete sources of change (Ng, 1992: 170–1). Moreover, by pointing the finger solely at the survival of traditional Chinese culture, the gender role framework can easily be incorporated back into the optimistic functionalist narrative. The stubborn persistence of gender inequalities in and outside the families can be seen as the swan-song of a dying culture, soon to be eradicated by the enlightened attitude and meritocratic practices of a new generation. Industrialization and its attendant imperatives are for the future. Chinese culture, and hence gender inequalities perpetuated on that basis, will in due course be swept back to their proper, archaic enclave.

This in a nutshell is the stalemate in women and family studies. The functionalist paradigm has been discredited by new-found 'facts', but the 'new orthodoxy' fails to connect with real world complexities and ignite further rounds of innovative studies. The trouble is not a question of data, but is thoroughly theoretical. The gender role socialization framework lacks a solid theoretical response to the functionalist paradigm. It lacks a detailed critique of the explanatory logic of the latter, and fails to advance an alternative view of social change capable of grasping the complex interplay of structure and agency over time.

What is needed is a systematic explanation, a theory, that can grasp the significance of the above-observed contradictory processes, take note of the advances that women have genuinely made, and still offer an explanation for the persistence and regeneration of gender inequalities in Hong Kong society. The way to do this is to put gender role socialization into context, to highlight the conflicting tendencies thrown up by the process of industrial development (both of these have been addressed in some detail in Leung's chapter), specify the mechanisms and agents involved, and see how household members respond to such challenges and construct their own identities (Ng, 1989; 1991a). This last point is especially worthy of note. Both existing frameworks have relegated questions of women's experiences, their pressure and resistance, and their gains and sacrifices to the background. The attempt to bring women back in must contain a serious engagement with the active and multifarious ways in which women have been involved in Hong Kong's postwar social change. It has to bring to the foreground women's contradictory experiences.

The following discussion will go on to show that many studies carried out over the years feed into such a reorientation. They usually come in three interconnected shapes: 1) rethinking the nature and history of industrialization, 2) discovering women's contribution to the household economy, and 3) examining women's contradictory identity.

## *Rewriting the History of Industrialization*

The emergence of a new understanding of industrialization in other areas of women's studies has been discussed elsewhere (Ng, 1991a; Lee and Ng, 1991). Here I will only reiterate the main points. Industrialization should not be seen as a uniform process which will generate similar outcomes everywhere. The expansion of economic opportunity and a more liberal social climate did provide an impetus for women's relief from household obligation and facilitate widened participation. However, as Thomas Wong's chapter on women and work in this book shows, even in the context of a free-for-all system like Hong Kong, obstacles to women's economic participation and career advancement can still be rampant. A general climate of meritocracy and market competition can perfectly co-exist with the most blatant form of labour market segmentation. Various forms of intended and semi-conscious discrimination against women can and do persist, and the systematic downgrading of women's contribution can even be an indispensable part of a strategy of industrial development that relies heavily on using cheap female labour in manufacturing (AAF, 1993: 2–6; Chan and Ng, 1994). As this book's introductory chapter argues, Hong Kong's export-oriented industrial capitalism owes much of its success to the availability of cheap labour. In this, Hong Kong women have made a significant, though seldom acknowledged, contribution.

Furthermore, important recent studies by Hall (1992), Hareven (1991), and others demonstrate that the same process of industrialization has in many places brought a fortification of the distinction between the public and private spheres of social life, and a redefinition of the role of women and men in the two spheres. The modern domestic ideology, championed by the rising middle class in the West in the nineteenth century, sought a new level of identification of women and 'their rightful place in the family'. Women were seen as primarily responsible for the newly important tasks of child care and household management, when both partners took on the all-important elevated appearance of the middle classes in the competition for social respectability and power. In that process of social aggrandizement, agents of the state, the media, and the ever more active welfare and education professionals all joined in to buttress that particular construction, albeit with varying degrees of conscious commitment. Hence a pull for women to be domesticated can and does exist side by side with the contradictory call for women's public participation. Many women will be torn by such ambivalent messages. Some will find being an 'angel in the house' a primary obligation that will forever tie them to the caring role inside their families (Ng, 1993).

How much of this 'ideological reversal' is occurring in Hong Kong? There is evidence pointing to the emergence and spread of a similar modern domestic ideology in the past two decades, though as of now what we know is more suggestive than definitive. It can be seen in the preference for neolocal, nuclear families of the younger generation, and in housing designs and interior decoration that put privacy, gentility, hygiene, taste and comfort to the forefront. It can be seen in the rise of a child-centred mentality in the modern family ideal, as reflected in the blossoming since the 1980s of clothes, toys and educational packages for children.

It is also reaffirmed by a series of state policies that over time shift their concern from addressing children as weak subjects to be protected (Employment Ordinance), to seeing them as assets to be cultivated (health clinics, compulsory education, Youth's Charter) (Ng, 1993). The role of women in this privatized, child-centred world is not difficult to delineate. Women are continually portrayed in advertisements, films and on television as contented moral guardians of juniors in the modern home — no doubt because the image reflects and reinforces popular imagination (AAF, 1993: 93–8). The 'husband-as-breadwinner and wife-as-dependent model' of the modern nuclear family is also explicitly codified as the normative basis of social policies in Hong Kong (AAF, 1990: 10–15).

This 'modern housewife' image differs significantly from the popular image of the so-called traditional Chinese wife.[4] The latter pays homage to a code of ethical and familial reality which stresses the continuity of the male line and landed assets. The heart of the former, on the contrary, belongs to the romance and glory of the modern (middle-class) home. If women today are confined to their familial caring role, the source for this image may well be a mixture of both the old and the new forms of domestic ideal. It is definitely not an archaic relic soon to be swept into the historical dustbin. Ascertaining the actual mix and the contradiction in ideal and experience that they may generate for women becomes a most important area for contemporary study. Some of the relevant findings will be discussed later.

## Economic Advancement and Household Economy

Industrialization does not bring unmitigated advancement for women. The actual outcome of the role of women in and outside families is the result of the resolution of the contradictory tendencies in the process of industrialization. It depends on the mode and stages of industrialization, on the contest between different projects of social construction, and on how women react to such possibilities and constraints and make their presence felt. In this sense, the best studies which tell the complex story of women's advance and retreat always link the active role women play in their families to the fluctuating fortunes engendered by Hong Kong's industrialization.

One major observation to emerge from recent feminist historical studies in the West is the significant economic contribution that women made to the household even before the onset of industrialization. Whether working in the fields, or as domestic servants in commercial towns, co-workers in family workshops, or shopkeepers-cum-accountants in merchants' households, different generations of women have been an indispensable component of a household strategy of survival and advance (Hall, 1992; Scott and Tilly, 1982; Laslett and Brenner, 1989). Even when the climate shifted at some points in the twentieth century to keeping women within their 'rightful' domestic place, working-class women continued to participate in many kinds of trade in order to make ends meet for their families, or to claim a place of their own in the public world (Gittins, 1985).

This is also, to a certain extent, true for women in the later years of imperial China. The family ideal, codified in élite documents, that sought the total domestic confinement of women, was never entirely successful. A fairly large proportion of women from peasant families had long been involved in farming and other gainful activities (Wolf, 1975: 8; Johnson, 1983: Chapter 1). Stacey made a clear case for regional difference in this regard: 'in the multiple-cropping rice regions of the South, however, female participation in weeding, transplanting, and harvesting the crops was more constant. In a few atypical areas, women carried almost exclusive responsibility for farm work' (Stacey, 1983: 23). Similarly, Topley found that 'women all over Kwangtung traditionally worked outside their home, and by this century women in other provinces were also working in cash-earning occupations' (Topley, 1975: 68). The study by Emily Honig, of Shanghai factory work from 1919 to 1949, provides ample confirmation that females, from an early age, were an integral part of the household's economic calculation. From the age of five or six, daughters were expected to help in the field and with housework in order to release their parents for work in the thriving industrial sector. Many learned to spin and weave in primitive home workshops. Most began their factory careers when they were nine or ten years old. In the years leading up to 1949, the majority of mill workers in Shanghai (then the largest industrial centre in China) were women. In fact, women accounted for two-thirds of the total industrial workforce in the city. The accounts from Honig made it clear that most of them were making a critical contribution to their household economies (Honig, 1986: 1; 166–71).

Such observations on women's economic contribution prior to industrialization compel us to rethink the role of women inside the family. Instead of seeing industrialization as single-handedly liberating women from domestic confinement, we need to assess the constraints and opportunities made available at successive stages of Hong Kong's particular mode of industrialization.

Official data from the 1930s to the 1950s show women to be participating in a broad range of economic activities, including commerce, personal services, transport and, increasingly, manufacturing (Levin, 1991: 185–9). This is not difficult to explain. The ravages of war, the nature of a migrant society, and the minimal support provided by the colonial regime put the question of collective survival on the top of the agenda for most families. Like families in pre-industrial Europe and industrializing Shanghai, families in Hong Kong acted then, as now, as collective resource-pooling and generating units, actively calculating the costs and benefits of different courses of action in the face of changing opportunities. Women played a big part in these household strategies.

In research into Hong Kong family history carried out by the present author, some of these issues have been tackled.[5] Respondents from the twenty-two families studied were mostly in their fifties and sixties. It was found that the women in the group had all been economically active in the 1950s, their prime years coinciding with the rudimentary but thriving industrial development at the time. None of them was an 'ideal typical housewife' of either the traditional or modern variants. Most reported on their 'take-for-granted' attitude to work, even though many were in work of an 'informal' nature, as domestic servants, shop assistants, street vendors, and family outworkers; miscellaneous work inside the home often took on some economic value. Only two withdrew from gainful activities permanently on marriage or giving birth to a child. Fourteen out of twenty-two had never interrupted their work at any time before their retirement. In some situations, such as when a husband died or was incapacitated by illness or accident, the wife took on the role of the chief provider and organizer of the household economy, allocating roles for offspring, mobilizing resources in and outside the families, and gradually bringing the families out of the crisis. They recounted their experiences with an understandable mixture of remorse and relief, yet it was clear such participation and contribution had also elevated their standing inside their families (Lee and Ng, 1991; Ng, 1994).

Industrialization does not automatically enhance the status of women in society. The recognition of their contribution was sometimes won on the back of major sacrifices. If times are rough, as they were in the 1950s, the sacrifice could be great indeed. Salaff's study on the life of twenty-eight 'working daughters' of Hong Kong during the 1960s and 1970s showed a different side of the same story. The industrial take-off during the 1960s was shown to have provided a different set of calculus for the families. The expanding economic opportunities had not broken down the Chinese family as predicted, Salaff argues, but had reinforced its 'centripetal' tendencies. The fate of household members was still tied to the overall strategy of survival and advancement of the larger unit. Most of the families studied responded to the new possibilities of social advancement by placing differential premiums on sons and daughters. Sons were seen as assets in which to invest; daughters as a tool for current economic gain. Many of the elder daughters of the families left school at an early age to lend a helping hand in household tasks, and relieve their mothers for full-time work. When they were between 12 and 14 years old, they themselves were ready for real economic work in one of the thriving factories of the time.

As the data from Salaff show, their contribution was often crucial to the survival of the families. When the overall dependency ratio of the families improved later, their income could be the basis for major purchase or investment that made for the collective upward mobility of the families concerned. The status of the working daughters experienced subtle shifts during these processes. As their economic contribution was recognized, they experienced a new level of freedom in terms of mate choice, friendship circles, and daily consumption, and could be influential in planning for the educational paths of younger siblings. However, the demands of the families still took precedence over their wishes if a clash occurred. Ultimately, their new-found respect inside the families was based on an irreversible truncation of their own material routes of social advancement (Salaff, 1976; 1981).

For those families which today still struggle at the lower end of the social hierarchy, this mix of enhanced economic opportunity and a household strategy, which places women at the back of the queue, continues, albeit in subtly different forms. We have seen how the Tuen Mun study confirmed the decisive influence that marriage and childbirth have on women's economic participation. Almost all the female respondents who were working at the time of the study had inferior incomes, employment status, and job security compared with their spouses. 40 per cent of those who were not working planned to work again due to economic necessity. Only a handful talked about their own career aspirations being the primary reason for their wanting to work again (Tuen Mun District Board, 1991: 16).

This continued submergence of female career interest in the working-class households of Hong Kong has been vividly revealed by Lui Tai Lok's study on outworkers. Outwork was shown to comprise a significant portion of female workers who were married and aged between thirty-five and thirty-nine. Most of them had children of pre-school age at home. Outwork was seen as the best means for them to fulfill the simultaneous need to care for the young and to add to the household coffers. Yet they openly acknowledged their truncated career aspirations, and their lack of interest in the things they did and in the absence of a long-term plan for themselves. A classic instrumental attitude to work went hand in hand with a deep sense of fatalism (Lui, 1991: 26–33).

This mixture of gains and losses, elation and sacrifice has also been found in the few studies of the middle class. Women from middle-class families obviously have more material and cultural resources at their disposal. It is safe to say, compared with their working-class counterparts, they have more say in their marriage, the number and timing of their children, and in enlisting domestic help when needed. In 1988, only 3.5 per cent of the families in Hong Kong employed domestic helpers. 78 per cent of the helpers were employed in families with monthly incomes above HK$30,000 (Hong Kong Census and Statistics Department, 1990). The economic restructuring and expansion in the past decade also facilitated their economic advance.

Cashmore's study of thirty-five 'successful career-women' in the late 1980s tells an ambivalent story. Aided by their liberal education or family background, they had all been able to break into traditionally male positions. They took pride in their achievements and no longer believed women to be severely disadvantaged in their rightful pursuit of a career. However, at the same time, they reported the existence of a male work culture and network that precluded their full participation. Many also expressed the pressure of being a mother and carer, and how ultimately they would put family obligation ahead of their careers (Cashmore, 1989).

These studies do not provide a comprehensive picture of women's family lives in the past forty-five years. However, together they confirm that there is much more to women's contribution and sacrifice in the process of industrialization than either the functionalist or gender-role socialization accounts allow. They address the contradictory possibilities of industrialization, show how household economic and social considerations mediated between the opportunities and the outcomes, and how and why women in different classes endured contrasting yet similar fortunes in all those years of uninhibited activities that brought us the Hong Kong miracle.

## Women as Gendered Subjects

Amidst the fervent charting of historical trends and structural underpinning, one must pause and ask the obvious question: how do women respond to all this?

The second wave of feminism in the West emerged on the crest of the debunking of the feminine mystique. On the surface, most women were contented with their lot. Deep down, however, there were other stories to be told (Friedan, 1963). Women in Hong Kong have been attributed simplistic personalities and attitudes. They are either portrayed as modernized, enlightened creatures deciding on their individual fate in the functionalist account, or seen as succumbing to the totalitarian domination of traditional culture in the 'new orthodoxy'. While the former notion is based mainly on conjecture and anecdote, the latter boasts a host of survey findings demonstrating the espousal of traditional female-denigrating views on the part of the female respondents themselves. Both views miss the essentially ambivalent nature of female experience and ideology.

In fact, contradictions abound in survey findings on women's attitudes to family life. Successive rounds of the social indicators surveys found women to be satisfied with their marriage and family life. Most of them believed sex discrimination was not a major social problem in Hong Kong. The successful career women in Cashmore's study deplored the 'traditional' Chinese value which suppressed female interests, but they all felt the value was a thing of the past as far as Hong Kong is concerned. In the Tuen Mun study, more than 70 per cent of the female respondents agreed that 'both women and men should have a say in public affairs, women should actively participate in them' (Tuen Mun District Board, 1991: 28). These findings seem to support the optimistic view of female advancement both in practice and in value.

However the same Tuen Mun survey also revealed that over 82 per cent of the female respondents agreed with the statement: 'taking care of my family is more important than developing my own career'; 63 per cent agreed with the idea of 'male in charge of the external world and women in charge of internal affairs' (Tuen Mun District Board, 1991: 28). In the Social Indicators Survey of 1986, over 80 per cent of the female respondents believed mothers to be the ideal carers for their children (Lau and Wan, 1987). Traditional sex-role socialization, on this evidence, is running wild.

This is not the place to lament the bluntness of the survey instrument as far as questions of moral and situated logic are concerned. Nor do we need to stress the arbitrary nature of much existing prognosis on women's value. The one simple, mundane observation — if we do not start from monolithic theories of progress or social domination — is that women's daily lives, like everybody else's, are full of conflicting currents and possibilities. Most women's views of themselves and society are mixed and contradictory. But they are not jumbled. One can indeed trace the source and pattern of such contradictory attitudes.

One possible line of fissure is the discrepancy between ideal construction and real-life experience. The classic case is captured by the notion of 'the housewife syndrome'. The 'modern, capable and contented housewife' is a powerful social construction circulating in the media, marriage manuals, school texts and policy assumptions. The real life of a typical housewife, as Ann Oakley clearly demonstrates, is more a series of endless chores, isolation and interrupted schedules (Oakley, 1974: 91–104). A typical survey question may tap the accepted construction, while the experience of drudgery will be revealed more subtly in the research context. There is, for example, a persistent discrepancy between the actual and the ideal forms of division of labour and power inside the families. The ideal expressed by the female respondents slants much more towards equal sharing than is actually the case in real life (Table 3.2). One can also see, for example during the interview process in the Tuen Mun study, the constant complaints from the women about the monotony of their daily lives, and the frustrated and fatalistic manner in which they said: 'of course it is me who does this, who else could it be?' The ambivalence was summarily captured when more than a few full-time housewives put down 'doing housework' as their most frequent form of 'leisure activity'.

The other source of contradiction could be among the social constructions themselves, and how they have been variously absorbed by the women concerned. Here the discussion has to be speculative pending new research efforts into this difficult area. One may speculate that the traditional and modern domestic ideals may each be exerting its powerful influence in different sections of the female population, with middle-class females more accepting of the latter. As we pointed out in a previous section, the modern domestic ideal provides a firm, sometimes 'scientific' justification for identifying women as the moral and physical nurturer inside the home. There are

*Table 3.2 Actual and ideal persons responsible for four types of family tasks (in percentage)*

|  | Wife | Husband | Tasks shared* | Others | (No.) |
|---|---|---|---|---|---|
| **Household chores** | | | | | |
| Actual | 72.1 | 3.6 | 13.6 | 10.8 | (390) |
| Ideal | 58.2 | 3.1 | 29.0 | 9.7 | (414) |
| **The making of important decisions** | | | | | |
| Actual | 13.7 | 32.3 | 47.0 | 6.9 | (387) |
| Ideal | 8.9 | 32.5 | 54.6 | 4.1 | (416) |
| **Supervision of children** | | | | | |
| Actual | 38.3 | 6.4 | 49.7 | 5.5 | (326) |
| Ideal | 25.8 | 8.6 | 62.8 | 2.8 | (395) |
| **Daily budgeting** | | | | | |
| Expenses | | | | | |
| Actual | 50.5 | 15.3 | 26.7 | 7.6 | (386) |
| Ideal | 41.3 | 15.2 | 39.6 | 3.8 | (414) |

\* Between husband and wife or among all members of the family
*Source*: Lee (1992): 13.
*Note*: Some of these figures have been rounded off for this table and thus do not add up to 100 per cent.

also a number of cultural and policy trends for the emergence and diffusion of this ideal. The pull of this ideal will come into conflict with the conception of meritocracy entertained by the educated section of the female population, as well as the actual taste of social advancement they experienced. Together they define the major ideational struggle among women in middle-class families (Ng, 1991b: 181).

Survey findings tend to show the less-educated, working-class segment of the population to be more 'traditional' in a range of values. Could it be that their subscription to the domestic ideal is more of the traditional variant, taking for granted that men should be in charge because that, seemingly, has always been the case, and forever will be so? How has the diffusion of the modern domestic ideal to the poorer section of the population affected their attitude to home ownership, decoration, provision for children's growth, the new significance of child care in a child-centred ideal, and the related tasks of home management? How would the necessity for most working-class women to bring some form of economic return to the household qualify their ideal and practices in being the angel of the house?

Contradictions are the prelude to sense-making, negotiation and resistance. Even under the most adverse, patriarchal climate of traditional Chinese households, women fought their own battle with *de facto* participation — fostering the uterine family, gossiping, mutual aid, and building networks of female support — and more openly in the form of marriage resistance and participating in feminist movements (Johnson, 1983; Stockard, 1989; Kazuko, 1989). Much remains to be discovered and written on these issues for women of today (AAF, 1992).

## Conclusions

Much of the above discussion is necessarily sketchy. However, we are beyond the frustrating stage of having to write a new research agenda in a void. The critique of the two existing frameworks is not intended to be a complete negation of years of research. It is by building on such abundance of existing theoretical and empirical work that one can ask for a different orientation of study.

The way forward is to see some of the gaps in evidence and arguments presented above as productive gaps. One may begin by offering deeper examination on the nature of industrialization. Then research efforts can concentrate on uncovering the hidden aspects of women's work over the course of the past 45 years and the relations they have with women's family roles and experience. We also need to reclaim the voice of women in different social locations, to see the contradictory social constructions they have to grapple with, and how they make sense of their own experiences, and devise their courses of action.

## Notes

1. Some of the figures often advanced in support of the functionalist thesis are:
   —— the overall number of births shows a continuous decline, from 86,751 in 1981 to 67,731 in 1990; the age-specific fertility rate falls for every age group in that same period;
   —— the median age of marriage for females rose from 23.4 in 1976 to 26.3 in 1990;
   —— the average family size fell from 3.9 in 1981 to 3.4 in 1991; the proportion of nuclear families among all families rose from 54.4 per cent to 61.6 per cent between 1981 and 1991 (Hong Kong Census and Statistics Department, 1991; *Hong Kong Women's File*, AAF, 1993: 62–7);
   —— evidence from surveys and other anecdotal sources also confirm the fact of husbands' increasing participation in housework, and the enhanced role of the female in family decision-making, especially for those who hold gainful employment (Wong, 1981);
   —— the female rate of economic participation shows a continuous rise from 36.8 per cent in 1961 to 49.5 per cent in 1991; not only are traditionally male occupations opening up for females, the latter are also making inroads into managerial and supervisory grades (Hong Kong Census and Statistics Department, 1991, 1992; Hong Kong Government Inter-departmental Working Group, 1992).
2. Association for the Advancement of Feminism, 1993: 70–80; 149–53 provides details of the sources and comprehensive summaries of the relevant findings.
3. In December 1992, the Legislative Council passed a motion, with almost unanimous support from those present, urging the government to extend to Hong Kong the United Nations Convention on the Elimination of All Forms of Discrimination Against Women. Feminist groups saw this as a significant landmark in the effort to put women's interest on the political agenda.
4. The image is of course a crude simplification of the reality of the Chinese wife through the centuries. It, for example, neglects

the often-commented difference among classes and localities, and the changes in status of the wife/daughter-in-law through the family life cycle. See Freedman, 1979: 245–6; Wolf, 1975: 89–90; Stacey, 1983: 38–59.
5. See Lee and Ng, 1991. The project aims to document and analyse some of the major paths of family advancement and retreat in post-war Hong Kong. The first stage of the study was completed in 1989 and consisted in the collection of life history data from male and female respondents of twenty-two families.

# References

Association for the Advancement of Feminism (1990), *Women and Hong Kong Welfare Policies*, Hong Kong: Association for the Advancement of Feminism.
—— (1992), *The Other Half of The Sky*, Hong Kong: Association for the Advancement of Feminism.
—— (1993), *The Hong Kong Women's File*, Hong Kong: Association for the Advancement of Feminism.
Cashmore, E. (1989), *The Experience of Successful Career Women in Hong Kong*, Hong Kong: Department of Sociology, University of Hong Kong.
Census and Statistics Department (1990), *Special Data Collected by the General Household Survey, Special Topics Report No. VI*, Hong Kong: Hong Kong Government Printer.
—— (1991), *Preliminary Report of Census 1991*, Hong Kong: Hong Kong Government Printer.
—— (1992), *Hong Kong Social and Economic Trends, 1980–1990*, Hong Kong: Hong Kong Government Printer.
Chan, K. W. and Ng, C. H. (1994), 'Gender, Class and Employment Segregation in Hong Kong' in S. K. Lau et al. (eds.), *Inequalities and Development: Social Stratification in Chinese Societies*, Hong Kong: Hong Kong Institute of Asia-Pacific Studies, The Chinese University of Hong Kong.
Freedman, M. (1979), *The Study of Chinese Society*, Calfornia: Stanford University Press.
Friedan, B. (1963), *The Feminine Mystique*, Harmondsworth: Penguin.
Gittins, D. (1985), *The Family in Question*, London: Macmillan.
Hall, C. (1992), *White, Male, and Middle Class*, Cambridge: Polity Press.
Hareven, T. (1991) 'The Home and the Family in Historical Perspective', *Social Research*, 58: 254–85.
Hong Kong Government Inter-departmental Working Group (1992),

*Findings of Working Group on Sex Discrimination in Employment*, Hong Kong: The Working Group.
Hong Kong Legislative Council (1992), *Minutes of debate on extending the United Nations Convention on the Elimination of All Forms of Discrimination Against Women to Hong Kong*, 16 December.
Hong Kong Young Women's Christian Association and Hong Kong Shue Yan College (1982), *Report on Working Mothers in Family Functioning*, Hong Kong: HKYWCA and HKSYC.
Honig, E. (1986), *Sisters and Strangers: the Shanghai Cotton Mills, 1919–1949*, California: Stanford University Press.
Johnson, K. (1983), *Women, the Family and Peasant Revolution in China*, Chicago: University of Chicago Press.
Kazuko, O. (1989), *Chinese Women in a Century of Revolution*, California: Stanford University Press.
Laslett, B. and J. Brenner (1989), 'Gender and Social Reproduction: Historical Perspectives', Annual Review of Sociology, 15: 387–404.
Lau, S. K. et al. (eds.) (1991), *Indicators of Social Development: Hong Kong 1988*, Hong Kong: Hong Kong Institute of Asia-Pacific Studies, The Chinese University of Hong Kong.
Lau, S. K. et al. (eds.) (1992), *Indicators of Social Development*, Hong Kong: Hong Kong Institute of Asia-Pacific Studies, The Chinese University of Hong Kong.
Lau, S. K. and Wan, P. S. (1987), *A Preliminary Report on Social Indicators in Hong Kong*, Hong Kong: Centre for Hong Kong Studies, The Chinese University of Hong Kong.
Lee, M. K. (1992), 'Family and Gender Issues' in S. K. Lau et al. (eds.), *Indicators of Social Development*, Hong Kong: Hong Kong Institute of Asia-Pacific Studies, The Chinese University of Hong Kong, pp. 1–32.
Lee, M. K. and Ng, C. H. (1991), *Class, Family and Social Life in Hong Kong, 1950–1980*, Research report presented to the Hong Kong Polytechnic Research Sub-Committee.
Leonard, D. and Speakman, M. A. (1986), 'Women in the Family: Companions or Caretakers?', in V. Beechey and E. Whitelegg (eds.), *Women in Britain Today*, Milton Keynes: Open University Press, pp. 8–76.
Levin, D. (1991), 'Women and the Industrial Labour Market in Hong Kong: Participation and Perceptions', in J. G. Scoville (ed.), *Status Influences in Third World Labour Markets: Caste, Gender and Custom*, New York: de Gruyter, pp. 183–214.
Lui, T. L. (1991), 'Waged Work at Home: Married Women's Participation in Industrial Outwork in Hong Kong' in F. M. Cheung et al. (eds.), *Selected Papers of Conference on Gender Studies in Chinese Societies*, Hong Kong: Chinese University Press, pp. 1–42.

Ng, C. H. (1989), 'Family Crisis, Whose Crisis?,' *Ming Pao Monthly*, January, pp. 3-10.
Ng, C. H. (1991a), 'Familial Change and Women's Employment in Hong Kong', in F. M. Cheung et al. (eds.), *Selected Papers of Conference on Gender Studies in Chinese Societies*, Hong Kong: Hong Kong Institute of Asia-Pacific Studies, Chinese University Press, pp. 43-54.
Ng, C. H. (1991b), 'Women's Employment and Family Change', in J. Cheng (ed.), *A New Hong Kong Era; the Symposium of 'I Love Hong Kong Campaign' II*, Hong Kong: Breakthrough Ltd, pp. 167-84.
Ng, C. H. (1992), 'Gender and Society', in M. K. Lee and S. L. Wong (eds.), *New Studies in Sociology*, Hong Kong: Commercial Press, pp. 165-82.
Ng, C. H. (1993), 'Popular Culture and the Modern Domestic Ideal', in C. H. Ng and M. H. Sze (eds.), *Popular Culture in Hong Kong*, Hong Kong: Joint Publishing, pp. 109-31.
Ng, C. H. (1994), 'Power, Identity and Economic Change: 25 Years of Family Studies in Hong Kong' in B. K. P. Leung and Wong, T. Y. C. (eds.), *25 Years of Social and Economic Development in Hong Kong*, Hong Kong: Centre of Asian Studies, University of Hong Kong, pp. 94-110.
Oakley, A. (1974), *Housewife*, Harmondsworth: Penguin.
Salaff, Janet W. (1976), 'Working Daughters in the Hong Kong Chinese Family: Filial Piety or a Transformation in the Family Power Structure?', *Journal of Social History*, 9: 439-65.
Salaff, Janet W. (1981), *Working Daughters of Hong Kong*, Cambridge: Cambridge University Press.
Scott, J. and L. Tilly (1982), 'Women's Work and the Family in Nineteenth-Century Europe', in E. Whitelegg et al. (eds.), *The Changing Experience of Women*, Oxford: Martin Robertson.
Smith, A. D. (1973), *The Concept of Social Change*, London: RKP, pp. 1-8.
Stacey, J. (1983), *Patriarchy and Socialist Revolution in China*, California: University of California Press.
Stockard, J. (1989), *Daughters of the Canton Delta*, Hong Kong: Hong Kong University Press.
Topley, M. (1975), 'Marriage Resistance in Rural Kwangtung' in M. Wolf and R. Witke (eds.), *Women in Chinese Society*, California: Stanford University Press, pp. 67-88.
Tuen Mun District Board (1991), *The Needs of Married Women in Tuen Mun, Research Report 1990*, Hong Kong: Tuen Mun District Board.
Wolf, A. (1975) 'The Women of Hai-shan: A Demographic Portrait'

in M. Wolf and R. Witke (eds.), *Women in Chinese Society*, California: Stanford University Press, pp. 89–110.

Wong, F. M. (1975), *'Industrialization and Family Structure in Hong Kong'*, Journal of Marriage and the Family, 37: 985–1000.

Wong, F. M. (1981), 'Effects of the Employment of Mothers on Marital Role and Power Differentiation in Hong Kong', in A. Y. C. King and R. P. L. Lee (eds.), *Social Life and Development in Hong Kong*, Hong Kong: Chinese University Press, pp. 217–34.

Yang, C. K. (1981), 'Introduction', in A. Y. C. King and R. P. L. Lee (eds.), *Social Life and Development in Hong Kong*, Hong Kong: Chinese University Press, pp. ix–xxv.

# 4 Women and Education in Hong Kong

*Choi Po-king*

Education has always been central in discussions concerning social inequality, whether structured on class, gender or race. This is due to two major reasons. In industrialized societies like ours, education has become an important means of social placement. The extent of participation in the education system is therefore taken as an indicator of certain groups' relative chances of upward social mobility. Also, formal education is undoubtedly a centre of cultural transmission to which almost all children are subjected in this age of universal education. The interest here lies in the kind of orientation, values, and world views that are inculcated in our children at a relatively impressionable age, that either justify and perpetuate present social arrangements, or present challenges to them.

This chapter proposes to address the relationship between education and gender on two levels: that of participation in the formal education system, and that of cultural transmission. Put in a simpler way, this chapter attempts to answer two questions. First, how many girls and women attend the various levels of the education system in Hong Kong compared to boys and men? Second, what are most of the students being taught in schools, colleges, and universities, both explicitly and implicitly?

Any discussion about the relationship between gender and education must go beyond these questions. It should not stop at the participation rates of the two genders in the education system, no matter how interesting and revealing these might be in themselves. On the contrary, it has to go one step further to identify the extent to which gender acts as a constraint on social placement and mobility. Similarly, it is not enough to present the kinds of gender-related orientations, values, and world views transmitted through our education system. It is also important to find out how thoroughly these ideas have been inculcated in young people who are recipients of such cultural transmission. This in turn hinges

## Table 4.1 Percentage of female students at various education levels, 1961–1990

|      | Kindergarten | Primary | Secondary* | Matriculation | Post-secondary (non-degree) | University |
|------|------|------|------|------|------|------|
| 1961 | 43.5 | 44.5 | 40.1 | 40.1 | 31.1 | 26.5 |
| 1971 | 45.8 | 47.7 | 42.7 | 35.1 | 26.8 | 31.8 |
| 1981 | 48.0 | 48.0 | 50.7 | 42.0 | 36.9 | 34.4 |
| 1986 | 48.5 | 47.7 | 50.2 | 44.4 | 50.1 | 39.3 |
| 1990 | 48.5 | 48.1 | 50.0 | 50.4 | n.a. | 42.3 |

* Secondary education includes day and night certification courses.
n.a. = Information not available.
Sources: *Education Department Annual Summary*, 1961, 1971; Census and Statistics Department, *Hong Kong Annual Digest of Statistics*, 1982, 1987, 1991; *Vice-Chancellor's Report, 1990/91*, The University of Hong Kong; student enrolment figures for The Chinese University of Hong Kong for the year 1990/1, by courtesy of the Registration Section of the University.

on the context, institutional and social, in which this process takes place. Unfortunately, the state of local research is such that considerable gaps of knowledge in these areas still exist, so this chapter can only aim at synthesizing available data, and construct plausible but tentative answers to the various questions outlined.

## Extent of Participation in Formal Education

### Participation and Segregation

As the past three decades have shown, enrolment at all levels of formal education has followed a general trend towards more equal gender participation (Table 4.1). Even at university level, where the participation of women is still below 50 per cent, the gap has been steadily closing in the last ten years or so.

This does not, however, shed much light on the state of gender equality, or indeed the lack of it. One has to look further into the sectors within each level to see if any gender segregation exists, and if it does, to what extent. Various writers have highlighted precisely this point, using figures from the mid-to-late 1980s (Pearson, 1990; Ou, 1990; Mak, 1992). Indeed, Ou pointed out that the level of gender segregation, or genderization of curriculum, as it is sometimes called, from the older to the younger age groups (between the ages of 45–54 and 15–24) is steadily rising. Using the differential participation rates of the two genders in various post-secondary curriculum made available in the 1986 by-census, Ou constructed an 'index of dissimilarity', which he found to increase steadily with younger age groups. He therefore observed that while new openings into service, or what he called tertiary, industries were available to young women, traditional and more prestigious professions and academic areas remained very much male-dominated.

One way of reviewing gender segregation in education is to examine the gender breakdown of enrolment figures among various fields of study in local universities. These are presented for the two older universities in Tables 4.2 and 4.3. The third university, the Hong Kong University of Science and Technology, only took in its first batch of students in the Autumn of 1991, and so the relevant figures were not available at the time of writing. All three universities differ in the structure of their curriculum, but they share an important common feature, namely, the requirement for applicants to apply directly to the faculties (Arts, Social Sciences, Engineering and so on) instead of to the university as a whole. Thus, if gender segregation exists — and we see from the tables that it does — then this segregation occurs very early on at the stage of admission.

In Tables 4.2 and 4.3, it can be seen that the fields of study remain sex-typed. Engineering, for example, has always been, and still is, a male-dominated field, just as education is female-dominated. As for the faculties of arts, the proportion of male students has been steadily declining, constituting only about 20 per cent of the population. Meanwhile, women's participation in other traditionally male-dominated fields such as architecture, dental studies and science has increased slightly, though the share still hovers around only 30 per cent or less. The greatest gain for women seems to have been in business administration, thus confirming the point Ou makes about the opening up of service industries to women. This

*Table 4.2  Percentage of women undergraduates in various faculties at the University of Hong Kong, 1971–1990*

|  | 1971 | 1976 | 1981 | 1986 | 1990 |
| --- | --- | --- | --- | --- | --- |
| **Faculty** | | | | | |
| Architecture | 17.1 | 14.3 | 20.0 | 32.8 | 28.7 |
| Arts | 48.0 | 70.8 | 65.3 | 67.6 | 79.6 |
| Dental studies | n.a. | n.a. | 14.1 | 14.9 | 31.5 |
| Education | n.a. | n.a. | n.a. | n.a. | 90.5 |
| Engineering | 2.2 | 0.8 | 2.4 | 1.4 | 6.2 |
| Law | 57.1 | 39.3 | 56.2 | 57.6 | 52.3 |
| Medicine | 20.0 | 17.2 | 16.1 | 14.6 | 27.8 |
| Science | 19.3 | 16.9 | 22.2 | 10.2 | 26.3 |
| Social science | 34.2 | 49.5 | 42.3 | 48.1 | 52.5 |
| Overall | 28.4 | 33.5 | 34.0 | 33.1 | 41.2 |

*Source:* Vice-Chancellor's Report, The University of Hong Kong, relevant years; *The Chinese University of Hong Kong Bulletin*, Winter 1976; *Vice-Chancellor's Report*, The Chinese University of Hong Kong, 1978–1982, 1985–1987; *Education Department Annual Summary 1971*; student enrolment figures for The Chinese University of Hong Kong for the year 1990/1, by courtesy of the Registration Section of the University.

gain at undergraduate level must, however, be weighted by the much less favourable career experience of women after graduation, both in terms of income and chances of promotion (AAF, 1993).

While a small proportion of students remain in the education system beyond the secondary level, the majority of them (around 70 per cent in the 1970s and 1980s) leave school after Form 5 (Choi, 1992). Among these, some take up technical and vocational training, while a small proportion might have taken this up earlier, in secondary-level technical and vocational schools. It is unfortunate that published official figures regarding gender participation in technical and vocational education are scarce, so it is very difficult to construct a complete picture. Nevertheless, segregation and a somewhat limited scope for female participation is apparent.

*Table 4.3 Percentage of women undergraduates in various faculties at the Chinese University of Hong Kong, 1971–1990*

|  | 1971 | 1976 | 1981 | 1986 | 1990 |
|---|---|---|---|---|---|
| **Faculty** | | | | | |
| Arts | 54.1 | 54.1 | 59.1 | 70.8 | 78.1 |
| Business administration* | 42.1 | 25.0 | 29.0 | 47.8 | 62.0 |
| Engineering | n.a. | n.a. | n.a. | n.a. | 9.0 |
| Science | 19.2 | 14.5 | 11.5 | 20.6 | 31.6** |
| Social science | n.a. | 38.8 | 45.7 | 57.6 | 58.9 |
| Medicine | n.a. | n.a. | 11.7 | 19.8 | 31.2 |
| Overall | 38.7 | 33.2 | 35.6 | 44.5 | 51.3 |

\* For the year 1971, the faculty was not yet separated from the Commerce and Social Science Faculty.
\*\* For the year 1990, the engineering programme was separated from the Science Faculty and set up as the Faculty of Engineering.
na = not applicable: faculty not yet established.

Table 4.4 shows that for secondary level technical/vocational training, there is a high concentration of girls in commercial classes providing training in basic clerical skills. As for technical and other vocational streams, the participation of girls is very low indeed, as is their participation in general. One can see, therefore, that for students who are not academically oriented, boys have a significant edge over girls in obtaining formal training in skills.

Owing to the lack of published data, one cannot complete the picture of technical/vocational training beyond the secondary level. From the meagre data that it has been possible to procure, it seems that the points made about secondary-level skill training apply also to this higher level. Table 4.5 shows that for 1972, the overall participation of female students in technical/vocational training was only slightly more than 8 per cent. The situation seems to have improved by 1982, perhaps with the addition of commercial and related courses, but the overall participation rate of female

*Table 4.4* **Percentage of female students in full-time secondary level technical/vocational (including commercial) education, 1972–1990**

|      | Technical/Vocational | Commercial | Overall |
|------|---------------------|------------|---------|
| 1972 | 24.0                | 99.5       | 31.7    |
| 1976 | 22.2                | 98.3       | 28.1    |
| 1982 | 28.9                | 95.5       | 32.6    |
| 1986 | 30.9                | 95.3       | 33.9    |
| 1990 | 34.2                | 93.3       | 36.8    |

*Source*: *Education Department Annual Summary*, relevant years.

*Table 4.5* **Percentage of female students in full-time post-secondary technical/vocational training, 1972–1990**

|      | Polytechnics | Technical institutes | Overall |
|------|--------------|----------------------|---------|
| 1972 | 17.0         | 8.0                  | 8.2     |
| 1976 | n.a.         | 11.4                 | n.a.    |
| 1982 | 28.7         | 28.2                 | 28.5    |
| 1986 | n.a.         | n.a.                 | n.a.    |
| 1990 | n.a.         | n.a.                 | n.a.    |

*Source*: *Education Department Annual Summary*, relevant years.
n.a. = information not available

students is still less than 30 per cent. Figures for 1993 given by Pearson in Chapter 9 demonstrate that Vocational Training Centre courses are predominantly male-centred (although open to both sexes) and that young men outnumber young women by 2.5:1 on average, the largest difference being 16.8:1 in part-time day-release technical courses.

## Table 4.6 Percentage of women students in teacher (primary) training, 1961–1990

|      | Full-time | Part-time | Overall |
|------|-----------|-----------|---------|
| 1961 | 63.2      | 55.8      | 58.4    |
| 1971 | 64.6      | 70.9      | 67.9    |
| 1981 | 69.8      | 64.1      | 67.3    |
| 1986 | 73.6      | 67.6      | 71.2    |
| 1990 | 74.7      | 70.8      | 72.9    |

Source: Hong Kong Statistics, 1947–1967; Education Department Annual Summary 1971; Hong Kong Annual Digest of Statistics, 1991.

For secondary school graduates who do not go on to higher education, there are two other types of formal training available — namely, nurse and teacher (primary school) training. As shown in Table 4.6, there is a steady trend of 'feminization' of teacher training, resulting in the parallel increase of women in primary school teaching. This is a point which will be reiterated later in the discussion on the authority structure in schools. Statistics regarding the nursing occupation are not available, but there is no reason to suppose that the situation there is any different.

## Gender: A Constraint on Life Chances

The phenomenon of educational expansion and hence the extension of formal education to girls and women is not unique to Hong Kong, and can be explained by the increased demand for skills and education brought about by the changing needs of capitalist production. At the same time, such extension is accompanied by genderization of fields of education or training, another development shared with other societies. It is clear, therefore, that capitalistic development does not displace gender differentiation. On the contrary, patriarchal domination in the form of sexual division of labour both within and outside the family, together with its associated ideologies, is clearly in operation. As a result, genderization of fields of training and study continue to preserve men's economic and social advantage (Stromquist, 1990).

Ultimately, the interesting question to ask is how sex interacts with class in determining the life chances of women in our society. More specifically, our concern for the participation of girls and women in the formal education system is meaningful only when compared with male opportunities.

Working on a 1981 census data set, Tsang (1993) constructed and tested, for youths aged between 15 and 27, a number of status attainment models, one of which takes into account sex as a structural constraint. His findings indicated that young women had to rely much more on educational qualifications than men to achieve a high socio-economic status. At the same time, they experienced more severe constraints in educational attainment with regard to their father's education, the number of siblings, and their father's socio-economic status. As for status attainment itself, women were again subject, to a significantly higher degree than men, to the indirect and total effects of all the family background variables used in the study. These included: their father's years of schooling and his socio-economic status, their mother's years of schooling, and the number of siblings.

Tsang's statistical analyses show that, as a result of their socio-economic background, young women in Hong Kong are subject to significantly heavier constraints than men in educational and status attainment. This explains the generally higher socio-economic status of young women, compared to men, among students in universities (Mak, 1992). For these women, it seems that their socio-economic background has compensated for their gender.

Tsang's quantitative research shows that, on an aggregate level, men are much less constrained than women by educational qualifications. Through qualitative research, we are in a better position to find out about the specific mechanisms which subject women to such constraints. Based on in-depth interviews of four young people three years after their graduation at Form 5, Lau (1992) discovered interesting forces at work: at a given level of educational attainment women's career prospects were depressed while men's were enhanced. Form 5 (the graduating year of the local secondary school, at around age 17) is a relatively low educational qualification in Hong Kong today, but in Lau's study, this seemed a much less inhibiting factor for the two young men than for the women. This gender discrepancy has arisen in a number of ways, including: more rigid job boundaries and specifications for women, inhibitions against young women forming 'vertical' work relationships with senior colleagues, and self-fulfilling expectations held towards women by seniors and by themselves.

Research pertaining to the relative mobility chances of women and the mechanisms involved is still too scanty to permit a thorough understanding of this issue, although Wong's work (Chapter 2) makes a significant contribution. More needs to be done in this, as in other areas, related to gender issues. Meanwhile, policy-makers and administrators should also be made more aware of gender as an important variable. In this regard, it is rather disheartening to find that it has become more, rather than less difficult to locate officially published figures relating to gender, which indicates a lessened, rather than heightened interest in this aspect.

## Cultural Transmission of Gender Inequality

It is necessary to probe more deeply into the process of education as a form of cultural transmission in order to discover the types of orientation, values, and world views which influence the younger generation and their attitude to the existing structure of gender inequality.

### Formal Curriculum and Textbooks

Gender segregation in fields of study clearly does not start at post-secondary levels, but is evident at a much earlier stage. The analysis presented in Table 4.7 of gender participation in various subjects in the Certificate of Education examination (the local school-leaving examination taken at around the age of 17) shows a clear pattern of gender segregation in the arts — including social sciences subjects — as well as in the science stream.

To appreciate the significance of this segregation, one has to bear in mind that the formal curriculum in local schools, and indeed the teaching and learning processes as a whole, are essentially examination-oriented. Furthermore, it is common practice for local schools to stream students into the

*Table 4.7  Gender ratios\* for subjects in the arts, science, and applied vocational streams, Certificate of Education Examination, 1976–1992*

|  | 1976 | 1982 | 1986 | 1992 |
|---|---|---|---|---|
| **Arts stream** |  |  |  |  |
| History | 0.65 | 0.49 | 0.48 | 0.47 |
| Chinese literature | 0.91 | 0.61 | 0.52 | 0.41 |
| Geography | 0.97 | 0.64 | 0.57 | 0.54 |
| **Science stream** |  |  |  |  |
| Physics | 3.35 | 2.85 | 2.52 | 2.09 |
| Chemistry | 2.82 | 2.63 | 2.38 | 1.98 |
| Additional mathematics | 3.41 | 2.83 | 2.40 | 1.95 |
| Biology | 1.10 | 1.10 | 1.41 | 1.58 |
| Human biology | n.a. | n.a. | 0.31 | 0.27 |
| **Applied vocational stream** |  |  |  |  |
| Principles of accounts | 0.50 | 0.36 | 0.42 | 0.43 |
| Commerce | n.a. | 0.29 | 0.44 | 0.43 |
| Electronics & Electricity\*\* | nil\*\*\* | 73 | 345 | 146 |
| Design & Technology | n.a. | 70 | nil\*\*\* | nil\*\*\* |
| Metalwork | nil\*\*\* | nil\*\*\* | nil\*\*\* | 93 |
| Home economics | n.a. | 0.01 | 0.01 | 0.01 |
| Needlework | 0 | 0 | 0 | 0 |

\* Number of male candidates for every female candidate.
\*\* This includes the subject Practical Electricity offered in 1976 and 1982.
\*\*\* This indicates that there were no female candidates taking the subject.
na = subject not yet introduced.

arts or sciences at the age of fourteen or fifteen (third or fourth year of secondary schooling). This streaming is usually done on the basis of examination results attained in the limited number of science subjects (such as integrated science and mathematics) and arts subjects (such as the languages and social studies) taken over two years. Very often schools will 'cream off' academically superior students for the more prestigious science stream, leaving the weaker students in the arts stream.

Since streaming is carried out at an early age, and provides only a very flimsy basis, there is considerable room left for non-academic factors, notably sex, to play a role. Teachers, for example, are far more likely to advise boys to enter the science stream, whilst discouraging girls, except for those with exceptionally good results. The effect of gender segregation in examination subjects means that from an early age, children will be impressed with the seemingly 'natural' fact that the two sexes are differently endowed for studies in the arts and sciences.

Nor is this 'natural endowment' for girls and boys in the pursuit of arts and science subjects a mere matter of dissimilarity. Any local schoolteacher, parent or student knows very well that school subjects are arranged in a kind of rank order which is informal, but nevertheless has real consequences. Luk (1991) differentiates between the 'incremental' and 'non-incremental' nature of science and arts subjects respectively. He notes that transition from the former to the latter at pre-college levels is relatively easy, whilst the opposite is difficult. As a result, secondary-school graduates from the science stream, who are predominantly male, have more options open to them when applying for admission into colleges and universities.

Apart from this instrumental advantage, pure and applied sciences generally enjoy much higher prestige than arts subjects in Hong Kong, as in most other societies. Critical theorists of education have attributed this to the technocratic-rational basis of most educational systems, which results in privileging natural sciences over arts and the humanities (Giroux, 1983). In the context of a Chinese society, such as Hong Kong, this discrepancy of status is probably augmented by the national experience of repeated military and political defeats since the last century, which then gave rise to an even higher prestige attached to modern science and technology. On an everyday level, the common opinion among teachers, parents, and students is that one needs greater intelligence to excel in science subjects, but only rote memory in the arts field. Gender segregation along these lines in local secondary schools therefore reinforces the poorer self-image and lower expectations generally held by girls. The psychological harm suffered by boys in the arts stream, of course, might also be considerable.

Various explanations have been put forward in other societies to explain this gender segregation of school subjects, though unfortunately no serious study of this issue has been undertaken locally. One explanation is differential teacher and parental expectations for boys and girls. The content of textbooks and classroom teaching is another explanation. They consistently construct a masculine image for science subjects, and a feminine image for the arts. Illustrations and images familiar to boys, such as those related to the military or team sports are used in science lessons and textbooks, while literature and the humanities are depicted as being more concerned with human relationships and emotions, an area deemed more appropriate for the female sex (Delamont, 1990). The anomaly that even in arts and the humanities it is men, and not women who are leaders in the field does not seem to affect the distinction between 'hard' (and therefore more demanding) and 'soft' (hence fit for the less intelligent) subjects at the secondary level or below.

Recent discussions in feminist studies point to deeply embedded affinities between masculinity (as seen and defined in Western cultures) and scientific pursuits. This might explain the differential attraction of science and arts subjects for male and female students, respectively. There is a common perception of a scientist, for example, as a powerful and yet distant person, which relates to the masculine self-image. Since girls and women are likely to have a different set of life experiences, including caring for others and transforming natural substances through activities like cooking, they are encouraged to see the world more in terms of links and continuities rather than separation and dualism (Jagger, 1990). It is likely therefore, that girls and women would have an aversion to science, as it is currently pursued, especially at pre-university levels where it is presented with an even higher degree of 'given-ness'. No study has been made locally of this particular issue, but one might imagine that the image of science as overtly masculine would be even more exaggerated in a Chinese society such as Hong Kong. The reason for this is that science and technology have been perceived, since the late nineteenth and early twentieth centuries, to be closely linked to national wealth and power (*fu-qiang*) in a generally acknowledged context of social Darwinism (Schwartz, 1964).

A closer look at the trend of gender segregation at the secondary level shows some interesting developments. Over the past decade-and-a-half gender imbalance has become steadily more marked in the arts subjects. Meanwhile, gender ratios for the more 'prestigious' science subjects — namely physics, chemistry, and additional mathematics — remain skewed, but there are signs that the gap is narrowing slowly but surely. In biology, the imbalance became more marked when human biology was offered as a new examination subject for arts students from the mid-1980s. As a result, human biology has become increasingly unpopular among boys. All this points to the extremely slow but steady increase of girls in the science stream, coupled, however, with the tendency for boys to avoid arts subjects to an increasing extent. Thus, it seems that the familiar scenario, whereby a minority of women strive to enter male-dominated fields, but with no concomitant change in the basic assumptions underlying existing gender divisions, is emerging in local secondary education also.

While there is a clear gender bias in the arts and sciences streams, segregation is very close to absolute in the case of some vocational subjects. These are 'male' subjects like electronics and electricity, design and technology, and metalwork, as well as 'female' subjects like needlework and home economics. There is no local anti-sex discrimination act or equal opportunities act such as those existing in many English-speaking countries, which prohibit schools from offering different subjects to males and females. While this differentiation is acknowledged as an illegal practice in other countries (Delamont, 1990), it is taken as a common, natural, and perfectly acceptable arrangement in pre-vocational and technical schools in Hong Kong, and would explain the low participation of women in technical and vocational education at the post-secondary level.

'Genderization' of school subjects is formalized in secondary schools, in particular, after streaming in the third or fourth year. Apart from the question of certain opportunities being closed to students of either gender, there is also the pedagogical effect to consider. There is no doubt that such institutionalized genderization of subjects leaves an indelible mark on the self-perceptions, aspirations and world views of innumerable young men and women who have gone through the schooling process.

Textbooks constitute another important channel of gender socialization, though in this area, only a limited number of studies are presently available. Luk and Yau (1988) studied the contents of history and social studies textbooks used in junior secondary schools, while Au (1993) analysed Chinese language, social studies and health education textbooks for primary schools. Both studies set for themselves the task of identifying the roles and images textbooks depict about gender, and their methods and parameters of measurement are similar. Their findings are consistent too, concurring on the passivity of women in contrast to the initiative and activity of men, the invisibility and domesticity of women, and the near monopoly of leadership by men in political, social and intellectual arenas.

Due to the aura of 'given-ness' and hence authority of textbooks, one can easily appreciate the influence these messages might have on students' world views and values. Nevertheless, in so far as students are not passive recipients, one has to consider the distance between the pedagogical messages and the perceived reality held by its users, in order to assess the long-term effects of such messages. In this regard, one would have to examine gender structures at work and in the family, as well as the prevalent attitude concerning gender relations in the media. This chapter confines itself to an examination of the school as the institutional context of cultural transmission, particularly its authority structure.

## Institutional Context of Cultural Transmission

Owing to the lack of observational or participatory studies of local schools, it is impossible to draw a clear picture of

*Table 4.8 Age and gender profile of teachers at various levels, 1991*

| Level of schooling | Total no. of teachers | % of women teachers | Mean age Men | Mean age Women |
|---|---|---|---|---|
| Kindergarten | 7,641 | 99.1 | 47.3 | 29.5 |
| Primary | 18,752 | 75.0 | 41.5 | 38.2 |
| Secondary | | | | |
|   non-graduate | 6,629 | 56.7 | | |
|   graduate | 11,190 | 45.1 | 34.9 | 34.0 |

Source: *Teacher Survey, 1991* (Education Department, Statistics Section, April 1992)

how gender affects social interaction in school. Nevertheless, it is possible to make use of available statistics to arrive at a general understanding of the authority structure of the school in relation to the gender factor.

The overall picture is a universally familiar one: there are more women teaching at the lower levels of the school system (Table 4.8). Kindergarten teachers, for example, are predominantly female (99.1 per cent overall, but 99.7 per cent if school heads are excluded). In primary schools, over 75 per cent of teachers are women, and this goes down to 56.7 per cent for non-graduate teachers, and 45.1 per cent for graduate teachers in secondary schools.

More concrete evidence can be found concerning status discrepancy between the genders in primary schools. The Education Department's *Teacher Survey, 1991* shows that the concentration of women is in the Junior Certificate Master/Mistress (CM) rank (80.7%), the initial teaching qualification giving a Teacher's Training Certificate, obtained on graduation from one of the four local teachers' training colleges. At the higher levels, women constitute half of the Assistant Master/Mistress (AM) posts, and account for only 33.3 per cent of the Senior Assistant Master/Mistress (SAM) posts.

Statistics regarding gender breakdown for various ranks among the secondary teaching force for 1991 are shown in Table 4.9.

## Table 4.9 Percentage of women teachers in secondary schools by rank, 1991

| Rank | % of women teachers |
| --- | --- |
| Principal I and II | 28.9 |
| Principal Graduate Master/Mistress (PGM) and Senior Education Officer (SEO)* | 33.6 |
| Graduate Master/Mistress (GM) and Assistant Education Officer (AEO) | 49.6 |
| Principal Assistant Master/Mistress (PAM)** | 33.3 |
| Senior Assistant Master/Mistress (SAM) | 39.0 |
| Assistant Master/Mistress (AM) | 52.2 |
| Certificate Master/Mistress (CM) | 62.4 |
| Private School Head | 12.5 |
| Private School Teacher | 32.7 |
| Other rank | 54.6 |
| Overall | 49.5 |

\* The counterparts of PGMs, SGMs, and GMs, who work in aided schools, are SEOs, EOs, and AEOs in government schools respectively. While their nomenclature differs, their ranks are actually equivalent. The ranks of PGMs and SEOs were added as from 1991 onwards, and these take up the role of assistant principals in the schools.
\*\* PAMs, SAMs, AMs, and CMs are equivalent in rank to those working in primary schools. In secondary schools, they teach in the junior classes, i.e., up to Form 3, the third year. The rank of PAM was added as from 1991 onwards.
*Source*: By courtesy of M. L. Lau (for Director of Education), Education Department.

This table demonstrates that secondary schools are essentially similar to primary schools in that women are concentrated in the lower ranks. This is true for both graduate teachers and non-graduate teachers. With the exception of a limited number of girls' schools which usually have a predominantly female teaching force, and therefore more women in important positions, most schools have male-dominated senior staff.

Gender discrepancy is greatest at the school principal level: only 28.9 per cent among them are women. Moreover, this ratio remained quite constant over the six years from 1985 to 1992 (Kingman-Lo, 1992). Given the lack of well-defined management structures in local schools, school principals, many of whom also double as supervisors representing school management committees, usually have thorough and wide-ranging powers within their schools (Hong Kong Education Department and Education and Manpower Branch, 1991). Together with the gender bias in school subjects and textbooks, this structure of male leadership is likely to impart a world view in which male authority is taken as given and natural.

Male leadership is also obvious in universities and colleges. In the two older universities, the gender ratio of the teaching force is about 85 per cent male versus 15 per cent female (Table 4.10). As one moves to the professorial ranks, the ratio becomes even more skewed: about 93 per cent versus 7 per cent. This is true even of the arts faculties, which have the highest concentration of women students.

In the two polytechnics, which, until the early 1990s, had a lower pay scale and slightly lower prestige, the gender gap is not as wide: about 75 per cent male to 25 per cent female (Table 4.11). At the professorial ranks, however, the gap is even wider than that of universities: about 97 per cent male to 3 per cent female. Meanwhile, the gap is smallest in the colleges of education: about 56 per cent male to 44 per cent female (Table 4.12). These colleges are much less prestigious as post-secondary institutions, and in the past three decades, women have been outnumbering men among the student population. Moreover, this gap is steadily widening, probably as a result of an increase in higher-education opportunities, making teacher education even less attractive to men.

*Table 4.10  Gender distribution of full-time teaching staff at the University of Hong Kong and the Chinese University of Hong Kong, 1992–1993#*

| Faculty | Reader/ Professor Male/ Female | Senior Lecturer Male/ Female | Lecturer Male/ Female | Total (%) Male/ Female |
|---|---|---|---|---|
| Architecture* | 4/0 | 6/0 | 41/5 | 51/5 (91.1%)/(8.9%) |
| Arts | 31/4 | 44/4 | 121/31 | 196/39 (83.4%)/(16.6%) |
| Business Administration** | 8/1 | 14/4 | 38/8 | 60/13 (82.2%)/(17.8%) |
| Dentistry* | 10/0 | 8/1 | 72/8 | 90/9 (90.9%)/(9.1%) |
| Education | 7/1 | 17/2 | 49/22 | 63/25 (71.6%)/(28.4%) |
| Engineering | 27/0 | 40/1 | 105/3 | 172/4 (97.7%)/(2.3%) |
| Law* | 3/2 | 12/16 | 44/19 | 59/1 (75.6%)/(24.4%) |
| Medicine | 78/17 | 58/83 | 327/110 | 463/10 (80.8%)/(19.2%) |
| Science | 38/0 | 25/0 | 97/1 | 160/1 (99.4%)/(0.6%) |
| Social Science | 37/1 | 38/8 | 125/27 | 200/30 (84.7%)/(15.3%) |
| Total | 243/18 (93.1%)/ (6.9%) | 262/39 (87.0%)/ (13.0%) | 1019/204 (83.3%)/ (16.7%) | 1514/261 (85.3%)/ (14.7%) |

* Only exists in the University of Hong Kong.
** Only exists in the Chinese University of Hong Kong.
# Due to technical difficulties, statistics for the Hong Kong University of Science & Technology are not available.
*Source*: The Chinese University of Hong Kong, Telephone Directory, November 1992, Information Office, CUHK; Calendar, 1992–93, (Part 2), Registry, The University of Hong Kong.

*Table 4.11 Gender distribution of full-time teaching staff at the Hong Kong Polytechnic and the City Polytechnic of Hong Kong, 1992–1993*

| Faculty/ Area of studies* | Reader/ Professor Male/Female | Principal and Senior Lecturer Male/Female | Lecturer Male/Female | Total (%) Male/Female |
|---|---|---|---|---|
| Applied Social Sciences and Law | 6/0 | 63/27 | 35/41 | 104/68 (60.5%)/(39.5%) |
| Commerce | 6/0 | 76/27 | 73/48 | 155/75 (67.4%)/(32.6%) |
| Design | 1/0 | 10/7 | 12/9 | 23/16 (59.0%)/(41.0%) |
| Health and Related Sciences | 0/0 | 24/13 | 20/39 | 44/52 (45.8%)/(54.2%) |
| Language Studies | 2/1 | 37/14 | 27/33 | 66/48 (57.9%)/(42.1%) |
| Science and Technology | 21/0 | 289/28 | 308/44 | 618/72 (89.6%)/(10.4%) |
| Total | 36/1 (97.3%)/(2.7%) | 499/116 (81.1%)/(18.9%) | 475/214 (68.9%)/(31.1%) | 1,010/331 (75.3%)/(24.7%) |

* For classification of departments into areas of study, please refer to appendix.
*Source*: The Hong Kong Polytechnic, Telephone Directory, 1992–1993; Chinese Polytechnic of Hong Kong, Telephone Directory, 1992–1993.

Throughout the education system therefore, male leadership predominates, and this is more so at higher levels and in more prestigious institutions. Besides being a manifestation of gender inequality in itself, this situation has at least two consequences. It reinforces the belief in male superiority along with textbooks, curricula, and pedagogy. It also reduces the possibility of the nurturing, within educational institutions, of a sensitivity to structured gender inequalities,

## Table 4.12 Gender distribution of full-time teaching staff at colleges of education, 1991

| Rank | Male | Female | Total |
|---|---|---|---|
| Vice-Principal | 8 | 6 | 14 |
| Principal/Senior Lecturer | 71 | 47 | 118 |
| Lecturer (Graduate) | 98 | 97 | 195 |
| Lecturer (Non-Graduate) | 27 | 13 | 40 |
| Total | 204 (55.6%) | 163 (44.4%) | 367 (100.0%) |

*Source*: Hong Kong Government Staff List, 1991, pp. 266–73.

and hence of a more desirable alternative in future. From the general neglect of the gender variable in the publication of official statistics, one might venture to say that such sensitivity is very low indeed.[1]

## Equality, Gender Roles, and Sexuality

The issue of gender inequality in the education system with respect to participation, curriculum, contents and pedagogy, and the authority structure of institutions has been examined. In this penultimate section, a crucial aspect in the process of growing up will be discussed. Namely, that of gender roles and sexuality. This is important, since gender roles and sexuality, as they are actually experienced by the individual, have serious repercussions on gender equality, not least in that structures of gender inequality are always explained in terms of allegedly 'natural' differences between the genders.

### Gender-Role Acceptance

The data concerning gender-role acceptance are drawn from past studies conducted by The Family Planning Association (FPA) of Hong Kong regarding the sexuality of secondary-school students and young people. The FPA, an organization which pioneered the promotion of contraception and sex

## Table 4.13 Gender-role acceptance of adolescents and young people in Hong Kong, 1981 and 1986

| Gender Role acceptance* | Secondary school students 1981 M | 1981 F | 1986 M | 1986 F | Young people aged 18–27 1986 M | 1986 F |
|---|---|---|---|---|---|---|
| Non-acceptance % | 1.4 | 17.9 | 1.4 | 16.4 | 4.6 | 30.8 |
| Acceptance % | 94.1 | 71.9 | 93.7 | 74.8 | 95.1 | 68.9 |
| Unknown** % | 4.2 | 8.3 | 2.1 | 7.8 | 0.3 | 0.3 |
| Head count | 1,888 | 2,029 | 788 | 756 | 613 | 692 |

\* Among secondary students, the question: 'If it were possible, would you consider altering your gender?' was asked. An affirmative answer is taken to indicate non-acceptance, and a negative one, acceptance. Among young people, the question whether they would rather be of the opposite sex was asked instead.
\*\* The answer 'no idea' was chosen.
Source: The Family Planning Association of Hong Kong, *Working Report on Adolescent Sexuality Study 1986*, 1986, pp. 57 and 101.

education, has been providing so-called 'family-life education' (sex education) to youths since 1967. In 1981, its Education and Youthwork Sub-Committee conducted its first survey of youths on various aspects, including familial and heterosexual interactions, growth experience and perceptions of sexuality. Respondents were drawn from students between Form 3 to Form 6 (14 to 17 years old). Five years later, the survey was repeated, this time with the additional sample of older youths (18 to 27 years old).

Gender-role acceptance among secondary students was operationally defined as a negative response to the hypothetical question: 'If you had the chance to change your sex, would you take it?' Young people aged 18 to 27 were asked instead whether they would rather be of the opposite sex. Results showed that a significant discrepancy existed between male and female adolescents, and young people.

Table 4.13 indicates that secondary schoolgirls had a much

lower level of acceptance than schoolboys, with a significant difference of around 20 per cent. What is even more revealing is that the level of non-acceptance of one's gender role was highest among young adult women studied in 1986. This was 30.8 per cent as compared to only 4.6 per cent among their male counterparts, 16.4 per cent among secondary schoolgirls in 1986, and 17.9 per cent among schoolgirls in 1981 (who would have grown into the same age group as the young women interviewed in 1986). For both males and females, ambivalence regarding one's gender role (the category 'unknown') seemed to decrease significantly with age, but sadly, for many women, this meant greater certainty in rejecting instead of accepting their own gender.

Without longitudinal and in-depth studies into the growth experience of young men and women, it is impossible to give a satisfactory account of the significant difference in the levels of acceptance between the two gender groups, and also between girls and young adult women. At this stage, one could only suggest areas in which answers could be found, and these include: experience and perception on the part of adolescent girls and young women of various social constraints (educational, occupational, and behavioural) specific to their gender, and of cultural restrictions on the female body and sexuality.

As yet, there are insufficient data regarding the above areas, but a tentative exploration will be attempted. Regarding cultural restrictions on the female body and sexuality, the *Adolescent Sexuality Study* (Family Planning Association, 1986) offers further details. In this study, questions were asked concerning boys' and girls' reaction towards selected physical signs of the onset of puberty: nocturnal emission for boys and menstruation for girls. From Table 4.14, it can be seen that there is a great discrepancy between boys and girls in their reaction towards such physical signs. While around 14 per cent of boys felt worried about nocturnal emission, more than 40 per cent of the girls felt worried about menstruation.

As stated in the original report, 'the experience (of nocturnal emission) is hardly equivalent to menstruation when its psychological and social significance is taken into account' (The Family Planning Association of Hong Kong, 1986). This terse statement summarizes a host of socio-cultural

## Table 4.14 Attitude towards onset of nocturnal emission (boys) and menstruation (girls), 1981 and 1986

| Attitude | 1981 Boys | 1981 Girls | 1986 Boys | 1986 Girls |
| --- | --- | --- | --- | --- |
| Not worried % | 74.8 | 50.1 | 77.6 | 53.0 |
| Worried % | 14.2 | 45.8 | 14.3 | 42.8 |
| No information % | 11.0 | 4.1 | 8.1 | 4.2 |
| Head count | 1,054 | 1,967 | 426 | 72.5 |

*Source*: The Family Planning Association of Hong Kong, *Working Report on Adolescent Sexuality Study 1986*, 1986, pp. 65, 67.

restrictions that impinge on the female psyche. One of these concerns female 'contamination' of the male world, as exemplified by existing beliefs in the polluting forces of menstrual blood in particular (the common description of it as being 'dirty') and of anything emanating from the female body in general.[2] The tenacity of beliefs about female contamination is such that girls and women are at present banned from subways or road tunnels which are under construction.[3]

No matter what the specific explanations concerning these socio-cultural beliefs are, the consequences are essentially the same, namely social exclusion and marginalization of girls and women. To this day, the Chinese word for 'woman' (*nui-yan* in Cantonese, or *nuu-ren* in Putonghua) still carries a negative connotation, which associates the person or object spoken of with undesirable qualities, including pettiness, trouble, and disrespect.

With such social exclusion and marginalization inflicted on the female sex, it is no wonder that many adolescent girls and young women find it hard to accept their gender role, and to come to terms with the physical signs of the onset of puberty. Sexual harassment and assault in its various forms, to which many women are subjected at various times of their lives, have not yet been mentioned. Sexual crime has the consequence of intimidating women, excluding them from male territory such as public places and the workplace, and ultimately degrading them.[4] Furthermore, everyday conversations (mostly but not exclusively male) and the media contain the ubiquitous message of women's bodies being sex-objects, which does not, in any way, add to the dignity of being a woman (AAF, 1993). Although very little research has been done into how this affects the psyche of growing girls, one could still venture to say that such messages would leave a less than desirable impression on them, particularly on their self-esteem. Turning sexuality into a commodity is likely to be internalized as part of young women's socialization to the extent that it may even pre-dispose some of them to participate in the commercial sex industry (Pearson and Yu, Chapter 9).

## *Female Chastity: Double Standards in Sexual Mores*

One crucial aspect of sexuality is the cultural image of female chastity — a double standard in sexual mores. In a recent study among university students, it was found that this image still exerts a relatively strong hold. In a 1991 questionnaire survey of 516 students (223 male, 293 female) of Chung Chi College, The Chinese University of Hong Kong, a stronger demand for female rather than male chastity was very much in evidence.

Table 4.15 shows that among university students, women were consistently more stringent in their sexual behaviour. Furthermore, while men were generally less strict about sexual mores, they were stricter when it concerned women. Nevertheless, the two genders seemed not to differ significantly as regards their expectation of their partners being virgins. For both genders, the proportion that held such an expectation exceeded 40 per cent.

## *The Teaching of Sexuality in School*

Having examined various contradictions in sexuality, it is necessary to ask how those who design the school curriculum address the issue of sex education.

In the highly academic and examination-oriented curriculum structure in Hong Kong, 'fringe subjects', like sex

*Table 4.15  Sexual mores held by university students, 1991*

| Sexual Mores | Yes | | No | | No definite answer | |
|---|---|---|---|---|---|---|
| | M | F | M | F | M | F |
| Expect partner to be a virgin at marriage % | 46.2 | 43.4 | 29.2 | 29.3 | 24.7 | 27.3 |

| | Not accept | | Accept | | No definite answer | |
|---|---|---|---|---|---|---|
| | M | F | M | F | M | F |
| Pre-marital sex for men % | 34.0 | 48.1 | 44.3 | 28.7 | 21.7 | 23.2 |
| Pre-marital sex for women % | 46.6 | 54.6 | 34.5 | 25.6 | 18.9 | 19.8 |
| Cohabitation for unmarried men % | 29.6 | 35.8 | 56.9 | 47.5 | 13.5 | 16.7 |
| Cohabitation for unmarried women % | 37.7 | 39.3 | 53.4 | 44.4 | 8.9 | 16.3 |

*Source*: Choi Po-King, 'Marriage and Sexual Norms Among University Students', *Gender Studies: News And Views*, No. 2, September, 1991 [in Chinese].

education and civic education are naturally given rather low priority. Nevertheless, the Education Department did issue a set of guidelines on sex education in secondary schools in 1986 (Hong Kong Education Department, 1986). This was followed by a few pamphlets introducing the subject to teachers (Hong Kong Education Department, 1990a, 1990c), as well as a four-volume teaching kit on sexual attitudes and values, all issued in 1990 (Hong Kong Education Department, 1990b). Furthermore, other teaching materials are available compiled by voluntary institutions such as the Family Planning Association of Hong Kong. For our purpose of identifying the general direction in which sex education in our schools might be heading, it is appropriate to base our review on the official guidelines and materials mentioned above.

The official sex-education materials manifest several major characteristics. First, there seems to be a major concern for preventing unwanted youth pregnancies. Probably as a result of this concern, the materials place a heavy emphasis on human reproduction, hence the frequent appearance (in written explanations and pictorial illustrations) of the female reproductive organs and functions. Meanwhile, there is also a puritan wariness of promiscuity and transient, non-committal sex, hence the frequent warnings against 'infatuation' and 'sex for sex's sake'.

With such an instrumental emphasis on youth control, it is hardly surprising that there has been no attempt whatsoever to discuss critically the prevailing socio-cultural context of the sexual act: gratification of male desire, women as sex objects, and male violence. Without this context, the frequent portrayal of reproductive organs, particularly those of the female, becomes a gross simplification. Worse still, the frequent display of female reproductive organs strengthens the conventional idea of the woman's body as the object of male-initiated sex. Admittedly, there is a brief mention of 'sexual exploitation', presumably by men of women. Unfortunately, it is here that the materials go wrong. Instead of acknowledging sexual harassment as a violation of the victim's rights, privacy and dignity, it is defined as 'coercion to fulfil one's sexual desires' (Hong Kong Education Department, 1986). This misrepresents the common understanding among psychologists and counsellors that in most cases of sexual assault, the perpetrators are not motivated by desire, but by the wish to overpower through violence.

The materials do attempt to move beyond the technical and seemingly neutral descriptions of sex and reproduction and discuss gender relationships, including gender-role stereotyping and the double standards behind the rule of female chastity. However, it is exactly here that the curriculum designers show great ambivalence towards gender inequality. Stereotyping is reduced to misinformation from 'the media', and the women's rights movement is mentioned in an offhand manner. In a chapter on gender attributes, students are asked to go through the exercise of assigning 'masculine' and 'feminine' labels to certain items of behaviour, thereby working to strengthen rather than challenge the existing myth about the 'naturalness' of gender difference. Instead of inviting them to challenge this myth, advice is frequently offered to students to 'accept' and 'respect' existing, dichotomized gender roles.

Given the compromising and uncritical nature of sex education, not to mention its low priority in the school curriculum, it is highly unlikely that students would be stimulated to evaluate critically the contradictions built into existing concepts of sexuality.

# Conclusions

Liberal thinkers have always placed great faith in the efficacy of a well-designed education system, and pedagogy in the elimination of various forms of inequality, including that structured on gender (Stromquist, 1990). This chapter has outlined the extent of gender inequality in the local education system with regard to patterns of participation, curriculum content and the authority structure of schools and universities. Generally, we have shown how education — its structure and content (both manifest and hidden) — works to reflect and uphold gender inequality in the wider society.

An awareness of such inequality and measures to overcome it would certainly go a long way towards achieving greater gender equality. In order for any strategy towards this end to be adequately designed and implemented, however, one has to have sufficient understanding of the intricate processes and mechanisms by which gender acts as a constraint — in school, the family and the workplace. As yet, available studies in Hong Kong are still far too scanty to provide an adequate picture. Much more has to be done.

We have seen the low level of official sensitivity towards the gender issue in education. Yet we should not lose sight of the profound importance of the education system in shaping the consciousness of our young people. Indeed, school is second only to family in its capacity to mould and fix each person's expectations about his or her own, and other people's, place in the world. In addition to this, so much of what happens in later life is playing out a script laid down in our early years. The most obvious example is, of course, in career choices and opportunities, but ideas about families and marital roles are also profoundly affected by what happens at school. The discussion in this chapter has shown that we cannot afford to be complacent about gender issues in our education system. Equal access to education does not mean equal educational opportunities. It behoves us, for many reasons, not to assume that because we have the former we also have the latter.

## Acknowledgement

The author acknowledges with gratitude the help of Ms Wai-chun Cheung in the preparation of the tables in this chapter.

## Notes

1. One of the most widely used government publications, *Hong Kong Annual Digest of Statistics*, stopped providing information on gender breakdown of enrolment in tertiary institutions from 1989. Meanwhile, similar information concerning enrolment in technical institutes and the two polytechnics for more recent years are no longer available in the Education Department *Annual Summary*. As for the institutes and polytechnics themselves, no information on gender participation has ever been made available. Information on gender breakdown is also meagre and sporadic in the annual *Teacher Survey* published by the Education Department.
2. In a press report of a case of pick-pocketing, two thieves who were caught in a busy shopping area complained of bad luck. This was not only because they were caught, but because they discovered what they had stolen from a woman's handbag to be a packet of sanitary napkins. The woman concerned was said to be 'very embarrassed'. See *Oriental Daily News*, 2 June 1989.
3. A common understanding among local journalists is that when press visits are arranged to subways or tunnels nearing completion,

only men should be sent because women colleagues will be refused entry outright. I was told recently by a senior teacher of a secondary school that he once wrote to the office of the Shing Mun tunnel (a road tunnel opened in 1990, linking two recently developed satellite towns, Shatin and Tsuen Wan) before it was open to public use, requesting a visit by a party of their students. An affirmative reply came, but with a clear statement that no girls should be allowed to join the visit. In a conversation over the phone, the officer-in-charge explained that it was because the range of hills through which the tunnel was built was a 'dragon's artery', (a geomancer's term) and the presence of women or girls would bring contamination or destruction. In the end, an all-male party from this co-educational school went, leaving the girls behind.

4. See *Women's Experience of Sexual Assault* [in Chinese], jointly published by the Coalition Concerned With Sexual Assault on Women and the Association for the Prevention of Child Abuse, November, 1992. In the reported questionnaire survey of about 455 women who were 21 years old, or above, it was found that 85 per cent of them had experienced sexual assault or harassment at least once in the past two years. The two most common experiences were obscene phone calls (49.2 per cent) and unnecessary physical touching or rubbing (47.9 per cent). See also Po-king Choi, et al., *Power and Dignity: Sexual Harassment on Campus in Hong Kong*, Occasional Paper no. 32, Hong Kong Institute for Asia-Pacific Studies, The Chinese University of Hong Kong, December 1993.

In the study on sexual harassment on campus, one woman respondent articulated her feelings of degradation whenever she heard men discuss the sexual prowess or physical features of women. Sexual harassment, involving such remarks by men in the presence of women, constituted to her an infringement of the dignity of women as a group.

# References

Association for the Advancement of Feminism (1993), *The Hong Kong Women's File*, Hong Kong: Association for the Advancement of Feminism, pp. 87–106 [in Chinese].

Au, Kit-chun (1993), *A Study of Gender Roles as Defined in Primary School Textbooks in Hong Kong*, Occasional paper no. 18, Hong Kong: Hong Kong Institute of Asia-Pacific Studies, The Chinese University of Hong Kong.

Census and Statistics Department (various years), *Hong Kong Annual Digest of Statistics*, Hong Kong: Hong Kong Government Printer.

Choi, Po-king (1992), 'Education', in Joseph Y. S. Cheng and Paul Kwong (eds.), *The Other Hong Kong Report 1992*, Hong Kong: Chinese University Press, pp. 249–79.

—— (1993), 'Women', in P. K. Choi and L. S. Ho (eds.), *The Other Hong Kong Report 1993*, Hong Kong: Chinese University Press, pp. 369–400.

Choi, Po-king, Au Kit-chun, Fanny M. C. Cheung, et al. (1993), *Power and Dignity: Sexual Harassment on Campus in Hong Kong*, Occasional Paper no. 32, Hong Kong Institute of Asia-Pacific Studies, The Chinese University of Hong Kong.

Coalition Concerned with Sexual Assault on Women, and the Association for the Prevention of Child Abuse, *Women's Experience of Sexual Assault*, November 1992 [in Chinese].

Delamont, Sara (1990), *Sex Roles and the School*, London: Routledge, 2nd edition.

Family Planning Association of Hong Kong (1986), *The Working Report on Adolescent Sexuality Study*, Hong Kong: The Family Planning Association.

Giroux, Henry (1983), 'Theories of Reproduction and Resistance', in The New Sociology of Education: A Critical Analysis, *Harvard Educational Review*, 53(3): 257–93.

Hong Kong Education Department (1986), *Guidelines on Sex Education in Secondary Schools*, Hong Kong: Curriculum Development Committee.

—— (1990a), *How to Introduce Physical Changes at Puberty to Students*, [in Chinese].

—— (1990b), *A Teaching Kit on Sexual Attitudes and Values*, Introductory Guidebook, and Parts I to IV, Social Studies & Health Education Section, Advisory Inspectorate, with the Secondary Curriculum Development Team (Social Studies).

—— (1990c), *Teaching Sex Education in School*, Curriculum Development Team (Social Studies).

—— (various years), *Annual Summary*.

Hong Kong Education and Manpower Branch (March 1991), The School Management Initiative.

Jagger, Alison M. (1990), 'Sexual Difference and Sexual Equality', in Deborah L. Rhode (ed.), *Theoretical Perspectives on Sexual Difference*, New Haven & London: Yale University Press, pp. 239–54.

Kingman-Lo, Ip-Shan (1992), *Hong Kong Secondary School Women Principals: A Study of Gender Bias*, unpublished M.Ed. dissertation, Hong Kong: The University of Hong Kong.

Lau, Chun-kwok (1992), *Occupational Differences Between the Sexes*,

unpublished M.Ed. thesis, Hong Kong: The Chinese University of Hong Kong.
Luk, Hung-kay (1991), 'Women's Opportunities in Tertiary Education in Hong Kong', in Fanny M. Cheung, Wan Po-san, Choi Hang-keung, and Choy Lee-Man (eds.), *Selected Papers of Conference on Gender Studies in Chinese Societies*, Hong Kong: Hong Kong Institute of Asia-Pacific Studies, The Chinese University of Hong Kong, pp. 271–6 [in Chinese].
Mak, Grace C. L. (1992), 'The Schooling of Girls in Hong Kong: Progress and Contradictions in the Transition', in Gerard A. Postiglione (ed.), *Education and Society in Hong Kong: Towards One Country and Two Systems*, Hong Kong: Hong Kong University Press, pp. 167–80.
Ou Hang-yue (1990), 'Higher Education and Gender Equality: The Case of Hong Kong', *Education Journal*, School of Education, The Chinese University of Hong Kong, pp. 107–13.
Pearson, Veronica (1990), 'Women in Hong Kong', in Benjamin K. P. Leung (ed.), *Social Issues in Hong Kong*, Hong Kong: Oxford University Press, pp. 114–39.
Schwartz, Benjamin (1964), *In Search of Wealth and Power*, London: Belknap Press.
Stromquist, Nelly P. (1990), 'Gender Inequality in Education: Accounting for Women's Subordination', *British Journal of Sociology of Education*, 11(2): pp. 137–53
Tsang Wing-kwong (1993), *Educational and Early Socio-economic Status Attainment in Hong Kong*, Occasional Paper, Hong Kong: Hong Kong Institute of Asia-Pacific Studies, The Chinese University of Hong Kong.
Yau-Lai, Betty Lai-ling and Luk Hung-kay (1988), *A Study of Gender Roles in Junior Secondary Chinese History and Social Studies Textbooks in Hong Kong*, Hong Kong: Institute of Social Studies, The Chinese University of Hong Kong [in Chinese].

# Appendix

Classification of Area of Studies in The Hong Kong Polytechnic and The City Polytechnic of Hong Kong: Applied Social Sciences and Law includes: Departments of Applied Social Studies in Hong Kong Polytechnic (HKP), Applied Social Studies, Economics and Finance, Law, Public and Social Administration, and Division of Humanities and Social Sciences in The City Polytechnic of Hong Kong (CPHK).

Commerce includes: Departments of Accountancy, Business Studies,

Hotel and Tourism Management, Management in HKP, Accountancy, Business and Management, and Division of Commerce in CPHK.

Design refers to the Swire School of Design in HKP.

Health and Related Sciences includes: Faculty of Health Sciences, Optometry and Radiography, Rehabilitation Sciences in HKP.

Language Studies includes: Departments of Chinese Translation and Interpretation, and English in HKP, departments of Chinese Translation and Linguistics, English, and the Language Institute in CPHK.

Science and Technology includes: Departments of Land Surveying and Geo-Information, Applied Maths, Applied Physics, Computing, Institute of Textile and Clothing, Centre for Maritime Studies, Faculty of Building and Surveying, Faculty of Applied Biology and Chemical Technology, and all the engineering departments in HKP, departments of Applied Science, Applied Statistics and Operational Research, Building and Construction, Computer Science, Electronic Engineering, Information Systems, Manufacturing Engineering, Mathematics, and Division of Technology in CPHK.

# 5 Political Participation

*Terry T. Lui*

On December 16, 1992, the Hong Kong Legislative Council passed a motion urging the British and Hong Kong governments to take action to extend to the territory the United Nations Convention on the Elimination of all Forms of Discrimination Against Women (CEDAW). The event marked an important victory for advocates of sexual equality, since it signified the formal endorsement of the principle of non-discrimination against women by the highest law-making body in the territory. However, the passage of the motion cannot in itself guarantee a fairer society. As the analysis in this chapter will show, the long-term prospects for sexual equality will have to depend on the active participation of women in local politics.

Such an argument is founded on a consideration of the political realities confronting women in Hong Kong. The first is that Hong Kong's political system is executive-led. Hong Kong's legislature, the Legislative Council can express its views on policy issues, but the ultimate decision-makers are often the senior public administrators in charge of the policy branches in the Government Secretariat (Lau, 1984; Miners, 1991). Hence, whether real changes in the direction of sexual equality through policy and legislative imperatives will be effected depends as much (if not more) on the commitment of top-level civil servants, as on the sentiments of legislative councillors.

The second consideration relates to the policy process. In common with legislatures elsewhere, the Hong Kong Legislative Council deals with many problems in society. In some instances, solutions to these problems involve a choice among conflicting values and interests. In other cases, implementation of the accepted solutions requires resources in excess of what the community can afford. Under these circumstances, the legislature has to establish priorities for actions and decisions. The Council may have recognized the need to address the problem of sexual inequality, but whether, and to what extent, the relevant policy measures will be adopted is inevitably a function of the relative importance that legislators attach to women's issues generally. This, in turn, depends as much on the legislators' subjective value stance as on the objective presence or absence of other competing concerns confronting the Legislative Council.

The third determinant of the prospects of sexual equality in Hong Kong pertains to the fact that the life-span of the present colonial government is limited. Under the terms of the Sino-British Joint Declaration, 1984, Britain's rule in Hong Kong will terminate on June 30, 1997 and China will resume sovereignty over the territory. The implication of this is that any obligation which the December 1992 motion has imposed upon Britain will theoretically be taken over by the new sovereign master, China. Hence, China's willingness to continue to uphold the spirit of CEDAW as it applies to Hong Kong will be of vital importance in shaping the future course of gender relations in the territory.

There is another aspect of the 1997 change of sovereignty which affects the success of the implementation of reform towards greater sexual equality, and it relates to the problem of 'competing concerns'. The issue of 1997 has brought about a turbulent environment, characterized by an unprecedented level of politicization in the community, and a gradual erosion of the authority and legitimacy of the colonial administration (Scott, 1989). Under these conditions, the government has to contend with a multitude of pressing concerns, some of which are of critical political significance. In the midst of these developments, policy-makers may be tempted to regard the question of women's rights and opportunities as a matter of secondary importance only.

The central question, then, is how supporters of the feminist cause can sustain the momentum and push the issue of sexual equality onto the policy agenda. This in turn is dependent on the type and degree of influence which women's concern groups and individuals can exert upon the authoritative policy-making machinery in the government. Not all of these groups or individuals necessarily comprise women, but since women are the major stake-holders in this political process, it is reasonable to assume that the level of political participation among women in Hong Kong, and the degree to which it is active and direct, will have an important bearing on the future of women's status in society.

In assessing the future of gender relations in Hong Kong, therefore, the question of women's political participation must be addressed. The following sections are designed to explore this subject in detail, but first it is essential that we define the term 'political participation'.

## The Concept of Political Participation

'Political participation' is a key concept in political science. It has been defined in many different ways. In essence, however, most conceptions stem from an understanding of politics as involving the 'authoritative allocation of values for a society' (Easton, 1971: 129) and the determination of 'who gets what, when, and how' (Lasswell, 1958). In a narrow sense, political participation refers to engagement in activities which are legally provided for 'within the system' and are 'aimed at influencing the government in some way' (Verba and Nie, 1972: 3, 29). Used in a broad sense, political participation encompasses all forms of mobilization of organizations and resources to engage in collective action — orderly or disorderly, legitimate or otherwise — for the purpose of affecting the distribution of power and benefits in a community (Gamson, 1975; Tilly and Gurin, 1990: 5–6).

The delineation between the narrow and broad senses of political participation is particularly useful in situations where legitimate channels for gaining access to government are limited. Under such conditions, the line between what is permissible 'within the system' and what falls outside that system can be more clearly drawn. In Hong Kong, the distinction is less helpful for two reasons. The first is that Hong Kong is a relatively free society where the right to express one's opinion is generally respected and sanctioned. There is not normally a perceived need on the part of interest groups to resort to extra-legal means to pursue their goals. Secondly, although Hong Kong people have become more politically active in recent years, most still appear to adhere to conventional modes of participation to influence government policy (Lau and Kuan, 1988, chapter 3). Mass mobilization and collective action are not a distinguishing feature of politics in the territory.

Our analysis will therefore be based on a simple conception

of political participation as comprising all actions taken by individuals or groups to engage in, or to impinge upon, the authoritative decision-making process in a polity. Participation can be direct or indirect. In the former case, the participant is personally involved in the political deliberative process, either as a member of the legitimate policy-making machinery, or as a lobbyist acting upon that machinery. Indirect participation, on the other hand, refers to those instances when the participant's goals are pursued through a mediator, whether it be a person, a political party, or a pressure group.

Political participatory activity can also be formal or informal. The key difference lies in whether the participant operates within the established institutions and procedures for arriving at authoritative decisions (for example, the system of election), or whether informal means are utilized such as public opinion, or the mass media, to exert pressure upon the political process.

On the basis of these concepts, a matrix can be constructed to categorize a number of activities which are often associated with political participation in many societies. Using the typology developed in Table 5.1 as a conceptual framework, an analysis of the level of women's political participation in Hong Kong can be presented.

## Women and Political Participation

There are many channels available for the people of Hong Kong to affect government policy. The following discussion focuses on those activities which represent the most common forms of political participation in the territory. These include: assumption of office in the public arena, membership of independent and advisory bodies, participation in elections, involvement in political organizations, and public expression of opinions on socio-political issues.

### *Assumption of Public Office*

In this context, 'public office' refers to all positions in the political and administrative systems which are charged with the responsibility of formulating, enacting, implementing or

## Table 5.1  A typology of political participatory activities*

|  | Formal | Informal |
| --- | --- | --- |
| Direct | – Assumption of public office<br>– Standing for public office<br>– Engagement in political party or interest group activities | – Expressing opinions on political and social issues in public<br>– Direct interaction with and lobbying of authoritative decision-makers in government<br>– Engagement in protest actions against the authorities |
| Indirect | – Voting<br>– Campaigning or canvassing support for political candidates<br>– Recruitment and training of political leaders<br>– Engagement in internal organization or co-ordination work to strengthen the capabilities of political parties or interest groups | – Organization of and involvement in public education programmes and other mobilization activities aimed at changing attitudes, shaping perceptions, structuring preferences and heightening the awareness of specific groups or constituents in the political community<br>– Responding to public opinion surveys on political and social matters |

* The activities listed above cover some of the most typical forms of political participation; they are not meant to be exhaustive. The categorization of some items may also vary across different societies as the line between 'formal' and 'informal' politics is often context-specific.

*Table 5.2 Percentage of female councillors at the three levels of the political system*

|  |  | Total number of councillors | Number of female councillors | Percentage of female members in the full council |
|---|---|---|---|---|
| Central Level | Executive council* | 16 | 4 | 25 |
|  | Legislative council* | 61 | 7 | 11.5 |
| Municipal Level | Urban council** | 40 | 7 | 17.5 |
|  | Regional council** | 36 | 1 | 2.8 |
| District Level | District Boards*** | 434 | 42 | 9.7 |

* Figures provided include the Presidents and all *ex-officios*, and are based on the membership lists as of 2 January 1993.
** Figures provided include the Chairmen and Vice-Chairmen, and are based on the membership lists of 2 January 1992 as shown in the *Official Annual Report, Hong Kong 1992* (Hong Kong: Government Printer, 1992).
*** Figures provided represent the gross total of the nineteen District Boards as listed in the *Civil and Miscellaneous Lists*, Hong Kong Government, 1 July 1991 (Hong Kong: Government Printer, 1991).

interpreting government policy. The discussion will therefore focus on the Executive and Legislative Councils, the two Municipal Councils, the District Boards, the civil service, and the judiciary.

The distribution of male and female councillors in the three tiers of the political system in Hong Kong is presented in Table 5.2. What clearly emerges is that there is an underrepresentation of women at all levels of government; particularly so in the Regional Council, and on the rural District Boards — the formation of which is rather heavily influenced by the male-dominated, New Territories-based advisory body, the Heung Yee Kuk.[1]

Women comprise a quarter of the membership of the highest policy advisory body, the Executive Council. However, Executive Councillors are all appointed by the Secretary of State in Britain upon the Hong Kong Governor's recommendation. Conventionally, appointments onto the Executive Council (and for that matter, the Legislative Council) tend to have been made primarily on the basis of the individuals' capabilities and expertise. The level of female representation in the Council is therefore subject, to some extent, to shifting policy concerns. Furthermore, female appointees have generally been highly accomplished in their respective fields; their very achievements and élitist image do not readily lend them credence as champions of the cause of the average woman in society (Studwell, 1992).

Apart from the fact that women constitute only a numerical minority in the formal political institutions, there is also the consideration that women's entry into politics is a fairly recent phenomenon. The Legislative Council had its first female appointee in 1966. That individual, Mrs Ellen Li Shupui, remained the only woman in the Council until 1972, when the number of women rose marginally to three. Between 1973 and 1980, the level of female representation in the legislature averaged 5 per cent of the full Council. That figure rose to 11 per cent from 1980 to 1988 when female legislators were increased from between one and three between 1973 and 1980 to between four and seven. The situation continued to improve slightly after 1988, as women began to occupy an average of around 21 per cent of the seats in the legislature. Unfortunately, as can be seen in Table 5.2, the overall percentage of female members has dropped again since 1991.

In the case of the Executive Council, the first woman, Mrs Catherine Joyce Symons, was appointed in 1976. Since then, the total number of female Executive Councillors has never exceeded four (or 27 per cent of the full Council).[2]

In respect of the administrative and judicial systems, the disadvantaged status of women can also be illustrated by the statistics provided in Tables 5.3 and 5.4. The figures in Table 5.4 show that the few women in the judiciary were concentrated at the lower levels of the hierarchy. This is also the case in the civil service, where the disparity between the

## Table 5.3 Percentage of women in the administration

|  | Total number | Number of women | Percentage of women |
|---|---|---|---|
| Policy secretaries and equivalents in the government secretariat* | 23 | 2 | 8.7 |
| Heads of government departments* | 59 | 5 | 8.5 |
| Administrative heads of independent offices and organizations* | 15 | 2 | 13.3 |
| Administrative Grade Officers** | 451 | 144 | 31.9 |

\* Figures are based on the *Civil and Miscellaneous Lists, Hong Kong Government, 1 July 1991* (Hong Kong: Government Printer, 1991) and *Civil and Miscellaneous Lists, Hong Kong Government, 2 January 1992* (Hong Kong: Government Printer, 1992).
\*\* Only the Administrative Grade is chosen for illustrative purposes as it is the most prominent grade in the civil service. Members of this grade are all occupants of key policy-making positions in the Government Secretariat and in departments. Figures provided here are based on Civil Service Branch, *Who's Who in the Administrative Service of the Hong Kong Government* (Hong Kong: Government Printer, July 1991).

number of male and female officials is much greater at the top (893 male versus 113 female at the directorate level) than at the bottom (46,016 males versus 31,308 female at the Master Pay Scale Points 1 to 25 level) (Civil Service Personnel Statistics, 1992: 12).

## Membership on Advisory and other Independent Bodies

Although political powers are highly centralized within the executive, governance in Hong Kong has been characterized by

## Table 5.4  Percentage of women in the judiciary

|  | Total number | Number of women | Percentage of women |
|---|---|---|---|
| Judges of the Supreme Court | 10 | 0 | 0 |
| Judges of the High Court | 22 | 0 | 0 |
| Judges of the District Courts | 34 | 5 | 14.7 |

Note: All figures are based on the *Civil and Miscellaneous Lists, Hong Kong Government, 1 July 1991* (Hong Kong: Government Printer, 1991) and *Civil and Miscellaneous Lists, Hong Kong Government, 2 January 1992* (Hong Kong: Government Printer, 1992).

the presence of a multitude of statutory and non-statutory boards and committees. Some of these organizations are advisory in nature; others undertake deliberative and executive functions in designated areas of public policy. A survey of the composition of these bodies can also serve as an indicator of the level of women's influence in the political arena.

There are over two hundred such organizations in Hong Kong (*Civil and Miscellaneous Lists*, 1 July 1991). A breakdown of the female membership on some of the more important ones is given in Table 5.5. With a few exceptions, women seldom comprise over one-third of the membership of these bodies. In most cases, the number of female members is under 25 per cent.

The various advisory and quasi-governmental organizations listed in Table 5.5 are not equal in terms of their power relationship *vis-à-vis* the administration. Given the colonial regime's longstanding concern for economic development in the territory, the most influential bodies tend to come from the business, financial, and industrial sectors, but it is precisely in these sectors that women's representation appears to be the weakest.

## Table 5.5 Percentage of female members in advisory and independent organizations

| Functional areas covered | Name of organization | Percentage of female members |
|---|---|---|
| Civil Service | – Public Service Commission | 0 |
| | – Standing Commission on Civil Service Salaries and Conditions of Service | 11 |
| | – Standing Committee on Directorate Salaries and Conditions of Service | 0 |
| | – Standing Committee on Disciplined Services, Salaries and Conditions of Service | 18 |
| Judicial and Legal Services | – Bilingual Laws Advisory Committee | 42 |
| | – Judicial Service Commission | 0 |
| | – Law Reform Commission of Hong Kong | 25 |
| | – Standing Committee on Judicial Salaries and Conditions of Service | 0 |
| | – Standing Committee on Legal Aid | 0 |
| Economic Services, Finance, Monetary Affairs, Trade and Industry, and Labour | – Business Council | 0 |
| | – Banking Advisory Committee | 0 |
| | – Deposit-taking Companies Advisory Committee | 0 |
| | – Exchange Fund Advisory Committee | 0 |
| | Securities and Futures Commission | 0 |
| | – Securities and Futures Commission Advisory Committee | 0 |
| | – Insurance Advisory Committee | 0 |
| | – Economic Review Committee | 0 |

## Table 5.5 (continued)

| Functional areas covered | Name of organization | Percentage of female members |
|---|---|---|
| Economic Services, Finance, Monetary Affairs, Trade and Industry, and Labour | – Federation of Hong Kong Industries General Committee | 3 |
| | – Industry Development Board | 0 |
| | – Hong Kong Productivity Council | 6 |
| | – Textiles Advisory Board | 12 |
| | – Hong Kong Trade Development Council | 8 |
| | – Trade Advisory Board | 13 |
| | – Consumer Council | 32 |
| | – Labour Advisory Board | 8 |
| | – Vocational Training Council | 6 |
| | – Panel of Arbitrators (Labour Relations) | 0 |
| Public Security | – Fight Crime Committee | 33 |
| | – Action Committee Against Narcotics | 25 |
| | – Police Complaints Committee | 27 |
| | – Independent Commission Against Corruption Complaints Committee | 25 |
| | – Immigration Tribunal | 28 |
| Infrastructure, Lands and Works, Planning and Environment | – Provisional Airport Authority | 0 |
| | – Transport Advisory Committee | 9 |
| | – Hong Kong Housing Authority | 10 |
| | – Land Development Corporation | 10 |
| | – Land and Building Advisory Committee | 7 |
| | – Town Planning Board | 0 |
| | – Environmental Pollution Advisory Committee | 13 |

## Table 5.5 (continued)

| Functional areas covered | Name of organization | Percentage of female members |
|---|---|---|
| Health and Welfare | – Hospital Authority | 24 |
| | – Medical Council of Hong Kong | 15 |
| | – Medical Development Advisory Committee | 23 |
| | – Advisory Council on AIDS | 22 |
| | – Hong Kong Council on Smoking and Health | 20 |
| | – Hong Kong Council of Social Service | 44 |
| | – Social Welfare Advisory Committee | 39 |
| Recreation and Culture | – Antiquities Advisory Board | 23 |
| | – Broadcasting Authority | 33 |
| | – Panel of Adjudicators (Control of Obscene and Indecent Articles) | 26 |
| | – Panel of Censors (Television and Entertainment Licensing Authority, Film Censorship) | 63 |
| Education | – Board of Education | 33 |
| | – Education Commission | 44 |
| | – Commission on Youth | 39 |
| | – Committee on the Promotion of Civic Education | 14 |
| | – Hong Kong Examinations Authority | 25 |
| | – Curriculum Development Council | 18 |

The statistics in this table are compiled on the basis of information in the *Civil and Miscellaneous Lists*, Hong Kong Government, 1 July 1991 (Hong Kong: Government Printer, 1991) and other public records, including newspapers and official publications of the relevant organizations. The numerical bases of calculations exclude government official representatives and other members who held offices on these organizations in an *ex-officio* capacity.

## Table 5.6  Percentage of female candidates running for political office, 1991

| Type of election | Total number of candidates | Number of female candidates | Percentage of female candidates |
|---|---|---|---|
| District Boards (March 1991) | 467 | 48 | 10 |
| Urban Council (May 1991) | 37 | 6 | 16 |
| Regional Council (May 1991) | 24 | 2 | 8 |
| Legislative Council (September 1991) | 54 | 6 | 11 |

*Source*: Figures obtained from the Registration and Electoral Office, Constitutional Affairs Branch, Government Secretariat (December 1992).

## Participation in Elections

The most conspicuous form of participation in elections is to stand for political office. Table 5.6 shows the percentage of female candidates running for positions in the three levels of government in the 1991 elections.

Voting is another common form of participation in elections. Table 5.7 shows the registration and turnout rates of male and female electors in 1991. One interesting phenomenon that emerges from a comparison of Tables 5.6 and 5.7 is that women are less forthcoming in standing for elections, but they are by no means less participative in registering as voters and casting their ballots. If we extend our analysis to cover other less visible forms of electoral activities, the imbalance between male and female involvement in politics becomes almost negligible. For instance, women have been as active as their male counterparts in campaigning work.[3]

## Table 5.7 Male/female voters' participation in elections, 1991

|  | Male | Female |
|---|---|---|
| Number of eligible voters* | 1,958,232 | 1,922,310 |
| Number of registered voters** | 1,004,026 | 895,707 |
| Percentage of registered voters against eligible voters | 51.3 | 46.6 |
| Number of actual voters in the 1991 Legislative Council Elections*** (direct elections) | 400,504 | 349,994 |
| Percentage of actual voters against registered voters | 39.9 | 39.1 |

* There is no official figure for the actual number of eligible voters. The statistics provided are compiled on the basis of information on the number of male and female residents aged 21 and above in the Census and Statistics Department, *Hong Kong 1991 Population Census, Tabulations for District Board Districts and Constituency Areas: Population by Age and Sex* (Hong Kong: Government Printer, 1991), p. 26. These statistics are not totally accurate as one of the requirements for eligibility to register as an elector (apart from age) is that electors must be permanent residents of Hong Kong, or have been resident in the territory for the preceding seven years. According to the *Hong Kong 1991 Population Census, Summary Results*, p. 42, around 85 per cent of the population fulfilled this criterion. It is possible that some of the individuals listed in this column might not have been eligible to vote in 1991.
** Figures obtained from the Registration and Electoral Office in October 1991. Note that the number of registered voters listed here, totalling 1,899,733, represents that which could be matched against the computer records at the Registration of Persons (ROP) Sub-division of the Immigration Department. The gross number of registered voters (some of whom could not be matched against the ROP records) was 1,916,925. The officially recorded voter turnout rate of 39.15 per cent was calculated on the basis of this gross number, rather than the number presented in this table.
*** Figures obtained from the Registration and Electoral Office. Only the turnout rates in the Legislative Council direct elections are recorded here as the level of turnout in that exercise was the highest among the three major elections held in 1991. The Legislative Council elections were also the most politicized.

## Involvement in Political Organizations

There are many different types of political organizations. Since it is not possible to conduct a comprehensive survey into the role and level of participation of women in all of these organizations within the confines of this chapter, only two kinds of organizations have been targeted for analysis: women's groups, and political parties.

Women's groups are selected for discussion primarily because they can be potent vehicles for reform. In Hong Kong, there are a number of such women's groups. The most notable examples include: The Hong Kong Council of Women, the Association for the Advancement of Feminism, the Hong Kong Young Women's Christian Association, and the Association of Women for Action and Research (AWARE). Women have been highly active participants in these groups, both at the initial stages of the organizations' formation and in their day-to-day operations. (For an account of the feminist movement in Hong Kong, see Chapter 10).

According to results of a study published in 1992, the development of women's groups in Hong Kong can be divided into five approaches: 'localization, diversification, politicization, co-operation and popularization' (Yau, Au and Cheung, 1992: 7). In other words, it was found that an increasing number of women representing different class and sectorial interests in the community ('localization' and 'popularization') were becoming more involved in a diverse set of activities premised on various practical and theoretical concerns ('diversification'). Furthermore, there was a growing trend towards more collaborative efforts ('cooperation') aimed at achieving their goals through changing the pattern of distribution of values and resources in society ('politicization'). The same study also concluded that women's concern groups adopted a 'community psychology approach' directed at 'educating the public, rallying the support of both sexes — especially those in positions of power — training women's leadership skills and strengthening the organization of women's groups' (pp. 28–9). It appears therefore that women in Hong Kong are likely to become even more politically aware and participative in the future.

The role of women in the polity must, however, be seen

## Table 5.8 Male/female participation as members of political parties

| Name of party | Total number of registered members | Number of female members | Percentage of female members |
|---|---|---|---|
| Democratic Alliance for Betterment of Hong Kong | 108 | 7 | 6.5 |
| The Liberal Democratic Federation of Hong Kong | 163 | 26 | 16 |
| Meeting Point | 149 | 25 | 17 |
| United Democrats of Hong Kong | 620 | 112 | 18 |

*Source*: Information obtained directly from the four parties in October 1992.

in the wider context of other forms of organized political activity. Since the late 1980s, Hong Kong has witnessed the emergence and proliferation of many groups which can be broadly labelled as 'political parties' (Lee, 1992; Louie, 1991). If one takes these groups as a basis for comparison, the under-representation of women in the political development of the territory is apparent. The disparity between the levels of male and female participation in the four major parties in Hong Kong is shown in Tables 5.8 and 5.9.

Women's groups and political parties are not necessarily competing organizational bases for the initiation and orchestration of policy changes. They can and do sometimes work together to achieve their common goals. However, under the existing political system, parties generally have more impact on government policy. The key point is that democratization (specifically, the advent of direct elections to the Legislative

## Table 5.9 Female membership in the central executive committees of political parties*

### Democratic Alliance for Betterment of Hong Kong

*Central Committee*
| | |
|---|---|
| Total number of office-bearers | 22 |
| Number of female office-bearers | 2 |
| Percentage of female office-bearers | 9 |

*Standing Committee*
| | |
|---|---|
| Total number of office-bearers | 7 |
| Number of female office-bearers | 1 |
| Percentage of female office-bearers | 14 |

### The Liberal Democratic Federation of Hong Kong

*General Committee*
| | |
|---|---|
| Total number of office-bearers | 26 |
| Total number of female office-bearers | 3 |
| Percentage of female office-bearers | 11.5 |

*Executive Committee*
| | |
|---|---|
| Total number of office-bearers | 7 |
| Number of female office-bearers | 1 |
| Percentage of female office-bearers | 14 |

### Meeting Point

*Central Committee*
| | |
|---|---|
| Total number of office-bearers | 28 |
| Number of female office-bearers | 3 |
| Percentage of female office-bearers | 11 |

### United Democrats of Hong Kong

*Central Executive Committee**
| | |
|---|---|
| Total number of office-bearers | 47 |
| Number of female office-bearers | 4 |
| Percentage of female office-bearers | 8.5 |

* Information obtained directly from the four parties in October 1992.
** Including the Chairman; Vice-Chairmen; Secretary; Treasurer; and members of the Executive Committee, the Central Committee, the Senate and the Disciplinary Committee.

Council since 1991) has made it possible for parties to put their own people into the central policy-making machinery. Women's groups, in contrast, still operate largely from the outside. Parties may embrace the values and concerns of women's groups,[4] but they also have other broader and more immediate political objectives. Seen from this perspective, the extent of women's involvement in the polity as a whole, and the degree of influence they can exert upon the system, still lag far behind their male counterparts.

## Public Expression of Opinions

Public expression of opinions can take two forms: participants can actively utilize various forums (for example, seminars and public meetings) or approach the mass media to communicate their views. At the same time, they may respond to instruments (such as opinion polls) designed by someone else aimed at informing or influencing government decision-making.

Given the extensive scope and the fluid nature of the empirical data relating to this subject, only rough indicators could be used to provide a general idea of the level of women's political participation in both forms of public expression of opinions. In the first instance, the author reviewed a selected sample of press clippings from two English-language newspapers in Hong Kong, the *South China Morning Post* and the *Hong Kong Standard*. The review, undertaken in June and July 1992, covered regular news reports, special feature reports, and articles and letters written by private citizens over the past decade. The results of the exercise confirm that women have been active in expressing their opinions on matters which affect their rights and interests directly. Some of the issues which attracted the most attention were: equal pay for equal work; equal job opportunities; discriminatory succession practices in indigenous villages in the New Territories; provision of child-care facilities for working mothers; domestic violence and sexual violence against women; discriminatory advertisements; the protection of children left unattended at home; education for children with special needs; control of prostitution and pornography; and the setting up of a special body within the government to address women's problems.

In March 1993, the author conducted a similar review of the Chinese newspapers.[5] The same issues were found to have dominated their coverage of the women's question. However, compared with their English-language counterparts, the Chinese papers seemed to place more emphasis on the part played by tradition — specifically, the concept of *nan zhu wai, nu zhu nei* (a man's responsibility lies outside the home, a woman's responsibility lies inside the home) — in constricting women's sex-role identification. The local-language press also appeared to be more concerned with the plight of women in the lower strata of society. The argument that runs through a number of commentaries is that sexual equality is harder to attain in the case of women who are not well educated, who come from a low-income background, who are not employed, or who take up unskilled and low-paid jobs in the labour market.

In many instances, the most vocal critics of the current state of affairs have been established women's groups. Like many other organized interests in society, these groups have become increasingly aware of the need to subsume their viewpoints within the broader legal and political framework. Their comments are therefore not only confined to the issues *per se*, but are also sometimes stated in the context of existing arrangements in the political system and relevant provisions in the Basic Law, and the Bill of Rights, as well as other legislation defining the status and entitlements of different categories of citizens in the polity.

The level of women's participation in politics is correlated with their interest in, and knowledge about, public affairs. An examination of the performance of female respondents to public opinion surveys reported in the English press suggests that women, especially those in the over-35 age bracket, appear to be generally less informed and less decided on various issues.[6] The percentage of 'no opinion', or 'don't know', responses is higher among women than men in many polls. The differences are particularly noticeable in relation to matters of a clear 'political' nature, such as the method for selecting the future Chief Executive and Legislative Councillors. However, the gap between the sexes tends to become narrower among the younger generation (that is, those between the ages of 15 and 34) of respondents.

## Constraints on Women's Political Participation

The foregoing account clearly shows that women in Hong Kong are not prominent actors in the political process. Their representation is particularly weak in the direct and formal realms of political participation. Women do not seem to be significantly more passive than men in voting or political campaigning. Women's groups have also been rather active in putting across their views and building up support for the long-term realization of their goals. However, the uneven presence of the two sexes in the central policy-making arena and in organized political groups means that the resources and opportunities available to women to effect policy changes are inevitably limited.

Viewed from a comparative perspective, the low profile of women in politics is by no means peculiar to Hong Kong. Empirical data in other — predominantly Western democratic — countries have shown that women are generally under-represented at the senior levels of the formal policy-making institutions (Hill and Roberts, 1990; Kahn, 1992; Martin, 1989; Studlar and Welch, 1987). The evidence also suggests that female citizens are no less active than their male counterparts in other indirect and informal modes of political participation (Verba, 1990). In this sense, the political behaviour of women in Hong Kong does not appear to be different from that of women elsewhere.

Various explanations have emerged in the West since the 1960s to account for women's lower level (or, some would argue, preference for different forms) of political participation. These explanations have tended to fall into three broad categories (Welch, 1977). First, it has been suggested that the psychological make-up and attitudinal orientation of women are different from men (Kathlene, 1989). Women are therefore less likely to be as ambitious or single-minded in their pursuit of political power (Diamond, 1977; Kirkpatrick, 1976). Adherents to this line of reasoning sometimes point to the inherent features of political life in contemporary society which are biased in favour of male participants (Bledsoe and Herring, 1990).

Second, it has been argued that women are confined within their traditional gender role as wives, mothers, and caretakers of their families. Consequently they have little time for meaningful engagement in politics (Campbell et al., 1964; Hills, 1982, 1983; Flora and Lynn, 1974). Third, some scholars have drawn attention to the fact that there are usually fewer women than men in those sectors of society (for example, the better educated and high-income groups) which are most conducive to participatory political behaviour (Pomper, 1975). Put in another way, most women lack the resources to compete successfully against men in securing party backing or voters' support in situations of political competition (Currell, 1978; Hills, 1983; Welch, 1978).

In Hong Kong, there is little evidence that boys and girls are exposed to two distinct patterns of political socialization. However, local feminist groups and concerned individuals have not failed to detect how sex-role stereotypes are reinforced in school textbooks and commercial advertisements that appear in the media (Choi, Chapter 4; Association for the Advancement of Feminism, 1987; Au, 1988; Ho, 1983a; Yau and Luk, 1988). There is therefore a subtle process of socialization which may shape the attitudes of men and women towards their roles in life (Cheung, 1986; Keyes, 1983, 1984; Lau, 1989). The divergence in the psychological dispositions of the two sexes may in turn affect their views of politics and power, thus explaining to some extent why fewer women than men are interested in pursuing a political career or participating in the formal realms of politics.

Apart from socialization, situational variables also appear to have limited Hong Kong women's prospects for political participation. The uneven distribution of household responsibilities — particularly child-rearing — between men and women in the territory is a well-documented fact (Association for the Advancement of Feminism, 1985; Cheung, 1979; Pearson, 1990). Familial obligations have become an oft-cited reason for the inconsequential number of women in political parties and public office.[7] Likewise, structural hindrances to women's successful engagement in politics are considerable. For example, women in Hong Kong have not enjoyed equal educational opportunities (Choi, Chapter 4; Tang, 1981). There are fewer women than men who are economically active (Census and Statistics Department, 1991: 50–3). Female members of the labour force sometimes suffer discriminatory treatment in their workplace (Cheung, 1981; Ho, 1983b, 1985). And as a corollary, women's chances of career advancement are usually restricted (Leung, Chapter 1; Ho, 1984; Lai, 1982).

Hence, it appears that the three sets of factors which have allegedly constrained women in the West are also applicable in a local context. One may even suspect that the problem of systematic discrimination against women has been exacerbated in Hong Kong by the traditional Confucian legacy which emphasizes differential sex roles and female subordination (Chiao, 1992). The relative importance of this cultural explanation, the exact way in which the various factors interact, and their respective influences on the political status of women in the territory, are all questions which would have to be more fully addressed and established on the basis of further empirical analyses.

For our present purpose, it would suffice to point out that the crux of the issue relating to women's political participation is that they have mainly been involved in those areas of activity which have only a marginal impact on public policy. For instance, voting and political campaigning are only indirect ways of impinging on the policy process. In Hong Kong, there is little evidence to suggest that women who cast their ballots or engage in canvassing activities in elections have necessarily been supportive of female candidates or of male candidates who are committed to the feminist cause. Women's groups have been playing a direct role in lobbying the government, but they tend to be working more at the peripheries than exerting their influence from within. Given the colonial legacy of a highly centralized system of political decision-making in the territory, external pressure groups do not normally play a decisive role in the formation of public policy. The 'community psychology approach' adopted by women's concern groups may help to redress the imbalance of political power in the future. However, such an approach takes time and patience. Its effect on immediate problems of sexual inequality is bound to be restricted.

Hence, as long as Hong Kong's political system remains tightly controlled from the centre, pressure group tactics alone are unlikely to bring about any real or long-lasting changes to discriminatory practices in society. It appears that the solution to the disadvantaged plight of women would have to rest on developments other than the mere adoption of CEDAW. One crucial development in this respect is for policy-makers to become more sympathetic towards the cause of women. The second development, which may be conducive to the first, is for more women to be selected into positions of political importance in the government. Unfortunately, the present political environment does not favour either of these developments.

## Women's Issues as a Policy Concern

As stated earlier, whether women's issues are included in the policy agenda, and the priority which is accorded to them, depend on the subjective value stance of policy-makers as well as the objective environment relating to the absence or presence of 'competing concerns'. At the moment there are few signs that women's rights and status are capturing the attention of senior bureaucrats and other decision-makers in government. Despite repeated appeals on the part of concerned groups and individuals, the administration has not acted promptly to set up a Women's Commission to advise the authorities on women's issues (*South China Morning Post*, 13 December, 1992). Its response to suggestions for legislation against sexual discrimination at work has long been a source of irritation for women's rights activists (*South China Morning Post*, 14 November, 1992). The majority of legislators have theoretically pledged their support for the feminist cause by voting in favour of the 16 December, 1992 motion. However, their long-term commitment to women's issues has yet to be demonstrated. At present, with Hong Kong's preoccupation with the 1997 transfer of sovereignty, women's issues do not seem to be high on the agenda of those in positions of power.

It might be expected, that with the settling of the major political debates surrounding the reversion of sovereignty, women's issues would stand a better chance of resolution after 1997. This belief may be further buttressed by the observation that China is itself a signatory to CEDAW, and that it has a more established social, political, and legal framework for the protection of women.[8] Nonetheless, such a view is overly simplistic because it omits a key political consideration. Sexual equality has been a central policy concern in China. It has served to legitimize Communist rule, as it represents an important aspect of the new socio-political order which the Communists have sought to install in mainland China (Croll, 1976, 1983; Johnson, 1983). Even then, as Jones (Chapter 6) points out, the reality is a long way from stated policy. Sexual equality in Hong Kong does not and will not acquire the same political status, especially since the intentions of the Chinese leadership in relation to the 1997 resumption of sovereignty have been to preserve the *status quo* in the territory, not to change it. To take the argument one step further, one may even question whether China would be prepared to concede to the demands of one category of activists (that is, the feminist groups), because doing so may encourage other interest groups to come forward. A politicized community comprising different sectorial groups who are fully aware of their rights and entitlements *vis-à-vis* the authorities is unlikely to meet with China's approval, principally because such a community may not be susceptible to centralized political control exerted from Beijing.

## *An Increase in Women's Representation in the Political System*

If the above analysis is correct, the case for an increased level of women's representation in the centre of political decision-making will become stronger. At the least, this can enable women to play a more direct participatory role in the political bargaining process; at the most, women can utilize their influence to change the perceptions and values of other actors in the polity. Nonetheless, the number of women in the central political institutions is dependent on many variables, not all of which are favourable to the feminist cause.

First, more women can theoretically be appointed into the Executive and Legislative Councils.[9] However, the limitations of the appointment system have already been noted. There is no clear ideological commitment on the part of the appointing authorities that more women should be selected into the Councils. Those who have been appointed are perceived as being too élitist to represent the interests of the common woman. Appointments are therefore not a satisfactory way to deal with the problem of women's disadvantaged presence in politics.

The functional constituency system in Legislative Council elections is biased against women. According to the White Paper on the Further Development of Representative Government in Hong Kong (1984), the purpose of the system is to give 'full weight ... to representation of the economic and professional sectors of Hong Kong society which are essential to future confidence and prosperity' (pp. 5–6). The 1988 White Paper on Representative Government also reiterated the same principle by laying down the guideline that 'functional constituencies should be substantial and of importance in the community' (p. 13). In essence, therefore, the concept of functional constituency representation excludes the right of non-working women to choose their representatives in the legislature. Furthermore, the élitist nature of the electorate in most constituencies, coupled with the fact that there are generally fewer senior female professionals in many of the recognized sectors, inevitably means that the number of women elected through this channel is likely to be small.[10]

This leaves direct elections as the most probable and reliable source for the emergence of policy-makers who are advocates of sexual equality. But certain prerequisites would have to be fulfilled. Clearly, more female candidates would have to present themselves for elections, either as independents or as representatives of political organizations. In both cases, in order to secure voters' support, candidates must have a good record of public service, or have the backing of a well-established political group. This implies that candidates must be active participants in political and community affairs before they stand for elections.

The statistics in Tables 5.6, 5.8, and 5.9 suggest that the preconditions for women's successful engagement in this form of electoral politics have not been met. As we have seen, there are many reasons for the relative passivity of women in these areas of political participation. Through a combination of socialization, situational constraints, and structural factors, female members of the community tend to be less-informed and less interested in politics. Unless these barriers to sexual equality are removed, women are not expected to fare well against their male competitors in political elections.

## The Future of Women's Political Participation

Despite the constraints identified in the last section, there is some cause for optimism. With the introduction of democratic reforms since the mid-1980s, a more liberal political environment has emerged. As groups and individuals become more vocal in discussing public affairs, the average Hong Kong citizen is continually exposed to views and ideas concerning questions of vital political significance. The level of political awareness in the community is bound to rise. Meanwhile, societal politicization has provided an opportunity for interest groups to develop. Against this background, women's rights activists have been making gradual progress towards the transformation of a polity which is at least willing to acknowledge the need for sexual equality.

There are other signs that women may be able to capitalize on the present situation to enhance their capabilities for a more active role in politics. Unlike other Western democratic countries where the right to vote in political elections was first granted to men and only subsequently extended to women, the franchise came late, but simultaneously, for both male and female citizens in Hong Kong.[11] Given that most voters are comparatively inexperienced, they may not have developed any deep-rooted prejudices which may adversely affect the prospects of female candidates running for public office. This view was partially borne out by a study of 812 voters in the Kowloon Central constituency in the direct elections to the Legislative Council in 1991 (Kwok, Leung, and Scott, 1992). In response to a question designed to test how the voters would choose between a male and a female candidate who were equal in all other respects, the majority of interviewees (59 per cent) stated that they had no preference.[12] The findings of the study as a whole indicate that the voters' choice of candidate was affected by other, non-gender-related considerations. Hence, if the mentality of the survey subjects in this constituency can be generalized, a candidate's sex may not be a decisive factor in his or her chance of winning an election.

Other social developments in Hong Kong may also be conducive to the long-term prospects of women's political participation in the territory. The expansion of free, compulsory education, the gradual entrenchment of meritocracy as a basis for the distribution of rewards in the community, the increase in the number of working wives, the reduction in the rate of fertility, and the general improvement in the economic conditions of most families (thereby making it unnecessary for parents to choose between sons and daughters in the provision of benefits) mean that gender differences are becoming less distinct. As women are increasingly involved in other spheres of social and economic activities, their desire for greater political participation will also be strengthened.

## Conclusions

Experience in other countries has shown that women's quest for political equality is often a long and arduous process (Andors, 1983; Campbell, 1987; Gelb, 1989; Randall, 1987; Rendel, 1981; Tilly and Gurin, 1990). In Hong Kong, that process has to some extent been boosted by the passage of the motion in the Legislative Council in December 1992. However, promises of support can easily degenerate into rhetoric in politics unless there is a commitment on the part of policy-makers to translate the spirit of CEDAW into action. The challenge for individuals and groups concerned with women's rights is how such a commitment could be secured and sustained.

The discussion in this chapter has shown that there are both opportunities for, and constraints against, the increased involvement of women in the political processes which is vital to the protection and promotion of women's interests in the territory. On balance, however, the constraints appear to outweigh the opportunities. Some of these constraints are inherent in the social and political systems which are biased in favour of an élite disproportionately represented by men. Meanwhile, the anticipated 1997 transfer of sovereignty has brought about dramatic changes in Hong Kong. Against this turbulent background, the problem of sexual discrimination has become buried beneath other concerns which are regarded by policy-makers to be of more critical political importance.

In the final analysis, the advancement of feminism is not simply a matter of political bargaining or strategic adjustments on the part of women's rights activists. It is related to the ethos of the polity. Notions of 'equality', 'fairness' and 'non-discrimination' are unlikely to have any real impact in a society which does not uphold the philosophy of equal respect for everyone. In this sense, the question of women's political rights is part of the broader issue of human rights. Unless the Hong Kong polity can develop a collective mentality which is conducive to the protection of the basic rights of individuals, irrespective of their sex, race, or other native characteristics, the achievement of sexual equality will remain elusive.

## Acknowledgements

The author is grateful to Sophia Lau, Elaine Chan, and Wilfred Lai, who assisted in the collection of material; Irene Tong and Ian Scott, who commented on an earlier draft of the chapter; and Y. L. Chan of the Registration and Electoral Office, Constitutional Affairs Branch, Government Secretariat, who provided useful data on the 1991 elections.

## Notes

1. Norman Miners, *The Government and Politics of Hong Kong*, 5th ed. (Hong Kong: Oxford University Press, 1991), pp. 177–80. In December 1991, there were altogether 148 Councillors in the Heung Yee Kuk; only four (or 2.7 per cent) were female. Under the present system, the Chairman and two Vice-Chairmen of the Heung Yee Kuk are ex-officio members of the Regional Council. Some Heung Yee Kuk members are also granted ex-officio seats in the rural District Boards. Jones (Chapter 6) gives a more detailed account of the role of the Heung Yee Kuk as a political pressure group, particularly in relation to the defence of male privilege in relation to the inheritance of land in the New Territories.
2. For an historical account of women's representation in the Executive Council, the Legislative Council, and the Urban Council, see Association for the Advancement of Feminism, *Hong Kong Women's File* [in Chinese], (Hong Kong: Association for the Advancement of Feminism, 1993), pp. 168–70.
3. Most candidates running for political office do not have official

name-lists of their campaign teams. However, telephone surveys conducted in June 1992 with assistants of the following candidates in the 1991 Legislative Council direct elections have revealed that most of their campaign teams comprised roughly equal numbers of men and women: Johnston Wong Hong-chung, Stephen Ng Ming-yum, Huang Chen-ya, Lau Chin-shek, Philip Li Koi-hop, Ng Kin-sun, Ronald Chow Mei-tak, Tai Chin-wah, Li Ting-kit, Tony Kan Chung-nin, Yeung Fuk-kwong, David Chan Yuk-cheung, Desmond Lee Yu-tai, John D. Young, and Peter Chan Chi-kwan.

4. A survey into the constitutions and other publications of nine major political groups in Hong Kong shows that some (for example, The Hong Kong Democratic Foundation and the United Democrats of Hong Kong) have included women's issues in their platforms. Out of the fifty-four candidates who contested the directly elected seats in the Legislative Council in 1991, forty-one addressed women's issues in their platforms. Among them, twenty-six were affiliated to political groups or trade unions. See *South China Morning Post*, 12 September, 1991.

5. Press clippings at the Resources Centre of the Association for the Advancement of Feminism in Hong Kong were used for this purpose. The clippings were extracted from over a dozen local Chinese-language newspapers.

6. The opinion polls covered a wide range of issues, including: decriminalization of homosexual acts among consenting adults; abolition of the death penalty; the acceptability of the Sino-British Agreement on Hong Kong's future and the Memorandum of Understanding on the Second Airport; democratization of the political system; building of the Daya Bay nuclear power plant; the Hong Kong government's handling of relations with China; repeal of the New Territories' exclusive male succession law; services in public hospitals; and the American involvement in the war against Iraq in early 1991.

7. Personal interview with Dr. Yeung Sum, Vice-Chairman of the United Democrats of Hong Kong, December 1992. See also *South China Morning Post*, 22 September, 1992.

8. The Constitution of the People's Republic of China makes provisions for women to enjoy equal rights with men in politics, economics, education, culture, society and the family. In October 1992, China introduced the Protection of Women's Rights Law which would serve to reaffirm the principle of sexual equality. See Katherine Forestier, '*Equality in the Name of the Law*' in *South China Morning Post*, 25 August, 1992.

9. The existing policy documents on constitutional reform in Hong Kong provide that there will not be any appointed members in

the Legislative Council from 1995 onwards. However, it is conceivable that a new body, the Election Committee, which will produce ten legislators to replace the appointed members in 1995, may eventually permit a new brand of political appointees to take up seats in the future Legislative Council.
10. In the 1991 Legislative Council elections, only one female candidate (out of a total of forty) contested a functional constituency seat. That candidate, Mrs Elsie Tu, secured the seat unopposed. But as she was running as a representative of the Urban Council, she cannot be regarded as standing for any 'professional' interests.
11. The argument is confined to elections to the District Boards and the Legislative Council. The elections to the Urban Council are excluded because the Urban Council is not regarded as a significant political institution. There are inequalities in the Heung Yee Kuk elections in the New Territories but the problem does not defeat the point made here.
12. Among those who had a preference, 30 per cent settled for a male candidate while 10 per cent chose a female candidate. The percentage of 'no preference' responses tends to increase among those survey subjects who were better educated. A total of 54 per cent of respondents with below primary-level education had no preference. The number of 'no preference' responses increased to 60.5 per cent among subjects with secondary to matriculation-level education, and then to 72.5 per cent among those with college-level education.

## References

Andors, Phyllis (1983), *The Unfinished Liberation of Chinese Women, 1949–1980*, Bloomington: Indiana University Press.

Association for the Advancement of Feminism (1985), *Women's Participation in Public Affairs: A Survey Report*, Hong Kong: Association for the Advancement of Feminism [in Chinese].

────── (1987), *Women and Media*, Hong Kong: Association for the Advancement of Feminism.

────── (1993), *The Hong Kong Women's File*, Hong Kong: Association for the Advancement of Feminism [in Chinese].

Au, Kit-chun (1988), *An Analysis of Sex-role Stereotypes in Primary School Chinese Language, Social Studies and Health Education Textbooks in Hong Kong* [in Chinese], paper presented at a Conference on Hong Kong: Cultural Tradition and Contemporary Education organized by The Chinese University of Hong Kong.

The Basic Law of the Hong Kong Special Administrative Region of the People's Republic of China (4 April, 1990).

Bledsoe, Timothy and Mary Herring (1990), 'Victims of Circumstances: Women in Pursuit of Political Office', *American Political Science Review*, 84(1): 213–23.

Campbell, Angus; Converse, Philip; Miller, Warren; and Stokes, Donald (1964), *The American Voter*, New York: John Wiley and Sons.

Campbell, Beatrix (1987), *The Iron Ladies*, London: Virago Press.

Census and Statistics Department (1991), Hong Kong 1991 Population Census, Summary Results and Hong Kong 1991 Population Census, Tabulations for District Board Districts and Constituency Areas: Population by Age and Sex, Hong Kong: Hong Kong Government Printer.

Cheung, F. M. (1979), 'Self-Perception, Cultural Norms and Development — Case Studies of 36 Chinese Women', *Journal of the Chinese University of Hong Kong*, 5(1): 355–62.

——— (1986), 'Development of Gender Stereotype', *Educational Research Journal*, 1: 68–73.

Cheung, M. T. (1981), 'The Career Women in Hong Kong', *Hong Kong Baptist College Academic Journal*, 8: 99–113.

Chiao, Chien (1992), *Involution and Revolution in Gender Equality, The Chinese Experience*, Hong Kong: The Chinese University of Hong Kong, Hong Kong Institute of Asia-Pacific Studies, Reprint Series No. 14.

Civil Service Branch, Government Secretariat (July 1991), *Who's Who in the Administrative Service of the Hong Kong Government*, Hong Kong: Hong Kong Government Printer.

——— (1992), *Civil Service Personnel Statistics, 1992*, Hong Kong: Hong Kong Government Printer.

Croll, Elisabeth (ed.) (1976), *The Women's Movement in China: A Selection of Readings*, London: Anglo-Chinese Educational Institute, Modern China Series No. 6.

——— (1983), *Chinese Women Since Mao*, London: Zed Books.

Currell, M. (1978), *The Recruitment of Women to the House of Commons*, paper delivered at the UK Political Studies Association Conference.

Diamond, Irene (1977), *Sex Roles in the State House*, New Haven: Yale University Press.

Easton, David (1971), *The Political System: An Inquiry into the State of Political Science*, (2nd ed.), New York: Knopf.

Flora, Cornelia B. and Lynn, Naomi B. (1974), 'Women and Political Socialization: Considerations of the Impact of Motherhood', in Jane S. Jaquette (ed.), *Women in Politics*, New York: John Wiley and Sons.

Forestier, Katherine (1992), 'Equality in the Name of the Law', *South China Morning Post*, 25 August.

Gamson, William (1975), *The Strategy of Social Protest* (2nd ed.), Belmont, California: Wadsworth Publishing Co.

Gelb, Joyce (1989), *Feminism and Politics: A Comparative Perspective*, Berkeley, California: University of California Press.

Government Secretariat, *Civil and Miscellaneous Lists, Hong Kong Government, 1 July 1991 and 2 January 1992*, Hong Kong: Hong Kong Government Printer.

Hill, Roberta and Roberts, Nigel S. (1990), 'Success, Swing and Gender: The Performance of Women Candidates for Parliament in New Zealand, 1946–87', *Politics*, 25(1): 62–80.

Hills, J. (1982), 'Women Local Councillors — A Reply to Bristow', *Local Government Studies (January/February)*, pp. 61–71.

—— (1983), 'Life-style Constraints on Formal Political Participation — Why So Few Women Local Councillors in Britain?', *Electoral Studies*, 2(1): 39–52.

Ho, S. C. (1983a), 'Sex Role Portrayals in Print Advertisements: The Case of Hong Kong', *Equal Opportunities International*, 2(4): 1–4.

—— (1983b), 'Women in Management: Challenges and Barriers', *Young Executive*, 4: 53–5.

—— (1984), 'Women's Labour-Force Participation in Hong Kong 1971–1981', *Journal of Marriage and the Family*, 46(4): 947–54.

—— (1985), 'The Position of Women in the Labour Market in Hong Kong: A Content Analysis of the Recruitment Advertisements', *Labour and Society*, 10(3): 333–44.

The Hong Kong Bill of Rights Ordinance 1990 (1990), Hong Kong: Hong Kong Government Printer.

Hong Kong Government (November 1984), *White Paper on the Further Development of Representative Government in Hong Kong*, Hong Kong: Hong Kong Government Printer.

—— (February 1988), *White Paper on the Development of Representative Government: The Way Forward*, Hong Kong: Hong Kong Government Printer.

—— (1992), *Hong Kong 1992*, Hong Kong: Hong Kong Government Printer.

Johnson, Kay Ann (1983), *Women, the Family and Peasant Revolution in China*, Chicago: The University of Chicago Press.

Joint Declaration of the Government of the United Kingdom of Great Britain and Northern Ireland and the Government of the People's Republic of China on the Question of Hong Kong (1984).

Kahn, Kim Fridkin (1992), 'Does Being Male Help? An Investigation of the Effects of Candidate Gender and Campaign Coverage on Evaluations of U.S. Senate Candidates', *The Journal of Politics*, 54(2): 497–517.

Kathlene, Lyn (1989), 'Uncovering the Political Impacts of Gender: An Exploratory Study', *Western Political Quarterly*, 42(2): 397–421.

Keyes, S. (1983), 'Sex Differences in Cognitive Abilities and Sex-role Stereotypes in Hong Kong Chinese Adolescents', *Sex Roles*, 9(8): 853–70.

—— (1984), 'Measuring Sex-role Stereotypes: Attitudes among Hong Kong Chinese Adolescents and the Development of the Chinese Sex-role Inventory', *Sex Roles*, 10: 129–40.
Kirkpatrick, Jeane (1976), *The New Presidential Elite*, New York: Sage.
Kwok, Rowena; Leung, Joan; and Scott, Ian (eds.) (1992), *Votes Without Power: The Hong Kong Legislative Council Elections 1991*, Hong Kong: Hong Kong University Press.
Lai, Wong May-ling, Catherine (1982), *Civil Service Attitudes Towards Women in Hong Kong*, Hong Kong: University of Hong Kong, Unpublished M.Soc.Sc. Dissertation.
Lasswell, Harold G. (1958), *Politics: Who Gets What, When and How*, New York: Meridian Books.
Lau, S. (1989), 'Sex Role Orientation and Domains of Self-esteem', *Sex Roles*, 21(5/6): 411–8.
Lau, S. K. (1984), *Society and Politics in Hong Kong*, Hong Kong: Chinese University Press.
Lau, S. K. and Kuan, Hsin-chi (1988), *The Ethos of the Hong Kong Chinese*, Hong Kong: Chinese University Press.
Lee, Jane (1992), *The Emergence of Party Politics in Hong Kong, 1982–92*, paper presented at an International Conference on 25 Years of Social and Economic Development in Hong Kong organized by the Centre of Asian Studies, The University of Hong Kong, 16–19 December, 1992.
Louie, Kin-sheun (1991), 'Political Parties', in Sung Yun-wing and Lee Ming-kwan (eds.), *The Other Hong Kong Report 1991*, Hong Kong: Chinese University Press, pp. 55–75.
Martin, Janet M. (1989), 'The Recruitment of Women to Cabinet and Subcabinet Posts', *Western Political Quarterly*, 42(1): 161–72.
Miners, Norman (1991), *The Government and Politics of Hong Kong*, (5th ed.), Hong Kong: Oxford University Press.
Pearson, Veronica (1990), 'Women in Hong Kong', in Benjamin K. P. Leung (ed.), *Social Issues in Hong Kong*, Hong Kong: Oxford University Press, pp. 114–39.
Pomper, Gerald (1975), *Voter's Choice: Varieties of American Electoral Behavior*, New York: Dodd Mead.
Randall, Vicky (1987), *Women and Politics*, (2nd ed.), Basingstoke: Macmillan.
Rendel, Margherita (ed.) (1981), *Women, Power and Political Systems*, London: Croom Helm.
Scott, Ian (1989), *Political Change and the Crisis of Legitimacy in Hong Kong*, Hong Kong: Oxford University Press.
Studlar, Donley T. and Welch, Susan (1987), 'Understanding the Iron Law of Andrarchy: Effects of Candidate Gender on Voting in Scotland', *Comparative Political Studies*, 20(2): 174–91.
Studwell, Joe (1992), 'How Democracy Has Deprived Women of a Right', *Sunday Morning Post*, 20 September.

Tang, S. L. W. (1981), *The Differential Educational Attainment of Children: An Empirical Study of Hong Kong*, Unpublished doctoral thesis, Chicago, Illinois: University of Chicago.

Tilly, Louise A. and Gurin, Patricia (eds.) (1990), *Women, Politics, and Change*, New York: Russell Sage Foundation.

Verba, Sidney (1990), 'Women in American Politics', in Louise A. Tilly and Patricia Gurin (eds.), *Women, Politics, and Change*, New York: Russell Sage Foundation, pp. 555–71.

Verba, Sidney and Nie, Norman H. (1972), *Participation in America: Political Democracy and Social Equality*, New York: Harper & Row.

Welch, Susan (1977), 'Women as Political Animals? A Test of Some Explanations for Male-Female Political Participation Differences', *American Journal of Political Science*, XXI(4): 711–29.

——— (1978), 'Recruitment of Women to Public Office: A Discriminant Analysis', *Western Political Quarterly*, 31(3): 372–80.

Yau, Betty L. L.; Au, Kit Chun; and Cheung, Fanny M. (1992), *Women's Concern Groups in Hong Kong*, Hong Kong: Hong Kong Institute of Asia-Pacific Studies, The Chinese University of Hong Kong, Occasional Paper No. 15.

Yau, L. L. and Luk, H. K. (1988), *A Study of Sex-role Stereotypes in Chinese History and Social Studies Textbooks in Junior Secondary Schools in Hong Kong*, Hong Kong: The Chinese University of Hong Kong, Centre for Hong Kong Studies, Occasional Paper No. 24 [in Chinese].

# 6 The New Territories Inheritance Law: Colonialization and the Élites

*Carol Jones*

This chapter explores the ways in which the socio-economic and political structures of colonialism in Hong Kong have shaped the law, as well as the law's silences, concerning women in Hong Kong. It examines the 'civilizing mission' role of the British Empire which elsewhere led the colonial powers to temper what they saw as the uncivilized (or even 'savage') customs and practices of the natives. Was this same 'mission' practiced upon the 'natives' of Hong Kong? Did it meet with local resistance? If so, the law should provide a valuable site of excavation for evidence of such conflicts.

In the Hong Kong of the 1990s, we still find laws on the books which insist that a man cannot be guilty of raping his own wife (a 300-year-old legal fiction which the Law Lords in the UK finally changed in 1992)[1]; the absence of anti-discrimination laws which means that employers can still select employees on the basis of age, sex, and, race — although this may be partially rectified before 1997 (Pearson and Leung, this volume); laws which, until 1994, prohibited women from inheriting land in the New Territories[2]; and, in urban and rural areas alike, a law which still insists that children below the age of majority must seek their father's, not their mother's, permission if they wish to marry[3].

Colonialism has often been portrayed as a relationship of domination and subjection between the colonizer and the colonized. This common but misleading view glosses over the subtleties of power relations and overestimates the position of the colonial government. In Hong Kong, the *realpolitik* of colonialism meant that the British administration quickly became dependent upon 'native' co-operation (of the local Chinese élites), to secure local compliance and permit effective administration of the colony. The hegemony of the colonial government has therefore never been quite as complete as some assume.

From the early days of the colony, the government declared

that it would not interfere with the 'good customs' and practices of the Chinese, an undertaking repeated in 1898 when the New Territories were leased to Britain from China. Repressive British rule in other colonies had proved ill-advised, with military expenditure threatening to undercut the rationale of colonization — that colonies should quickly become a source of gain rather than drain for the 'home' economy. This required low-cost strategies to ensure political stability, and the Hong Kong government's promise not to interfere with native customs reflected this. It was an approach which has been especially evident in laws relating to women, for it is here that we find powerful segments of the colonized population (for example, the merchant, business and landowning groups) contesting the government's right to administer Chinese society by challenging its *locus* to regulate the private life of the Chinese family. Debates concerning the regulation of the Chinese family and consequently Chinese women have, therefore, also been debates about the reach of the colonial state.

With respect to women and the family, law not only reflects dominant social values, it is also constitutive of this dominance. For example, the law's traditional distinction between the public and the private realms has typically been regarded positively, as a limit on state intervention in a citizen's private and domestic life. But this protection of domestic bliss also shields domestic abuse. The law's refusal to enter the marital bed is based on the belief that a sexual relationship between a man and his wife belongs to the private realm. But this leaves married women unprotected against physical and sexual abuse, rape and even sexual torture by their husbands. The public/private divide effectively allows the power of the husband and father to go unregulated. By remaining silent, the law thus sustains and constitutes patriarchal power within the household.

In Hong Kong, this public/private distinction has not only sustained male power in the household, but also differences between the colonizing population and the colonized. For many years, Hong Kong law has permitted club members and private landlords and landowners to select new members and residents on the basis of sex, race, and class (employers are also able to advertise jobs on the basis of race and sex). So, for example, membership of the Hong Kong Club, established in 1846, provided one means of status differentiation (Chan, 1991: 36). It was deliberately established as a gentlemen's club, which excluded ladies (Criswell, 1981: 207). Today, women are still only permitted to become associate members, with limited access to facilities. The Club was for the exclusive use of the colonial male élite.

In modern Hong Kong, segregation of women from men, of the 'lower classes' from the élites, and of the colonized from the colonialists, still continues. It is sanctioned by the conventions of society and by regulations governing private clubs and housing developments. In 1993, for example, a sign appeared in a prestigious apartment block, Tregunter Towers, announcing to those using the elevators that 'No dogs or Filipinas' were allowed. Recreation clubs persist in restricting the entry of maids (*amahs*). Formerly these maids were mainly Chinese, but nowadays, they are usually Filipina. This spatial separation of populations was and is legitimated in law on the grounds of privacy, since the regulations made by landlords or club members are intended for their private properties. In these ways the public/private distinction divides the sexes within the society of the colonized and the colonizer, as well as dividing the colonized from the colonizing populations.

In early Hong Kong, the promise to respect Chinese customs also contributed to this policy of separate development, with a Chinese Protectorate being set up to administer the affairs of the Chinese population. One might view this as a positive attempt to respect Chinese customs and practices; alternatively, one might see it as a particular form of apartheid. Likewise, in the name of cultural sensitivity, whenever an issue of custom has arisen, advice has been sought on the proper interpretation of Chinese law from a small number of expatriate and local 'China experts' — all of them male, all of them adamantly patriarchal, and all of them competing to be the authentic 'voice' of the local population. The differences of the Chinese were further emphasized by the Chinese élites themselves, as they sought to develop their own power-base and identity in colonial society.

This combination of factors has produced a policy of appeasement whenever the co-opted Chinese élite has objected to legal reforms which might benefit women. Combined with the *laissez-faire* principle of non-intervention in Hong Kong law (as well as its fabled 'free-market' economy) the power of these élites has been maintained in both the private realm of home, and the public place of work thus permitting Chinese patriarchal customs to flourish, despite widespread evidence of the harm they cause to women.

Given this background, it becomes less surprising that Hong Kong law has never reflected the kind of principled moral endorsement of women's rights that we find in American or British law. The idea that the law should embrace women as full and equal members of society has only become an important issue since the late 1980s. In the 1970s, a series of legal reforms and a concerted campaign by dispersed women's groups contributed to the final demise of concubinage, customary marriage, and a series of other customary family-law provisions, which placed many Chinese women firmly at the bottom of a highly patriarchal society. Moreover, since the 1970s, legislative changes have also improved the status of married women seeking divorce or separation, the issue of domestic violence has slowly arrived on the legal agenda, and tax law has finally acknowledged the right of a married woman to separate taxation.

## Patriarchal Values

In response to this litany of shortcomings, it is frequently argued that women's rights have no place in Chinese culture. Defenders of this conservative version of Chinese culture accuse the British of imposing foreign laws and values upon what is essentially a Chinese society (whatever that may mean). Closer inspection reveals, however, that Hong Kong law regarding women is not so much the product of a conflict between colonizer and colonized, as a product of values shared between them — a point that Pearson and Yu (Chapter 9) make with regard to the use of women for commercial sex. Principal amongst these shared values is a commitment to patriarchal values and the patrilineal distribution of wealth.

The initial introduction of British law to Hong Kong resulted not in a conflict with local practices, but a reinforcement of pre-colonial forms of patriarchal power. Though Britain and China may be very different in some respects, both societies have patriarchal values deeply embedded in their laws. If we look, for example, at the legal status of a woman in Victorian society and that of a woman in pre-colonial Hong Kong, we find that both were defined by their relationship to men (daughter, wife, mother). Women in both jurisdictions were regarded as chattels: rights over them were transferred on marriage from the father to the husband and any other man who damaged these exclusive rights of possession faced a legal penalty. Any property these women might have owned in their own right before marriage automatically became the property of their husbands upon marriage. Their chief duty as wife was to produce a male heir, and failure to do so provided grounds for divorce.

In both jurisdictions men had sole rights of divorce and rights of the custody of the children — the law presumed both women and children to be the property of the man, or, in the event of his death, of his family. In both societies, the law allowed (and in Qing law sometimes even insisted) that wives could legitimately be beaten by their husbands, whilst consent to sexual intercourse upon marriage was taken as consent for life — thus no husband could ever be guilty of forcing his wife to have sex against her will. In both societies, there was also a strong double-standard of sexual behaviour: adultery on behalf of the wife constituted automatic grounds for divorce; but the law expected her to tolerate the same behaviour by her husband (Watson, 1984: 1). Indeed, the legal regulation of prostitution in both British and Hong Kong Chinese society institutionalized male sexual infidelity. The law in both societies clearly regarded women as non-persons. The power of the male head of the household (the paterfamilias) over everyone within his domain was thought to provide the best guarantee of order in the family, in society, and in the Empire. The social and economic position of men and women was legally structured to preserve these arrangements. For colonizing and colonized women, the experience was one of common oppression.

In modern Hong Kong, these pre-colonial forms are privileged by a new Orientalism which identifies 'Chineseness' with conservative traditions. This has acted as an ideological barrier against the introduction of modern British laws favouring women. The Chinese and expatriate (male) business and commercial élites also argue that anti-discriminatory workplace legislation would push up the costs of production if employers were forced to pay women workers equal pay for equal work, ultimately damaging Hong Kong's competitive edge. Patriarchal values are thus as important to industry as they are to landowners, partly because they deny the market-value of female labour.

Those who wish to continue the legal prohibition on women inheriting New Territories land form a wealthy landowning élite which has hitherto been recognized as the sole legitimate voice of the people of the New Territories. This voice — the Heung Yee Kuk — is a wholly male voice. It was first recognized as an advisory body by the government in 1926. Women have never gained equal representation on this council, which rules through a system of elected elders and rural committees, dominated by men. There are few women on the rural committees, since normally only family heads are allowed to elect village representatives, and family heads are male: 'At its head is an élite of 131 council members, most of them big landowners. Six of their number ... are also members of the Legislative Council, while their representatives dominate the government-appointed bodies that administer the area' (*South China Morning Post*, 21 October 1990).

In return for the Heung Yee Kuk's assistance in governing the area, the administration practically left them to run the New Territories: 'They provide local leadership and the government depends upon them for support' (*South China Morning Post*, 21 October 1990). The Heung Yee Kuk argues that allowing women to have an equal voice and/or to inherit New Territories land would lead to the destruction of village life. 'Doing nothing' to interfere with these customs and practices, whilst at the same time making the Heung Yee Kuk the voice of the New Territories, meant that the women of the New Territories could be evicted from homes and land (in which they had made a lifetime's investment) by sons, cousins, or grandsons who intended to sell the property before emigrating to Canada, Australia, or America. Non-intervention meant that these women were forced to rely on their menfolk to make some provision for them — perhaps granting them the privilege of staying in their homes until they died, or using some of the revenue from the land to provide them with a dowry or an education, none of which they were entitled to as a right, and all of which kept them in a position of economic and social dependence. The silence of government was taken as its consent to these practices and perpetuated a system of settled inequalities and continued discrimination.

## The Position of Women in the New Territories

The struggle to change discriminatory inheritance laws in the New Territories provides a paradigm case for our understanding of how vested interests and dominant values have intersected colonial rule to reproduce this system of settled inequalities.

The New Territories comprise all of the outlying islands, together with the land between the urban areas of Kowloon, and the border with mainland China. The territory of Hong Kong consists of 1,094 square kilometres, of which 952 square kilometres (or 88 per cent) comprise the New Territories; 41 per cent of the territory's population lives there (Hong Kong Government, 1992). Originally, Hong Kong island was ceded to the British in 1842, whilst the New Territories were leased in 1898 for a period of ninety-nine years. It is this leasing arrangement which prompts the return of Hong Kong to mainland China in 1997. Kowloon and New Kowloon were developed principally in the 1950s and early 1960s. The islands, such as Lantau, Cheung Chau, Peng Chau, and Lamma, remained populated by a scattered indigenous population dependent upon fishing and agriculture. The largest of the islands, Lantau island, is, however, destined for rapid change as it will accommodate Hong Kong's new international airport. The mainland section of the New Territories has also become one of the most populous areas of Hong Kong, with over two million people living in a series of modern, densely populated high-rise new towns.

Some of the old walled villages of the New Territories still remain, and it is here that most of the 50,000 indigenous people claim to live, though, in practice, many male heirs to land now live overseas. The definition of the 'indigenous population' in law refers to those who can trace their ancestry in the New Territories back through the male line to before 1898. These include what Baker has called the 'Five Great Clans' of the New Territories (Tang, Hau, Pang, Liu, and Man); most were Cantonese, but at least one has Hakka origin (Baker, 1966: 27). These five clans secured for themselves the best agricultural land in the area, and '... the best land of the New Territories was, and still mostly is, in the possession of these five clans, and certainly in the local situation it was these five clans which wielded power' (Baker, 1966: 30). Baker describes how (in the nineteenth century) being wealthy and large, these clans could command arms and men to protect their interests and control the New Territories; they also made use of networks of contacts to bring in support even from Government (Baker, 1966: 39). Clearly, those who lacked land — i.e. women, as well as some of the lesser lineages and the fishing communities or boatpeople — lacked this kind of wealth and power.

The 1990s has seen a powerful alliance of these old interests against new attempts to modify their control over the affairs of the New Territories. Their resistance to proposals enabling women to inherit land was rooted not only in self-interest (i.e. keeping control of very valuable land) but also in opposition to any curtailment of this control. This opposition itself is nothing new. The proposal to allow women to inherit simply provided another, particularly potent, focus for opposition; it also revived old questions about the ungovernability of the New Territories.

Despite the fact that urban sprawl and modern ways of life now mean that the New Territories are firmly part of twentieth-century Hong Kong, the principal law that governed the area until 1994 was the New Territories Ordinance 1910, consolidated by Cap. 97 of the Laws of Hong Kong. This law was the main obstacle to female inheritance of land. In addition, it is sometimes claimed that the prohibition on female inheritance was a custom protected by a declaration, made during the 1898 handover of the New Territories, that the British administration would not interfere with the 'good customs' of existing New Territories residents. It is likely that such a declaration was made in order to forestall 'native' opposition to colonial rule, an aim which appears to have been shared by the Chinese in their many invocations to New Territories residents to obey their new rulers.

The spirit of the New Territories Ordinance seems to have been to preserve the way of life of indigenous residents of the New Territories, although it also included a clause which allowed land to be exempted from the customary law rules otherwise preserved by Part II of the Ordinance (Part II, Section 7 (2) and (3) — still in force). This in itself provides us with some evidence that it was never the original intention of the government to prevent any break with pre-colonial customs and traditions.

'Land', as defined by the New Territories Ordinance, includes any undivided share in land and interest in land (for example, rent or profit) (Cap. 97, Part I, s.2 1984). Part II of the Ordinance applied to the New Territories only and it was primarily this which secured the exclusive right of males to inherit Part II land. Women (widows, wives, daughters, sisters) were not entitled to inherit New Territories land except where land had been exempted from customary law under Section 7.

Although the exemption clause in the New Territories Ordinance had existed since 1910, the Hong Kong government never drew it to the attention of aggrieved women, nor did its officers encourage New Territories men, who wished their wives or daughters to inherit, to have their land exempted. As with so many legal rights, the right to exemption remained a dead-letter because most rights go unclaimed. In the New Territories, however, the District Officers also seem to have played an important part in organizing local-level negotiations and compromises. Since customary law is meant to be flexible, this kind of negotiation makes perfect sense within a customary law tradition. However, it also stopped cases from proceeding to court with the result that relatively few disputes were heard by the courts. One knock-on effect of this has been that those cases which have proceeded to court have been judged on the basis of a very narrow reservoir of case-law and limited understanding of customary law. Thus there was a two-tier operation of law: one at the grass-roots level, negotiated by District Officers on the basis of their understanding of customary law coupled with expediency;

and another at the level of the formal legal system, where judicial decisions have tended to confuse custom with precedent, and, as a consequence, fossilize practice.

The kind of confusion which the courts have caused may be seen in the case of Tang Kai-chung and another versus Tang Chik-shing and others[4], in which the court decided that it must recognize and enforce Chinese customary rights in relation to *Tso* land in the New Territories. This decision has generally been taken to imply that it is mandatory to apply Chinese custom to all cases involving all New Territories land, a view which fails to understand the differences in the land, of which *Tso* land is a very particular type[5]. In numerous other kinds of 'Chinese custom' cases, judges have decided not to apply customary law because to do so would lead to injustice or oppression[6].

There was a common misapprehension that the New Territories Ordinance applied only to indigenous residents. Indeed, many of the government's own administrators also seem to have held this view. In fact, the New Territories Ordinance itself never referred to indigenous residents at all. It applied to all persons living on New Territories land, whether they lived in rural villages or in high-rise apartments. Given that there existed an exemption clause, and given that much of the development in the New Territories was government-led, it was generally assumed that the government automatically exempted most of the land in the New Territories, leaving only isolated pockets of indigenous residents covered by the customary law on succession. During the development of New Kowloon exemptions were, in fact, sought by developers, with the result that most of urban Kowloon is exempted.

However, research (Jones, 1991) has revealed that only fifty-four plots of land in the New Territories were exempted, none of which included major residential developments, including the new towns. Selby (1991) has argued that exemptions have been made as a matter of policy to Housing Authority land used for the building of flats under the Home Ownership scheme but these exemptions were not, in fact, made. It would therefore seem to be the case that large urban areas remained unexempted and fell under Part II of the Ordinance, which meant that, in theory at least, customary law still applied to all of the two million New Territories residents. Alerted to this fact, the government at last began to grant exemptions to all new developments in 1993, and brought forward the New Territories Land (Exemption) Bill which retrospectively exempted the urban areas of the New Territories from customary law. This Bill introduced a new distinction between rural and urban land in the New Territories and would have exempted urban land from the operation of Part II of the New Territories Ordinance (and thus from the application of Chinese customary law in matters of inheritance), while leaving rural land covered by the Ordinance (and thus preserving customary law discriminating against women in matters of inheritance).

Christine Loh, a Legislative Councillor, introduced an amendment to the Bill which was intended to exempt both urban and rural land from the operation of the New Territories Ordinance, thereby making it possible for all women to inherit land. Those who wished to leave land only to their sons or to their customary heirs could still do so by making a will to that effect. This amendment was intended to bring the law into line with the guarantees of equality and non-discrimination on the grounds of sex contained in article 26 of the International Covenant on Civil and Political Rights. This article guarantees equality before the law and equal protection of the law and requires legislative protection against discrimination on various grounds including sex. This guarantee was incorporated as part of Hong Kong law in 1991 by article 22 of the Hong Kong Bill of Rights. However, although article 26 of the Covenant requires the elimination of discriminatory inheritance laws, the Bill of Rights has been held by the Court of Appeal not to apply to legal relations between private parties. Accordingly, it may not have been possible to invoke article 22 of the Bill of Rights directly to challenge the discriminatory aspects of Chinese customary law relating to inheritance in the New Territories.

Despite opposition from the Heung Yee Kuk and other vested interest, Loh's amendment was accepted and became part of the New Territories Land (Exemption) Ordinance (No. 55 of 1994), which came into force on 24 June 1994.

In addition to the New Territories Ordinance prohibiting female inheritance, it was and is government policy to allow males the right to build what is known as a 'small-house' of specified dimensions within or near the village confines. However, it has become a common practice for men to use their 'small-house' concession to build 'Spanish-style' villas for sale or rent to outsiders, undercutting the original 'conservation' rationale of the policy. Since the 'small-house' policy is a male-only privilege, women are denied the opportunity to build their own house either for their family or for profit. This puts women at a distinct economic disadvantage given the high sale and rental values of land and property — scarce and highly desirable commodities in the Hong Kong real estate market. Although the legal situation regarding the inheritance of land has changed, the policy regarding land grants to build 'small-houses' has not.

It is difficult to justify the existence of feudal laws in modern Hong Kong where the general mood is towards equality and fairness. Moreover, even within the New Territories, the kind of society in which older laws 'made sense' has changed beyond all recognition. Much of the agricultural land has been developed for housing; some is used as storage space for containers or scrap metal, vast swathes of which now scar the former rural landscape. Waves of migration have also undercut old extended family ties, whilst the new towns have brought a rapid influx of urban inhabitants with modern ideas. Within the walled villages themselves, houses are increasingly rented to outsiders. Despite these changes, when faced with criticism from the United Nations Committee on Economic, Social and Cultural Rights, the government still felt able to justify continuing its discriminatory 'small-house' policy in the following terms:

> A violation of the principle of equality and non-discrimination under the International Covenant on Economic and Social Rights arises if there is differential treatment of equal cases without there being an objective and reasonable justification, or if proportionality between the aim sought and the means employed is lacking. The Small-House Policy has an objective and reasonable justification. It is intended to maintain the quality of housing by promoting the cohesiveness of indigenous culture of the New Territories by preserving the links that indigenous villagers have with their own villages. (Appendix 1 to Legco Paper No. PL 81/94–95, 12–1–95).

The law too has played its part in this transformation. Reforms introduced in the 1970s — such as the Marriage Reform Ordinance, the Intestates Estates Ordinance, and the Probate and Administration Ordinance — put an end to customary forms of marriage, to concubinage, and to the practice of posthumous adoption to preserve the lineage. These 1970s legislative reforms were clearly an interference with Chinese custom in family life. Why did the government change its policy of non-intervention in the 1970s; and why did it choose to legislate for radical changes in 1970 and not before — or even after?

Part of the explanation lies with social, economic, and political events in Hong Kong during the 1960s, and the restructuring of power which followed in the 1970s. In the aftermath of the 1966 and 1967 riots, the Hong Kong government acknowledged that it faced a problem of legitimacy (Scott, 1989). Throughout the 1960s, Hong Kong underwent massive economic restructuring, resulting in significant changes in the demographic and social structure of Hong Kong society. It was no longer sufficient for the administration to sit back and let free-market forces govern. The old-style colonial administration also faced opposition (albeit short-lived) from a population increasingly politicized by events in mainland China, principally the Cultural Revolution.

In the aftermath of the 1966 and 1967 riots, it became necessary for the government to re-negotiate its legitimacy. The new-style colonial government had to be seen to be modernizing, making progressive policies, ensuring economic performance, and consulting its subjects on important issues. Re-fashioning some of society's social and political structures was part of this project, persuading the people of Hong Kong that theirs was a good society in which to live. Thus, from 1970 onwards, there was an intensification of legislative activity, providing everything from free primary and secondary education, to the introduction of District Boards. Media propaganda and street-level festivals were used to establish a new image of Hong Kong as an integrated modern society.

It was in this process of hegemonic restructuring that radical reforms to Chinese customary law took place. However, many of these reforms specifically did not apply to those living on Part II New Territories land. Preserving the New

Territories way of life had become something of a romantic obsession with expatriate colonial administrators. It was their attempt to preserve the New Territories life against the more radical reforms which mistakenly extended the reach of customary law beyond that originally intended in the New Territories Ordinance itself.

This British reverence for Chinese tradition stems from a combination of factors. It was the result of the 'Little England' values of the original District Officers and the shift to 'native rule' in late Victorian colonial policy. This policy, initiated in Africa by Lugard in his Political Memoranda, required massive amounts of information to be collected by District Officers about the customs of the 'natives'[7]. It encouraged District Officers to develop friendly relations with those who were powerful locally, cultivating them as official intermediaries. District Officers tended to do this rather well, sometimes overstepping the proprieties of colonial life by 'going native', i.e. becoming fluent in Cantonese, taking Chinese wives, living in rural villages, etc. Arriving in the New Territories, many of these District Officers would have been delighted to find a lifestyle so reminiscent of the 'Little England' rural idyll romanticized by Victorian political and intellectual life. This romanticization, coupled with the Victorian values of family and patriarchy, and the need for order in the Empire, predisposed these 'sentimental imperialists' towards tradition rather than modernity, to stability rather than change, doctrines forever close to the heart of British conservatism.

Throughout the Empire, 'native rule' required notes on local customs to be both detailed and prolific. But these observations were written for a particular purpose, at a particular time and for a particular audience made up of those who wished to know how 'different' foreigners were from themselves, principally in order to govern them more effectively. Knowledge was the key to 'native rule' but its collectors tended to set forever in tablets of stone the customs of those observed. The processes of rational administration by the colonial authorities itself distorted certain features of local customary law. In particular, the machinery of rational administration petrified the social order of the New Territories (Chun, 1990: 401).

Expatriates dominated colonial administration in Hong Kong until the restructuring and localization policies of the

1970s brought a new breed of District Officer, Hong Kong born and bred, and committed to the modernization of Hong Kong as an adjunct to its economic restructuring. For these officers, change was good, and the break with tradition an important part of the modernization process. Sentimental protection of customary practices did not form part of their mind-set — indeed it contradicted their mission. Their presence brought about an ambivalence in the colonial policy towards Chinese law and custom, an ambivalence also felt by some expatriates within government who had begun to realize its mistaken extension of the reach of customary law to the urban areas of the New Territories. The rise of these urban areas, administered by a new breed of administrators, weakened the power-base of the Heung Yee Kuk itself.

Since its recognition as an advisory body in 1926, the Heung Yee Kuk has acted as official interpreter of local custom and as a conduit for the transmission of government policy down to the grassroots of New Territories society. The new breed of local administrators could perform this function equally, if not more effectively, lacking as they did any vested interest in the preservation of the status quo. Moreover, the Heung Yee Kuk's interests were, and are still, increasingly at odds with the modernizing measures of these administrators, resisting any attempt to change the New Territories inheritance laws or to bring some of the more wayward practices of the New Territories into line with government law and policy.

In the 1990 debate about whether or not the Bill of Rights would end male-only succession in the New Territories, the Heung Yee Kuk exploited tensions in Sino-British relations and mobilized political opinion in Beijing against such a change, arguing that it interfered with Chinese custom. In 1994, when the issue of women's land rights resurfaced, they once again employed this strategy. It would be ironic if China, which itself confirmed the right of women to inherit in its 1930 Civil Code, could be persuaded to uphold Qing dynasty practices. The Heung Yee Kuk has also found support amongst expatriate former District Officers who see themselves as trustees of Chinese rural life.

In the 1970s, a number of legal reforms stripped the law prohibiting female inheritance of its former societal underpinnings. Paradoxically, these modernizing reforms also inadvertently resulted in the position of New Territories women becoming far less equitable than before.

Prior to 1971, a New Territories woman could still have probated a will and obtained a valid grant of administration. Her title to land would have been valid in any contest with a male claiming customary law rights. The 1971 reforms reversed this position so that her title would fall before the customary rights claim of the nearest male heir. This had important consequences for women. Section 13 of the New Territories Ordinance gave the District Court and High Court power to recognize and enforce any Chinese custom or customary right regarding New Territories land. Prior to June 1994 when amendments excluding the application of Chinese customary law to succession in the New Territories were passed, this power applied to proceedings relating to testate and intestate succession. Section 17 (repealed with effect from 24 June 1994) dealt with the registration of successors to a deceased landowner where no probate is granted. This stated that, if no grant of probate or administration of the estate of the deceased was made by the High Court within three months after death, the Land Officer must ascertain and register the name of the person who was entitled to succeed. If a grant of probate or administration was made by the High Court within three months of the death, 'the grantee therein named shall be registered as the successor'. If a grant of probate was not made, or letters of administration not granted, within three months of the death, customary law would apply.

In 1991, Selby recognized that it was 'almost impossible' to obtain a grant within this time period: 'This can give rise to a situation where a woman has obtained probate on a valid will bequeathing property to her, but the Land Officer is bound by customary law to register the land in the name of a male heir' (Selby, 1991: 75). The net effect was to make non-exempt New Territories land subject to customary law, i.e. male-only succession. In fact, this position was known to the Hong Kong government in 1988, and was acknowledged in an unpublished report of a Working Party on these issues[8]. Its conclusion, however, was that such things were custom, and that law could not change custom. Such a position reveals the continuing misunderstanding of, and ambivalence by the government towards, Chinese customary law. In 1971, the state used its formal legal powers to totally abolish several kinds of customary law. Nevertheless, in the 1980s, we find Selby writing that, whilst the situation of women in the New Territories had led to dissatisfaction amongst women excluded from a share of the estate of the deceased, even the most reasonable demands for equality for women 'cannot be entertained without going against custom' (Selby, 1991: 77). This begs the question of what exactly government lawyers understand customary law to be.

The situation of New Territories women was in fact far worse than Selby's 1991 article suggested, for whilst the Wills Ordinance allowed a New Territories resident to make a will, section 75 of the Probate and Administration Ordinance specifically exempted Part II land. In effect, any woman who inherited New Territories land under a will did not have good title, was not entitled to have the will probated, and could legally be ousted at any time by the nearest male customary heir under customary law. It was a matter of legal debate whether probate could be granted at all, let alone within the three months required by the New Territories Ordinance. This situation has now been remedied by the New Territories Land (Amendment) Ordinance, which applies the general law governing succession to land in the New Territories.

The same situation existed regarding letters of administration. The exclusion of Part II land under Section 11 of the Intestates Estates Ordinance 1971 meant any woman who was given a grant of administration with regard to Part II land did not have valid title and could be challenged by any male claiming to be the next male customary heir. The Law Reform Commission recommended the repeal of Section 11, arguing that:

> We consider it difficult to justify in this modern age the preservation of two systems of inheritance of (land)... within one jurisdiction.... Further, the cutting out of the daughters and the restriction on the rights of a widow of a deceased Chinese intestate are considered by us to be wrong in principle and out of touch with modern thought in Hong Kong (Law Reform Commission, 1986: 12.6).

The reforms of the 1970s preserved the customary law of succession but took away most of the relationships upon which it depends (Evans, 1973: 44). Attitudes and practices within the New Territories itself have also been changing. Women in the New Territories are now more likely to be given a share of the proceeds from customary land trusts (CLTs), a change more in keeping with the views of 'the present generation of CLT members and managers' (Selby, 1991: 69)[9]. Selby does not give us the empirical evidence for this conclusion. In any event, privileges are not legally enforceable rights. They are 'private law'; which may be withdrawn at any time without legal redress; and also perpetuated the economic dependency of New Territories women.

A survey of New Territories inhabitants in 1990 showed that the majority were in favour of changing the law prohibiting female inheritance (*South China Morning Post*, 30 July 1990), a finding increasingly supported by the newly-organized grass-roots movements amongst indigenous women who have at last found their voice. This view was also supported by the former Commissioner for Administrative Complaints, Mr Arthur Garcia, who drew attention to inequities in the New Territories law (Commissioner for Administrative Complaints, Case C45/53/91).

## The Force of the Cultural Argument

The view that those who try to improve the position of women in Hong Kong are meddling Westerners recurs in several episodes of Hong Kong's legal history. We see this argument raised in the law reforms regarding *mui tsai*, and, later, in the reform of licensed prostitution (Jaschok, 1988: 8; Gronewold, 1985: 46; Miners, 1987: 157). Supporters of these practices persistently argued that the British did not understand Chinese customs, nor the place of women in Chinese society. The evidence shows, however, that there was in fact a real divide within local Chinese opinion on these issues (Smith, 1981: 91; Jaschok, 1988: 149). However, the Hong Kong administration relied upon:

> ... those 'respectable' Chinese whom it recruited as its advisers. Then as now, these were the wealthy merchants, landowners and professionals. They did not represent the masses of the people. Their role as leaders of the Chinese community was, however, seldom challenged by the silent majority. It was a surprise to them and to the Government

when an aggressive opposition suddenly emerged . . . (Smith, 1981: 92).

Resisting 'foreign' interference in Chinese culture has thus been a long-established strategy of some segments of the Chinese élite and the colonial administration. Talk of protecting Chinese culture conveniently overlooks the part played by local Chinese in the campaigns for change. It glosses over the fact that Chinese custom and culture is itself a contested domain. In the early days of colonialism, the government's policy of non-interference stemmed from a fear of jeopardizing the support of powerful segments of the Chinese élite. Towards the end of the nineteenth century, the theory of 'indirect rule' encouraged the government to foster 'native' support and collect information about its colonized people. The principal source of intelligence about the 'natives' was again those who were powerful locally. These two factors have combined to produce a lasting susceptibility to élite interpretations of Chinese culture. This susceptibility was, and is, increased by the fact that the British administrators themselves have had little understanding of how customary law works. British administrators have generally adopted a rather fixed and legalistic interpretation of Chinese custom and law, so much so that the order they reproduced in the early days of the colony has itself come to be seen as 'authentic native' tradition.

Moreover, given the provisions of the Basic Law, this petrified comprehension of Chinese custom is set to continue long after 1997. Yet one of the features of customary law is its ability to bend and change with circumstance. Indeed, to begin with, the Chinese themselves did not have a custom of memorializing in written form successions to property; 'nor did they as a practice bother to register conveyances of sale with provincial authorities' (Chun, 1990: 413). One of the attractions of customary law is that it lends itself to multiple interpretations, the negotiation of which facilitates compromise and resolution of disputes. British attempts to protect custom, far from preserving indigenous tradition, have artificially constructed a version of Chinese tradition which now handicaps any challenge to those with a vested interest in the status quo.

This illusion of tradition, what Hobsbawn and Ranger (1983)

call 'the invention of tradition', has been perpetuated by scholars, administrators and lawyers alike (Chun, 1990: 402). Indeed, the position of District Officer as arbiter of customary law has meant that he could negotiate disputes at grassroots level, very often mistaking any solution which found agreement between all parties 'as *ipso facto* in accordance with local custom' (Chun, 1990: 414). Chun goes on to argue that, 'to claim, as the government did repeatedly, that it modified customary practice "on the ground" as a means of preserving intact in the long run its traditional essence as a system of law grossly understates the nature of radical change that took place' (Chun, 1990: 417). Indeed, the dearth of legal challenges to the New Territories inheritance law was in no small part due to the fact that District Officers 'ironed out' disputes by persuading women to accept some compromise solution to their claims. Nelson also argues that in tidying up Chinese customary law, the British administrators became 'more Chinese than the Ching' (Nelson, 1969: 33). This led to a fossilization of Chinese society in the New Territories (Huang, 1982: 56).

Custom and culture are not fixed and immovable things; domains were contested often, and historically were annexed by the more powerful clans, 'to browbeat weaker groups into acknowledging their largely spurious claims to landownership' (Nelson, 1969: 4), and, in the 1990s, annexed by the Heung Yee Kuk for similar purposes.

Wesley-Smith has argued that in administering the New Territories, the Hong Kong government has selected either 'law' or 'custom' whenever its political purpose was best served (Wesley-Smith, 1994: 214). Similarly, different groups have used different interpretations of Chinese custom to serve their own ends. Thus it was, and still is, argued by the Heung Yee Kuk that the patrilineal distribution of property protected by male-only succession is essential to the stability and well-being of the New Territories 'way of life'.

Will the end of colonial rule bring China's more enlightened laws on women's equality to Hong Kong? The experience of women in China offers little room for optimism, for, although China's laws promise equality, traditional patriarchal practices persist (Wolf, 1985; Ocko, 1991). As Ocko points out, this raises questions about the role of law as a guarantor of women's rights. Nevertheless, the Heung Yee Kuk has proved itself able to exploit fissures in Sino-British relations in order to preserve laws upholding male dominance. The mingling of the two economies has also encouraged more co-operation between the male commercial and landowning élites of both Hong Kong and mainland Chinese society amongst whom we can expect to find a strong degree of shared patriarchal values. However, modern Hong Kong has a population which has undergone rapid politicization, starting with the 1984 signing of the Joint Declaration, the 1989 June 4th incident in China, and the 1990 enactment of a Bill of Rights. In this climate, the claims of the Heung Yee Kuk to political legitimacy have weakened, as indeed have any claims based on traditions associated with Empire, be it Chinese or British. As Chun points out, the kind of functionalist arguments used to preserve traditions are characteristic of the hegemony of the state (Chun, 1990: 418), but the fact is that in the 1990s, the state in China and in Hong Kong itself is engaged in re-negotiating its legitimacy. This means that increasingly, government is concerned with new constituencies, and the Heung Yee Kuk's case may receive a less sympathetic hearing than it once did.

## Conclusions

Faced with arguments which deter change on the basis that it undercuts traditional culture, the academic must look at who is interpreting the nature of Chinese culture, how and when they are interpreting it, and why. Culture is not the privileged interpretation of dominant groups. Examining the history of women's issues in Hong Kong alerts us to the fact that a highly conservative version of culture has suited the interests of both the colonized and colonizing male élites. Additionally it alerts us to the fact that questions about the status of women in society are inextricably also questions about the ownership of property and the exercise of power within that society. In the New Territories, one consequence of the law's support of patrilineal descent has been the production of misogyny as a cultural form.

Nowhere has this been more apparent than in the reaction

of the Heung Yee Kuk to the recent legislative proposal enabling rural women to inherit property. The female Legislative Councillor who tabled the proposal to change the inheritance laws in the New Territories, Christine Loh Kung-wai, met with threats and intimidation, including the threat (made on television) of rape. This is the traditional Chinese punishment for women who reject patriarchal control, and also a very brutal, male, method of mocking the status of women who claim to have an identity of their own. Other female activists and intellectuals were warned not to venture into the New Territories for fear of personal violence. Only with a large-scale police presence or the Heung Yee Kuk's protection, it was claimed, would they be safe. The message here is clear: women — even educated women — need male protection. The protection of the Heung Yee Kuk, like rape, is an organized male attempt to control women. There can be no clearer indication of how the old New Territories property law was constituted by and constitutive of, coercive forms of male domination.

Law is symbolic. Battles over inheritance and anti-discrimination laws reflect wider contests between competing groups in Hong Kong society over changes in Chinese identity and claims to 'Chineseness'. These are, in part, also battles over how society treats people, both in the private sphere and in the public domain of work. They alert us to the use of 'culture' and 'tradition' as political resources and legal discourses of power.

The continued presence of laws — and silences in the law — which discriminate against Hong Kong women can be explained by the colonial administration's past reliance upon élite views of Chinese custom, and by the colonial bureaucracy's incomprehension of the flexible nature of customary law. Benign imperialism and political compromise preserved a feudal law which prohibited female succession, and failed to pass laws prohibiting sexual discrimination until the last decade of the twentieth century.

The accusation of cultural imperialism has often been used by sections of the Chinese élite to de-legitimize opposition to the status quo. It has also been used by successive colonial administrations to secure the support of this élite. Where a selective interpretation of Chinese culture by dominant groups comes to be regarded as the sole interpretation, its effect is to silence all opposition within and without Chinese society. In the debate on the Bill of Rights, the Hong Kong Foundation (a regrouping of Heung Yee Kuk members together with local businessmen and politicians) claimed that it was a 'charter filled with alien ideas', based upon values which were essentially Western, rooted in Western culture and derived from Christian philosophy (*Hong Kong Standard*, 6 January 1990).

Thus the full rhetoric of cultural imperialism was directed against those who challenged the status quo. Supposed conflicts between East and West, Christian and Confucian, were exploited to the full by the Hong Kong Foundation, for whom the Bill of Rights was inimical to local traditions as well as to business interests. Exactly how inimical is revealed by the complacency of the government in the area of equal pay laws. Hong Kong capital has resisted equal pay just as it has resisted collective bargaining, fully paid maternity leave, and pension rights. Clearly the 'economic miracle' of Hong Kong also depends in part upon the law's support for a system which reproduces a submissive female workforce. In 1992, the *Report of an Inter-Departmental Working Group on Sex Discrimination* concluded that the low level of complaints about workplace discrimination meant that 'the problem is not serious in Hong Kong' (1992 Report: 3). It failed to consider whether this indicated an absence of accessible channels for complainants.

It may also be that, because Hong Kong women share a common work experience, they reason that 'everyone goes through life the same way, why should I be different?' (Levin 1991: 208). This is what Lockwood calls 'conditional fatalism', the perception 'that privations are due to forces over which people believe they have little or no control' (Lockwood, 1982: 101–18). Lack of control over one's life is a common experience of colonized peoples deprived of a political voice. In one sense, it could be argued, the experience of Hong Kong women parallels the experience of Hong Kong people more generally.

## Notes

1. R. v. R. (rape — marital exemption) (1992) 1 *Appeal Cases* 599.
2. New Territories Ordinance 1910, Part II, consolidated in Cap. 97 Laws of Hong Kong. The law changed in June 1994 when the New Territories Land (Exemption) Ordinance was passed.
3. Marriage Reform Ordinance 1971, Section 14. See also Pegg, L. (1986) *Family Law in Hong Kong*, Singapore: Butterworths, p. 16.
4. Tang Kai-chung and another v. Tang Chik-shing and others, Action No. 2071 of 1966, (1970) *Hong Kong Law Reports* pp. 276–322.
5. For a description of *Tso* land see Wong, B. (1990) 'Chinese Customary Law — An Examination of *Tsos* and *Tongs*' in *Hong Kong Law Journal* pp. 13–30.
6. See, for example, Wong v. Wong (1957) *Hong Kong Law Reports* 420, and Khoo Hooi Leong v. Khoo Chong Yeok (1930) *Appeal Cases* 346.
7. Lugard, Frederick, *Revision of Instructions to Political Officers on Subjects Chiefly Political and Administrative: 1913–1918 Political Memoranda* (1970), London: Frank Cass and Co. Ltd.
8. Report of the Working Group on the New Territories Ordinance (Cap. 97), April 1989, unpublished. Some, but not all, of the findings of this report are given in Selby (1991).
9. For a fuller description of CLTs see Selby (1991).

## References

Baker, H. D. R. (1966), 'The Five Great Clans of The New Territories' *Journal of the Hong Kong Branch of the Royal Asiatic Society*, 6: 25–47.

Chan, W. K. (1991), *The Making of Hong Kong Society*, New York: Oxford University Press.

Chun, A. (1990), 'Policing Society: the "Rational" Practice of British Colonial Land Administration in the New Territories of Hong Kong c. 1900', *Journal of Historical Sociology*, 3(4): 401–22.

Crisswell, C. (1981), *The Taipans: Hong Kong's Merchant Princes*, Hong Kong: Oxford University Press.

Evans, D. M. (1973), 'The New Law of Succession in Hong Kong', *Hong Kong Law Journal*, 3(1): 7–50.

Gronewold, S. (1985), *Beautiful Merchandise: Prostitution in China 1860–1936*, New York: Harrington Park Press.

Hobsbawn, E. and Ranger, T. (1983), *The Invention of Tradition*, Cambridge: Cambridge University Press.

Hong Kong Government (1992), *Fourth Annual Report of the Commissioner for Administrative Complaints, (Case No. C45/53/91)*, Hong Kong: Hong Kong Government Printer.

Hong Kong Government (1992), *Annual Digest of Statistics*, Hong Kong: Hong Kong Government Printer.

Hong Kong Bill of Rights Ordinance (Cap. 383), 8 June 1991, Hong Kong: Hong Kong Government Printer.

Huang, Shu-min (1982), 'Hong Kong's Colonial Administration and the Land Tenure System', in Huang Shu-min (ed.), *Rural Hong Kong: The Anthropological Perspectives, Papers in Anthropology No. 6*, Iowa State University Department of Sociology and Anthropology.

Intestates Estates Ordinance, 1971, *section 11, Cap. 73 Laws of Hong Kong*: Hong Kong Government Printer; Annotated Series, annotated by D. M. Evans, (1974), Hong Kong: Hong Kong Law Journal Limited.

Jaschok, Maria (1988), *Concubines and Bondservants*, Hong Kong: Oxford University Press.

Jones, C. (1991), 'Prohibition on Female Inheritance of Land and "Small Houses" in that Part of Hong Kong Known as the New Territories', in C. Howarth, C. Jones, C. Petersen, and H. Samuels, *Report to the United Nations on the Implementation of the International Covenant on Civil and Political Rights in Hong Kong*, Hong Kong: Hong Kong Council of Women.

Kirk-Greene, A. H. M. (ed.) (1970), *Lord Lugard: Political Memoranda*, London: Frank Cass and Co. Ltd.

Law Reform Commission of Hong Kong (1986), *Report on Law of Wills, Intestate Succession, and Provision for Deceased Persons' Families and Dependents*, Hong Kong: Government Printer.

Levin, D. (1991), 'Women and the Industrial Labor Market in Hong Kong: Participation and Perceptions', in G. Scoville (ed.), *Status Influences in Third World Labor Markets*, New York: Walter de Gruyter, pp. 183–214.

Lockwood, D. (1982), 'Fatalism: Durkheim's Hidden Theory of Order', in Anthony Giddens and Gavin MacKenzie (eds.), *Social Class and the Division of Labour*, Cambridge: Cambridge University Press.

Miners, Norman (1987), *Hong Kong Under Imperial Rule 1912–1941*, Hong Kong: Oxford University Press.

Nead, L. (1988), *Myths of Sexuality*, Oxford: Basil Blackwell.

Nelson, G. H. (1969), 'British Land Administration in the New Territories of Hong Kong, and its Effects on Chinese Social Organization', Conference Paper for The London-Cornell Project for East and Southeast Asian Studies, Ste. Adele-en-haut.

New Territories Ordinance 1910, *Laws of Hong Kong Cap. 97 1984, Part II*, Hong Kong: Hong Kong Government Printer; (original Ordinance is No. 34 of 1910).

Ocko, J. (1991), 'Women, Property, and Law in the People's Republic of China', in Rubie S. Watson and Patricia Buckley Ebrey (eds.), *Marriage and Inequality in Chinese Society*, Berkeley: University of California Press, pp. 313–45.

Peak District Reservation, No. 4 of 1904: An Ordinance for the reservation of a residential area in the Peak District. See also the *Hong Kong Government Gazette*, 24 March 1888, p. 295: The Regulation of the Chinese Ordinance Probate and Administration Ordinance, 1971, section 75.

Scott, Ian (1989), *Political Change and the Crisis of Legitimacy in Hong Kong*, Hong Kong: Oxford University Press.

Selby, S. (1991), 'Everything You Wanted to Know About Chinese Customary Law (But Were Afraid to Ask)', *Hong Kong Law Journal*, 21(1): 45–77.

Smith, C. T (1981), 'The Chinese Church, Labour and Elites and the *Mui Tsai* Question in the 1920s', *Journal of the Hong Kong Branch of the Royal Asiatic Society*, 21: 91–113.

Watson, Rubie S. (1984) 'Women's Property in Republican China: Rights and Practice', *Republican China*, X(1a): 1–12.

Wesley-Smith, P. (1994), *The Sources of Hong Kong Law*, Hong Kong: Hong Kong University Press.

Wills Ordinance No. 32, 1970, Hong Kong: Hong Kong Government Printer.

Wilmhurst, D. J. (1980), 'The Erosion of Customary Succession in the New Territories', Memo to Registrar General, NT Section.

Wolf, M. (1985), *Revolution Postponed: Women in Contemporary China*, Stanford: Stanford University Press.

Wang, B. (1990), 'Chinese Customary Law — An Exemption of *Tsos* and *Tongs*', *Hong Kong Law Journal*, pp. 13–30.

# 7 Women and Crime in Hong Kong

*Jon Vagg*

In Hong Kong, as in most countries, women comprise a small proportion of detected offenders and generally commit minor crimes. Seen against the background of male-dominated, armed robberies in the early 1990s, women offenders typically do little harm and attract little attention.

Yet a focus on women and crime reveals three otherwise hidden problems. First, in the decade leading up to 1992, the rate of female juvenile delinquency rose faster than the equivalent rate for males. While the numbers have remained small, the rate of increase has given rise to concern. Second, as Lee (1989) has argued, definitions of delinquency and responses to offenders are gender-biased, especially in the case of younger age groups. Female juvenile delinquents are subjected to a patriarchal form of 'welfare protectionism' which judges them primarily in terms of their sexuality and their 'need' to be 'protected from themselves'. This is partly a ramification of the Chinese patriarchal tradition discussed in the introductory chapter of this book, and partly an aspect of the sexist ideology prevalent in modern capitalist societies. Indeed, other contributors to this volume (Jones, Pearson and Yu) point out that men from Hong Kong and the United Kingdom frequently share a world view in attitudes towards prostitution. In this context, it is worth noting, as Pearson and Yu's chapter on commercial sex points out, that women who have shaken off the yokes of this protection and attempted to make a living through prostitution are generally denigrated, while their male clients are seldom subjected to such moral censure. It is obvious that sexual mores are applied with much greater stringency to women than to men. Finally, this bias towards the protection of young girls, however well-intentioned, blurs the boundaries between the treatment of young female offenders and young females who are 'at risk' of offending, who are often described in Hong Kong as 'pre-delinquents'.

This chapter deals with these issues in the following way.

The extent and type of female offending is examined with more specific consideration being given to the issues surrounding young female offenders. The criminal justice system and its response to female offenders and 'pre-delinquents' is surveyed, whilst consideration is given to women as victims rather than offenders. This section argues in particular that certain female offenders are also victims, and should be treated with more sympathy than societal attitudes and the current correctional system engender. The concluding section draws these separate issues together and argues for a change in thinking in Hong Kong, particularly regarding the treatment of young female offenders.

## Female Offending: Type and Extent

Over half of all crimes are never solved, and we can say nothing about the sex of these undetected criminals. Figures for detections and convictions are not routinely broken down by gender. Consequently, the only useful published information at the 'front end' of the criminal justice system is that on police arrests. Whilst arrest is not synonymous with guilt, we can treat these figures as a reasonable proxy for the gender breakdown of offenders.[1]

In 1991, the police arrested 38,300 males and 5,679 females, that is, 6.8 males for every female arrested. However, women were less likely to be suspects in violent crimes; twelve males were arrested for every female (violent crimes include murder and manslaughter, woundings and serious assaults, kidnapping, robbery with firearms, blackmail, arson, and rape). For property offences, women were less likely to be involved in burglary (one female arrested for every twenty-three males) and proportionately more involved in shop theft (one female for every 1.7 males). Men thus outnumbered women even for the offence regarded as most 'typically female', namely shoplifting. The only offence in which females outnumbered males — presumably this reflected patterns of childcare — was 'cruelty to children'. However there were only seventy-nine arrests in total for this offence.

A breakdown of arrests by age indicates that for all detected offences, arrests were distributed in the same way across age groups for both sexes. When the breakdown is done by offence group, however, it does appear that in one case only — arrests of persons aged between 31 and 60 for shoplifting — is there a near-equality between the sexes, with 918 males and 864 females arrested.

These figures should not be taken to minimize the danger posed by some female offenders, or their professionalism. Anecdotal evidence indicates that women have been involved in armed robbery gangs, in a variety of support roles.[2] There is also evidence to suggest that some women are involved in serious 'white-collar' crimes.[3] Yet we still need to ask why there is such a discrepancy between male and female offending rates. The single major factor seems to be socialization. As Downes and Rock (1988: 287) comment, the available evidence indicates that girls in Western societies are subjected to more intense informal and family-based social controls than boys. Women are, Downes and Rock suggest, 'oversocialized', and the external controls in childhood become internal, psychological inhibitors of deviance in adulthood. Although data on Hong Kong are not conclusive, it would certainly support the contention that this 'over-socialization' of girls is at least as common in the territory as it is in Europe or America.[4]

Recent English studies of female offenders (Carlen, 1988; Worrall, 1990) have thus investigated whether, and why, such dense social controls were absent in the lives of female offenders. They conclude that female offending is associated with resistance to patriarchal social controls, and with situations in which social controls are overwhelmed by more immediate considerations. Carlen in particular indicates that a childhood experience of foster care or institutionalization tends to lead to a reaction against paternalistic discipline, and that the stronger the attempts to impose such control, the stronger the reaction against it. The end-point of this sequence is, of course, crime. She also asserts that where women are emotionally involved with male drug-users, alcoholics, gamblers, or offenders, they often also become involved as accessories to crime, or engage in crime to support their partner's habit or to cover household expenses. Such patterns may not be automatically applicable to Hong Kong, but in the absence of clear data they are at least plausible hypotheses. The experience of the women described in Pearson and Yu (Chapter 9) certainly supports the view that emotional involvement with male drug-abusers, etc. provides an entry into the world of commercial sex.

## Offenders and 'Pre-delinquents'

While crime rates in Hong Kong are low by international standards, reported crime figures and victim surveys confirm that they rose very quickly in the early 1980s. After a period of stability from 1986 to 1989, reported crime figures began to rise quickly again from 1990. For reasons which have yet to be fully explained, the arrest rate for females rose to a peak in 1987 and then dropped, only to turn upwards again from 1990. However, despite these fluctuations, we can safely say that females, and young females in particular, have come to represent a larger proportion of all arrested offenders.

Lee (1992) has shown that the rate of female offending in Hong Kong almost doubled, from 115 to 204 arrests per 100,000 females per year, between 1981 and 1991.[5] The juvenile arrest rate also doubled in the same period, from 458 to 919 arrests per 100,000 juveniles. It is hardly surprising therefore that the arrest rate for female juveniles increased by about two-and-a-half times.[6] Lee also notes that over this ten-year period, female juveniles seemed to become involved in progressively more serious, sophisticated, and violent crimes; and when caught, they tended to be more manipulative in their dealings with the police.

What are these young female offenders like? In Hong Kong, most studies have been small-scale or exploratory pieces of research dealing either with offenders who have committed specific crime types, or who were selected on sentence criteria (for example, committal to a particular type of custody). These studies show there to be associations, for both boys and girls, between delinquency and poor school performance, truancy, exposure to delinquent peers, parental criminality, poor parent-child relationships (a catch-all description covering a variety of problems), broken homes, and low family income. Many offenders are described as having low self-esteem or poor ego-strength, or as being excessively 'pleasure-seeking'. Early or extensive dating or sexual experience is also related to offending, though this is almost always seen as more significant for girls than it is for boys. It is, however, clear that none of these factors in themselves are good predictors of offending — hence recent interest in multi-factor models[7] — while some have much closer associations with each other than with offending. This is the case, for example, with broken homes and family income.

While such studies give us an overall picture of offenders' characteristics, few provide any fine-grained information on individual offenders and therefore tell us little about what the offending means to the offender. In this connection, Chow's (1992) study is an important work despite the inclusion of only six female offenders in her sample.[8] They cannot be seen as statistically representative of all young female offenders — for one thing, they were all interviewed in custody and are by implication among the more serious of the young female offenders. Yet her cases do tell us something about how and why they came to offend and what significance the offences had for them. Brief pen-pictures of these six are:

**Case 17.** Age 16, on probation in a girl's home for breach of a probation order originally imposed for theft and forgery of documents. Her parents divorced when she was young and she was brought up by her maternal grandparents who were ineffective in controlling her. At school she was below average. At about the age of 14 or 15 she began to cohabit with her boyfriend, became pregnant and had an abortion.

**Case 18.** Age 21, in a Training Centre for an offence of robbery. Her father deserted the family when she was born. Her mother 'didn't care' about her, and she became hostile to her mother and ran away from home. She spent much of her time with an uncle — a triad member involved in drug-trafficking. She herself became a triad affiliate. Although clever, her secondary schooling was disrupted by frequent moves, punishments for breaching school rules on dress, and truancy. She had been involved in, though never arrested in connection with, gang fights. By the time of the offence she was working as a dance hall hostess and prostitute.

**Case 19.** Age 17, sentenced to a Training Centre for blackmail and breach of a previous probation order. She had one previous conviction for theft. She came from a harmonious family (though her father was frequently away on business) though parental supervision was 'inadequate'. Her school performance deteriorated in Form 2 when she acquired a boyfriend. In school she was punished for breaches of rules on dress and hairstyle.

**Case 20.** Age 19, sentenced to a Training Centre for breaching a probation order by running away from a home (no indication as to what offence the order had been imposed for). Her father deserted the family before she was born. She has half-siblings, was not supervised by her mother, and lived first with her mother, then with grandparents, and ultimately in an institution for deserted children. Her school performance was poor, perhaps due to frequent changes of school. She described herself as having an unhappy, lonely childhood, and at the time of the interview had found some happiness in recognizing herself as homosexual and finding a girlfriend.

**Case 29.** Age 15, on probation for offences of threats and blackmail. Her father died when she was five; as a result she was brought up by her mother in very poor circumstances. She rebelled against her mother's strictness and lived separately from her mother (in rented accommodation with other young friends) from Form 2 onwards. She was below average at school, associated with 'dubious peers', and had played truant since Form 1. She had previously been the subject of a Care and Protection Order imposed for engaging in underage sex (which she denied) and for running away from home. She had been working in an amusement ground, claimed she was a triad affiliate, and had allegedly been offered (but had refused) work as a dance hall hostess. However, family circumstances clearly do not determine future delinquency. Her sister had not been involved in delinquency and was working as a secretary.

**Case 30.** Age 16, on probation (in a social welfare home) following a conviction for possessing dangerous drugs, and with a previous conviction for trafficking in drugs. She came from a harmonious home, though her father had often been absent in China and was retired at the time of the interview. Both parents were chronically ill and she had experienced little supervision. She had run away from home during Form 1, lived at the house of a friend, and while still in her early teens had cohabited with a boyfriend. Although above average at school she had 'dubious peers', had played truant since Form 1, and had been involved in triad activities. Prior to conviction she had worked as a dance hostess in a night club.

These six cases depict individuals who, in the context of Hong Kong, may be seen as relatively serious offenders. Nonetheless their criminal careers are relatively short, and the offences which had led to their sentences were, with the possible exception of Case 30, relatively trivial despite the labels given to them. Blackmail and robbery usually referred to the intimidation of other girls, either by violence or by threatening to inform authorities about their wrongdoing, and the amounts of money involved were not large. Moreover, in at least three of these six cases, part of the current trouble stemmed not from criminal activity but non-compliance with orders made for previous delinquent acts.

To echo Carlen's (1988) argument, these girls' offending seems less important than their long track records of 'predelinquency' and conflict with authority, whether in the shape of parents, schools, social workers, or criminal justice agencies. How such conflicts developed is a difficult question. However, it is noteworthy that four of the six came from single-parent families; five said they experienced little effective parental control (and the sixth rebelled against overcontrol); and five had either run away from home or lived away from the parental home (and in one case, had been partly raised in an institution). The information on school is ambiguous. Some did badly in school and might have associated with 'bad elements' as a result. Others did poorly, despite their intelligence, because their motivation had been sapped either through punishment, boyfriends, or involvement with 'dubious peers'. Finally, for girls in this situation, as other economic alternatives may begin to foreclose on them, the 'skin trades' (i.e. various forms of prostitution) are frequently close at hand even for those aged 15 or under.

These observations are, in Hong Kong terms, more applicable to 'advanced' offenders than the 'beginners'. What then, of the younger girls, whose involvement in delinquency is only in its beginning stage? Lee's (1992) study of juvenile female delinquents in the New Territories concludes that the majority of juvenile (that is, up to age 16) girls involved in crime are engaged in shop theft, begin offending at about the age of 13 or 14, are likely to become so involved through 'dubious' associations made in places such as video game arcades, often commit offences in groups rather than individually, and commit them partly because of greed, but largely because it 'adds colour' to their lives. Lee sees this situation largely in terms of Sutherland's 'differential association' theory (Sutherland and Cressey, 1955), which suggests that individuals are influenced by their associations with peers. This may well be the case once the girls begin to acquire closer ties to already-delinquent peers, but raises the question of why this particular avenue is chosen to add colour to lives that, by implication, the girls see as colourless and uninteresting.

In short, it seems that while 'pre-delinquent' activities may emerge out of poor school performance or home environment, resulting in conflicts with authority, the reverse may also be true; conflicts can emerge out of the poor application of authority, and result in pre-delinquency. By no means all the girls who engage in pre-delinquency follow it through to a lifestyle that involves offending. In many respects it is hard to pursue the path of persistent opposition to authority. But where girls feel 'locked into' such conflicts, a delinquent lifestyle, and very likely the commission of offences, is often the result. The reasons why girls may feel locked into such an oppositional attitude may well have to do with the reactions of authority figures to delinquency, and it is worth noting in this connection that for girls in particular, the responses to both delinquency and pre-delinquency tend to be very similar.

The observations above suggest two primary explanations for offending among juvenile and young females. Young girls appear to commit acts of pre-delinquency and relatively minor delinquency (probably under the influence of more advanced delinquents) as a way of enriching life experience. We should not be dismissive or cynical about such a claim; it is a genuine desire for these girls. Such girls may grow out of delinquency for a variety of reasons. However, we must explain why some girls do not grow out of, but into, lifestyles which include continued delinquency and offending. Poor school performance and lack of parental supervision both seem to be associated with this, but the decisive factor is most likely a feeling of continuing conflict with authority.

It is important to recognize that it takes two parties to make a conflict; the reaction of authority figures to perceived pre-delinquency is thus as important as the initial problem. Yet even for 'committed' delinquents, crime may not be the central characteristic of their lifestyle. As Chow's data indicates, even relatively hardened young female offenders do not have long criminal records. The more important issue seems to be an attitude of continuing conflict with authority, which makes a vicious circle of offending, a penal reaction, and further criminality as a reaction to 'punishment' or 'treatment', more likely.

## Punishment and Treatment

It has been noted above that female offenders tend to have shorter criminal records, and commit less serious offences, than males. In addition, the view that delinquency is a symptom of a personal, perhaps psychological, problem that should be treated seems to be invoked much more often for females than males. The consequence is that female delinquency is more commonly regarded as the province of the Social Welfare Department rather than the Correctional Services. Although one has to exercise caution in interpreting the available data, it seems likely that the lower rate of use of imprisonment for women, the generally shorter sentences, and the smaller proportion of female than male offenders who receive training centre sentences, may be explained by these factors.

In 1990, fewer than one in five arrested females (17 per cent) ended up in Correctional Services custody, compared with over one-third (35 per cent) of arrested males.[9] Even these figures substantially over-estimate the likelihood of Hong Kong resident offenders being sent to jail, since they include convictions for illegal immigration. In 1990 the ratio of male to female illegal immigrants was lower than for offences in general — about two to one. It therefore follows that a higher proportion of female than male receptions into prison were for immigration offences.[10] While the likelihood of resident male offenders being given custodial sentences was less than the proportion of one in three cited here, the corresponding figure for females would have been very much less than the ratio of one in five.

Equally, females sentenced to imprisonment appear to be given lighter sentences. In 1990, 62 per cent of females, but only 44 per cent of males, sentenced to imprisonment had sentence lengths of less than twelve months.[11] The 'illegal immigration' factor appears here, too, since persons convicted for this offence typically receive sentences of about fifteen months. The implication is that if one disregards the illegal immigrants and considers only Hong Kong resident females, the proportion of females receiving sentences of a year or more would be much lower than the aggregate statistics indicate.

If women and girls appear to be less deeply involved in the 'hard end' of the correctional system, the other side of the picture is that they are more often dealt with by the Social Welfare Department. The Social Welfare Department mandate in relation to offenders is primarily directed at juveniles and young persons; and while the Department manages several homes — that is, custodial facilities — for juveniles, it also administers non-custodial forms of treatment, such as probation and community service orders. In addition, the social welfare task extends beyond offenders to include juveniles and young persons at 'risk' of offending — the so-called 'pre-delinquent' youngsters who form the target of so much government-subvented outreach work. And as stated earlier, the boundaries of pre-delinquency in the case of girls include 'moral welfare' concerns such as early sexual experience and vulnerability to exploitation. They thus include matters such as running away from home, which are widely held to indicate such vulnerability. The end result is a blurring of the boundaries between the treatment of offenders and that of 'pre-delinquents' who have not committed offences.

To concentrate on the use of Social Welfare correctional homes is, admittedly, to discuss only one part of the whole picture. It is, however, the part that includes the most troublesome youths. In 1991/2, Social Welfare correctional homes of all kinds admitted 2,489 males and 1,706 females between the ages of seven and twenty-one.[12] By no means were all these admissions for offences. Most were for the care and protection of girls who were, for example, runaways out of parental control.[13] While the admission of males still outnumbered females, it is significant that the sex ratio — roughly three boys to every two girls — was much less biased towards males than were arrest statistics.

Two factors can combine to explain this phenomenon. First, one might expect that attention to pre-delinquency would lead to less gender bias, as one would see in the response to offending. Offending among females is comparatively rare, but pre-delinquency much less so. Second, however, the definition of pre-delinquency — and thus one of the motivations for committal to an institution — almost certainly varies between boys and girls. Girls who run away from home may be perceived as at greater 'risk', a view which reflects, probably rightly, the prevalence of males prepared to exploit young girls not least for the purposes of prostitution. More attention may also be paid to sexual promiscuity in girls than in boys. Early or extensive sexual experience in girls is widely regarded as reprehensible for a variety of reasons, and an indication of an unruly attitude; in boys, by contrast, it is simply not an issue. Lee (1989) in particular criticizes both Hong Kong law and the juvenile courts for their persistent gender bias. She argues that care and protection orders for girls are often justified in court on the grounds that the girls place themselves in 'moral danger' by associating with bad elements or running away; and that any known sexual experience is often depicted in court as an example of wilful and self-damaging behaviour — behaviour which indicates that the girl must be 'protected from herself'. Such rhetoric is rarely heard in the case of boys.

The implication of this line of argument is that the criminal justice system sets different 'thresholds' and criteria for intervention in the lives of girls and boys. It may be argued that since the girls are more vulnerable, and more likely to be exploited by males, sex differences in the application of measures for care and protection are justified. This is a legitimate argument in principle; the problem lies with its practice. The system of care and protection, however well-motivated, is often perceived by the girls as a new form of punishment. It involves forms of authority similar to those they have already rebelled against. The system designed to engender trust, co-operation, and behavioural reform, can thus also perpetuate resentment and rebellious behaviour.

What then of the conditions in the institutions for females? It is often said in Western countries that women are marginalized within the prison system, and their particular problems are not properly addressed. Problems often mentioned in this connection include inadequate medical treatment, a lack of resources for drug rehabilitation, and difficulties with visits created by the allocation of women to prisons long distances away from their homes, families, and children (Carlen, 1983, 1990). However, such arguments are probably not applicable to Hong Kong. They are predicated on the idea that substantial resources are made available to the correctional authorities, but are disproportionately allocated to male establishments. The facilities and privileges open to male prisoners are thus more advanced than those for females.

In Hong Kong, it is probably fair to say that the Correctional Services Department is doing the best it can with the resources at its disposal. It undoubtedly also perceives itself as moving rapidly towards a liberalization of the conditions of imprisonment for females and males alike. In recent years, an experimental programme of more extensive visits for women with children has been implemented. Nonetheless, prison conditions for males and females alike are comparatively basic and spartan. The majority of inmates sleep in dormitories rather than single-occupancy cells, and they are allowed few personal possessions (though the list has been liberalized in recent years). Discipline remains comparatively tight and quasi-military. It is, however, fair to say that, in a situation where overcrowding is now common in penal establishments, the main female establishment — Tai Lam — is exceptionally overcrowded and that the conditions there have attracted criticism from women's groups.[14]

A slightly different issue exists in relation to the Social Welfare custodial institutions. Again, it is true that improvements have been made, such as the opening of new accommodation for sentenced girls whose probation order includes a condition of residence in a home. The Ma Tau Wai girls home is now primarily a remand home. However, girls may be held on remand not only in relation to an offence, but also pending a care and protection order resulting from pre-delinquency. Even though the two groups, offenders and non-offenders, are apparently separated, they undergo a regime which is similar in most respects. This of course would provide some justification for any feeling among the non-offenders that they were being, in effect, punished even though they had committed no offence.

## Women as Victims and Female Offenders as Victims

While the main thrust of this chapter has been directed at offenders, we should not forget that women — including of course female offenders — can also be victims of crime. Here, a clarification of the notion of crime victims and, by implication, the concept of victimization, would help towards understanding the discussion that follows. According to the legal definition, crime victims are persons who have suffered harm, loss, or damage through acts or omissions which are in violation of criminal laws. But there is a broader, so-called social process definition which considers crime victims to be those who have suffered any form of damage or pain arising out of an offence (Chan, 1991). This second definition suggests that what happens to victims at the hands of other people, including social control and criminal justice agencies, may amount to a 'secondary victimization'.

Several recent Hong Kong studies have made important points about the victimization of women.[15] The key issues are that spousal violence is grossly under-reported and facilities for battered spouses inadequate; that victims of sexual offences frequently do not report their victimization to the police, and may even be blamed for their victimization by their families; and that while some form of victim assistance does exist in Hong Kong, the facilities for both battered women and victims of sexual assaults — both psychological counselling and refuges — are meagre and overstretched (Chan, 1991).

These are of course important issues which demand not

only attention, but also action. However, these observations lend themselves to an argument which, whilst controversial, must be taken seriously. Many female offenders, especially young female offenders, have been victimized (in the widest sense of the word) by others, and their own offending is the result of this. Many more have become involved in delinquency as the result of conflicts with parents or school authorities, but the type of delinquency in which they become involved often makes them into victims. This book's chapter on commercial sex, for example, shows how women prostitutes often become victims of their delinquency. In the Hong Kong context these points are still controversial, as the next section will indicate. Yet they underline the need for an altogether different approach by agencies such as the Social Welfare and Correctional Services Departments.

Offending tends to be closely associated with, and is often a consequence of, a track record of conflict with authority. How that conflict arises may vary; inadequate parental controls, schools that handle poor students poorly, and sheer willfulness on the part of the girl, have all been claimed to play a part. It is not my intention to argue that parents and schools should not have authority. But authority must be seen as legitimate, and its exercise justified, if it is to be obeyed. Authority figures must handle conflict sensitively in order to retain their legitimacy and to avoid an escalating spiral of punishment calling forth more disobedience and delinquency.

Unfortunately, Hong Kong people (and institutions) seem generally to hold fairly conservative, authoritarian views on social deviance of all kinds, and in particular to have a highly punitive attitude towards delinquents and offenders; one explanation for this has been that deviance is regarded as a transgression of that cardinal Confucian virtue, filial piety.[16] There are no compelling reasons to regard such attitudes as unique either to Confucianism or to Hong Kong, but they are nonetheless prevalent in the territory.

Equally unfortunately, such attitudes are likely to inflate the significance of conflicts with authority, and do not lend themselves to the sympathetic consideration of persons in opposition to authority — including of course, pre-delinquents and offenders. Ever-increasing levels of punishment are more likely to be seen as the appropriate response to continued delinquency, yet under the conditions outlined earlier in this chapter, they may well result in a spiral of increasing delinquency. Many younger female pre-delinquents, and those at the beginning of their offending career, seem to have become enmeshed in such a cycle. Even though their own actions give that spiral a further twist, the situation appears to the girls very much like a trap, and very much like victimization. Much the same argument could of course be applied to boys. Yet the difference between boys and girls in the definitions of pre-delinquency, and the threshold at which the criminal justice system is used to intervene, make the issue more pressing in the case of girls.

This is, of course, to use the concept of 'victimization' in a broad and vague manner. In Hong Kong, the term is usually given a much narrower, and morally loaded, sense. As Chan (1991) notes, victim assistance in Hong Kong largely takes place within a welfare model; help is provided on the basis of needs rather than rights, is conceived of as a form of charity or humanitarian aid, and most importantly, deals only with 'deserving' cases. The 'disreputable victim' is not deserving of help. A female victim, even of a serious crime such as rape, who has an offending record or whose social status is damaged by work in an area such as prostitution, would almost certainly be seen as someone who 'had it coming'. Even more importantly, a girl who suffers a sexual assault late at night, while probably viewed with more sympathy, might also expect her status as a victim to be doubted. Why was she not at home at that hour? Was she associating with 'bad elements'? In short, the victimization might become an occasion for 'treatment' for an 'underlying problem' of pre-delinquency.

The advantage of widening the sense of 'victimization' in the way indicated above is that it allows us to see the inappropriate or overly punitive use of authority as giving rise to a feeling of being victimized. The offence is simply one aspect, not necessarily the most important, of the lifestyle that is the response to feelings of victimization. This view may seem to place the responsibility for the offence on society rather than the offender, but it is not intended to do so; it is simply a way of recognizing that offending takes place in a social context, and that individuals not only act, but also react to the way that others treat them. Nor does it deny the role of free will; it simply recognizes that free will is exercised in the context of an unequal, sometimes unreasonable and uncaring, and often pressured, social framework.

Two further points can be made in connection with this view of 'offenders as victims'. First, what are we to make of those girls who actively seek out their involvement in delinquency: for example, the schoolgirls who, in Grindrod's (1989) phrase, have 'worked out Hong Kong's priorities early' and become involved in part-time prostitution? The girls seem often to be involved for no more complex reason than greed, in the face of a highly materialistic and consumer-oriented society. One limit that we might impose on the victim-centred view, then, is that the lighter the burden that social structures place on the offender, and the more life alternatives she has available to choose from, the more she can be held responsible for her actions. Even here we should be careful. Anomie, lack of structure, and loose social relations create just as much pressure towards delinquency as over-structured, conflict-ridden social situations, where the only escape is into low-paid factory or clerical work. Second, while a victim-centred view may apply in principle to any delinquent or offender, it is clearly more palatable in relation to lesser delinquency and persons in the earlier stages of a delinquent career. The more persistent and serious the delinquency or offending, the more reasonable it is to say that the offender acts from commitment rather than reacts to the pressures of a situation.

While accepting these limits, a victim-centred view nonetheless offers a way forward in seeking to break the cycle of conflict, punishment, and offending which seems to occur at the beginning of female criminal careers. One way to resolve conflicts with authority, and to seek ways out of pragmatic but 'disreputable' life choices, is to allow the delinquent to define herself as a victim and to address the question of how that victimization took place. This does not have to be an exercise in self-pity, nor does it have to minimize the role of the offender's own choices. But it does allow discussion to take place on key issues such as legitimacy, justice, and the exercise of authority, and on processes of exploitation.

None of this may be news to social workers and outreach teams. But in Hong Kong, outside such circles, this kind of approach and the changes of attitudes towards offenders that it requires has remained largely unexplored.

## Conclusions

It has often been remarked that if men behaved like women there would be a great deal less crime. A smaller proportion of females than males offend, and they tend to commit less serious offences. The more intensive network of social controls that surrounds females makes them less likely to offend than males. Women who offend are typically those for whom these controls are weak or absent; but the reasons why they offend are generally similar to those that are given for males.

There is more concern about pre-delinquency in girls than in boys however, particularly in relation to staying out late, running away from home, and so forth. The particularly patriarchal nature of society means that such incidents are more quickly and readily regarded as 'troublesome' in girls, with action taken to 'protect them from themselves'. However well-intentioned this may be, it quickly puts girls in a position of conflict with authority — a conflict they cannot win. Also, the available evidence suggests that such conflicts are precursors to 'harder' delinquency and offending. Every punishment calls forth a stronger reaction, which in turn leads to harsher punishment. The key to preventing female delinquency seems therefore to lie in the more sensitive application of authority to prevent an escalation of conflict. Such conflicts and responses to them can put younger girls, in particular, in a position of vulnerability. The likelihood of their being exploited, particularly in relation to prostitution, is high. The girls may see such activities as a rational way to survive. This in no way alters the fact of their exploitation. A final and rather separate point, however, is that despite their small numbers, hardened and professional female offenders do exist. They too may well have a background of vulnerability and exploitation, yet the seriousness of their offences makes it difficult to respond to such factors in a sensitive way.

The treatment of female offenders and delinquents is a somewhat complex issue. Delinquency, and indeed pre-delinquency, is often dealt with by way of custody in a girls' home. Moreover the parameters of pre-delinquency differ from those of boys because of the inclusion of concern about their 'moral welfare'. Since some girls may be sent to such a home as the result of a conviction for an offence, there is a blurring of the boundaries between the responses to crime and to pre-delinquency. At the other end of the spectrum, prison is used less often and for shorter periods than for males, though this may be due to the generally less serious nature of female offending. Women in prison suffer many of the same problems as do men, not the least being overcrowding. However, the relatively small size of the female prison population, and the existence of only two female correctional establishments, means that the separation of different categories of inmates proceeds more by the imposition of discipline than by physical segregation of the different groups.

Returning to the issue of younger female delinquents, the assertions that continued delinquency may be a consequence of a conflict with authority, and that continued delinquency renders them vulnerable to exploitation, can lead us to the conclusion that they may be just as much victims of their circumstances as they are offenders. This view tends to be overshadowed in Hong Kong by the relatively widely held authoritarian and punitive attitudes towards deviance in general. But it is an important concept to grasp because it offers one avenue for limiting the extent to which conflicts with authority can escalate into criminality. It amounts, in effect, to a proposal to treat delinquency and the beginnings of an offending career as an opportunity to discover the kinds of conflicts the delinquents feel they are locked into, and to try to offer ways of mediating solutions. This ultimately means that formal institutions will need to accept that they need to be more flexible in the ways that they exercise their authority — in schools, for instance, considering how to motivate poor performers, and whether issues such as dress or hairstyle rules are really relevant to the core issue of education.

Understanding a problem does not equate to solving it. However, the tool-kit of concepts presented here — conflict with authority, victimization, mediation, and rule-guided rather than rule-following authority — are all useful in helping us to rethink how we should be dealing with female delinquents.

## Notes

1. With one exception: since male police officers cannot search female offenders, one would expect proportionately fewer females than males to be arrested for offences which may involve a stop and search, such as possession of an offensive weapon. This has been noted as a problem in other countries such as the USA, where there have been reports of, for example, men involved in shooting incidents and passing their guns to female accomplices who carry them away from the incident in their underclothing (Kaiser, 1969). Hong Kong arrest data contain a number of other known biases; for example they refer to police arrests only, and thus exclude arrests carried out by the ICAC, Customs and Excise, and the Immigration Department. However these are unlikely to affect the conclusions drawn in the text.
2. See, for example, the arrest of a woman along with four men in a police raid on an armed robbery gang's hideout in Tsuen Wan (*South China Morning Post*, 3 December 1992). See also the report of the arrest of nine members of another gang — five men and four women — in the *South China Morning Post*, 19 January 1993. One of the women was found to be carrying a loaded gun and a live grenade in her bag.
3. For example, a women was involved as the intermediary between a hotel employee with access to credit card data, and a major credit card fraud syndicate. Other recent 'white-collar' crimes by women include corruption in the case of an immigration officer, and fraudulent health insurance practices by a female medical practitioner (ICAC press releases of 29 September, 16 July, and 6 August 1992 respectively).
4. For broader discussions of the role of women in Hong Kong society, which nonetheless include reference to the socialization of girls and their status within families, see Pearson (1990), and Salaff (1981).
5. In the peak year, 1987, there were 218 arrests per 100,000 females (Lee, 1992).
6. This figure is calculated from the information given in Lee (1992). Although Lee's study is primarily concerned with the

New Territories, he provides some territory-wide statistics. To set these figures in perspective, the overall arrest rate for both males and females, territory-wide, rose by only about one-third over the decade. Total arrests were 577 per 100,000 population in 1981, and 766 in 1991, a rise of 32 per cent (Lee, 1992: 65). Various explanations for this apparent rise in female criminality have been offered, ranging from a breakdown in family structures to changes in police arrest practices. In the absence of proper studies, such explanations must be treated with caution. However, repeated victim surveys, while they cover personal and household crimes only and exclude 'victimless' crimes and the victimization of businesses, incidate that levels of criminality in fact fell significantly between 1982 and 1989 (Census and Statistics Department, 1990). This makes it likely that some, if not most of the rise in arrest rates has been the result of changing arrest practices.

7. See, for example, Cheung and Ng (1985).
8. Cases 17, 18, 19, 20, 29 and 30 in the published text of the dissertation. The comments made here are, however, based on a re-analysis of Amy Chow's original data. I am grateful to Amy Chow for making her data available to me; my own use of these cases is rather different from hers.
9. These and subsequent figures are taken or calculated from Section 18 (Law and Order) of the Annual Digest of Statistics 1991 (Census and Statistics Department, 1992).
10. In 1991 it was even lower, at about 1.3 to one.
11. The comparison can only be approximate. First, it can only be made for sentences of imprisonment because Training Centre sentences are indeterminate; that is, their duration is determined (within legal limits) by an institutional board which considers factors such as the inmate's response to training. Second, while there are three types of Correctional Services custody for females — prison, training centre, and drug addiction treatment centre — detention centre orders constitute a fourth option which can be used for young males.
12. Figures cited in Social Welfare Department (1992) for new admissions (excluding re-admissions).
13. A breakdown of new admissions in Ma Tau Wai Girls' Home for the period 1 April 1991 to 31 March 1992, indicates 131 admissions on remand for offences and 24 as a condition of probation (presumably following a conviction), but 681 on remand while a care and protection order was sought and 66 under the terms of such an order (Social Welfare Department, 1992).
14. See for example, the *South China Morning Post*, 8 March 1993,

which reported that Tai Lam, with 60 per cent overcrowding, was the most crowded institution among the eleven adult correctional institutions, and that convicted women were being held in Victoria Prison, which had previously been used for male and female Vietnamese boat people and illegal immigrants. The report also states that the Hongkong Association of Business and Professional Women, which expressed concern over the conditions in female establishments in 1992, was trying to 'monitor the situation'.
15. These include Chan (1991), Cheung, Andry, and Tam (1990) and Yeung (1990).
16. For a fuller discussion, see Lau and Kuan (1988). Some comments on punitiveness and criminal justice policy are also made in Vagg (1994).

## References

Carlen, P. (1983), *Women's Imprisonment*, London: Routledge and Kegan Paul.
────── (1988), *Women, Crime and Poverty*, Milton Keynes: Open University Press.
────── (1990), *Alternatives to Women's Imprisonment*, Milton Keynes: Open University Press.
Census and Statistics Department (1990), *Crime and its Victims in Hong Kong 1989*, Hong Kong: Hong Kong Government Printer.
────── (1992), *Annual Digest of Statistics 1991*, Hong Kong: Hong Kong Government Printer.
Chan, W. T. (1991), 'Victims of Crime', in H. Traver and J. Vagg (eds.), *Crime and Justice in Hong Kong*, Hong Kong: Oxford University Press.
Cheung, F.; Andry, R.; and Tam, R. (eds.) (1990), *Research on Rape and Sexual Crime in Hong Kong*, Hong Kong: Institute of Asia-Pacific Studies.
Cheung, Y. W. and A. M. C. Ng (1985), 'Social Factors in Adolescent Deviant Behaviour in Hong Kong: An Integrated Theoretical Approach', *International Journal of Comparative and Applied Criminal Justice*, 12, (1): 27–45.
Chow, A. M. (1992), *A Psychological Study of Young Offenders in Hong Kong*, Unpublished M.Ed. Educational Psychology dissertation, The University of Hong Kong.
Downes, D. and Rock, P. (1988), *Understanding Deviance*, 2nd ed., Oxford: Clarendon Press.
Grindrod, B. (1989), 'On the Game', *Lawyer*, December, pp. 7–9.

Kaiser, L. (1969), *The Vice Lords: Warriors of the Street*, New York: Holt, Rinehart and Winston.
Lau, S. K. and Kuan, H. C. (1988), The *Ethos of the Hong Kong Chinese*, Hong Kong: Chinese University Press.
Lee, M. S. Y. (1989) *Care and Control of Juvenile Delinquents in Hong Kong*, Unpublished M.Phil. thesis, The University of Hong Kong.
Lee, T. Y. (1992), *Female Juvenile Offending in the New Territories 1981–1991: Changing Patterns of Criminality and their Causes*, Unpublished M.Soc.Sc. dissertation, The University of Hong Kong.
Pearson, Veronica (1990), 'Women in Hong Kong', in Benjamin K. P. Leung (ed.), *Social Issues in Hong Kong*, Hong Kong: Oxford University Press.
Salaff, Janet (1981), *Working Daughters of Hong Kong*, Cambridge: Cambridge University Press.
Sutherland, E. and Cressey, D. (1955), *Principles of Criminology*, 5th ed., New York: Lippincott.
Social Welfare Department (1992), *Annual Departmental Report 1991/2*, Hong Kong: Hong Kong Government Printer.
Vagg, Jon (1994), 'Crime and its Control in Hong Kong: Recent Developments and Future Prospects' in Benjamin K. P. Leung and Teresa Y. C. Wong (eds.), *Twenty-five Years of Social and Economic Development in Hong Kong*, Hong Kong: Centre of Asian Studies, University of Hong Kong.
Worrall, A. (1990), *Offending Women: Female Lawbreakers and the Criminal Justice System*, London: Routledge.
Yeung, C. (1990), 'Wife Abuse', *The Hong Kong Journal of Social Work*, 25: 29–37.

# 8 Women, Health, and Medicine

*Linda C. L. Koo*

The health status of women worldwide is inversely associated with their degree of poverty, powerlessness, and number of pregnancies (Population Crisis Committee, 1988). These lifestyle characteristics have improved in recent decades for Hong Kong women so that their health status has been uplifted. The majority of women who lived in Hong Kong in the 1950s and 1960s were born in the rural areas of China. They were illiterate, unskilled, and frequently pregnant as they attempted to fulfill the Chinese cultural ideal of having numerous sons. As Hong Kong's economic and social environment developed into a more wealthy, modern, and industrialized one, the availability of health care, education, and jobs, as well as the infusion of ideas on gender equality imported from both Communist China and the West, led to great improvements in women's health. To describe these changes, morbidity, mortality, and other statistics have been gathered from government sources to illustrate the health status of Hong Kong women in contrast to women in other countries, women in the past, and men in Hong Kong.

## How Healthy Are and Were Hong Kong Women?

### Infant and Maternal Health

The health of infants has traditionally been recognized in public health as a useful measure of the health status of a community. This is because this age group is the most vulnerable to variations in nutrition, sanitation, basic medical care, and immunization. When resources are scarce, they are the first to become ill and die. Since healthy mothers are more likely to have healthy children, infant mortality is also an indirect measure of women's health status.

As can be seen from Figure 8.1, Hong Kong's infant mortality rate dropped from a high of 66.4 per 1,000 live births

Fig 8.1 Trends in maternal and infant health in Hong Kong, 1955–1990

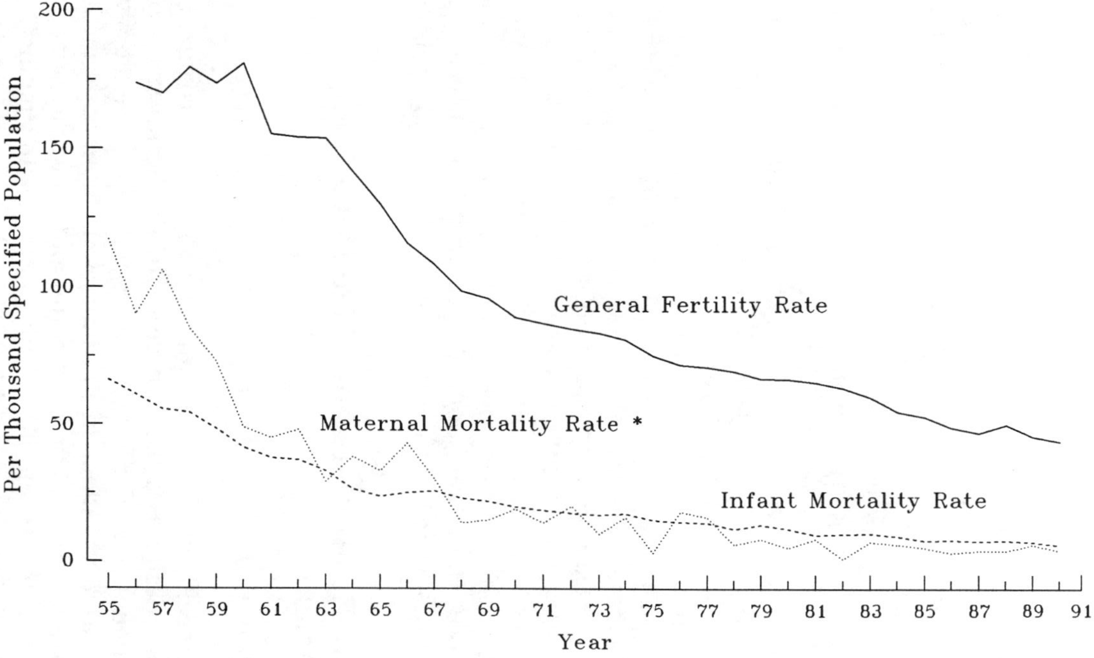

* per 100,000 live births

Sources: Department of Health,
Census and Statistics Department

in 1955 to 5.9/1,000 in 1990. There are few reliable statistics preceding the 1950s for Hong Kong, but an impression of what probably happened in Hong Kong in the first half of this century can be obtained from Singaporean statistics. Singapore's infant mortality was estimated to be 280 in 1928, 130 in 1939, 300 in 1944, 100 in 1950, 50 in 1955, 25 in 1966 (Williams and Jelliffe, 1972: 65), and 7.4 in 1987 (WHO, 1988). By comparison, the more recent data from Hong Kong which overlap Singapore's indicate their parallel trends, i.e., infant mortality in Hong Kong was estimated to be 92 in 1951, 66 in 1955, 25 in 1966 (Colbourne, 1976: 19), and 7.5 in 1987 (WHO, 1988).

The historically wide fluctuations in Singapore's infant mortality prior to 1950 were likely to have similarly occurred in Hong Kong since both areas shared common historical forces. Both were urban island states populated by Southern Chinese migrants, colonized by the British, and suffered from Japanese military occupation during World War II. When Colbourne compared the historical disease patterns in Hong Kong with Singapore, he commented (1976: 8) that 'it is interesting to note the similarities of the causes of death in the two cities at similar times'. Even since Colbourne's publication, health indices for both societies continue to be similar, for example, life expectancy, mortality rates, cancer trends, etc.

When infant mortality exceeds 100, as was frequent in pre-1950 Hong Kong, and is still the case in Bangladesh where the rate in 1986 was estimated to be 133 (ESCAP, 1986), most infants die from such preventable causes as diarrhoea, enteritis, pneumonia, and influenza. By contrast, since the 1970s, congenital anomalies is the single largest contributor to infant deaths in Hong Kong, a pattern typical of wealthy developed countries.

It can be inferred that before the 1950s, the health profile in Hong Kong was typical of underdeveloped countries where infectious diseases like malaria, tuberculosis, pneumonia, diarrhoea, enteritis, smallpox, plague, etc. were the major causes of mortality (Phillips, 1988). At that time, infants died so commonly that, even among male babies, births were not registered with the Hong Kong government until the children had survived the first month. For females, births were usually not registered at all (Phillips, 1988: 26–7).

The current infant mortality rate of 5.9 per 1,000 live births in Hong Kong in 1990 is among the lowest in the world, comparing favourably with the recent estimations by the World Health Organization (WHO, 1991) of 4.6 in 1989, Japan; 5.3 in 1989, Iceland; 8.4 in 1989, the United Kingdom; and 10 in 1988, the USA. Hong Kong's infant mortality is lower than many Western countries because there is wide coverage of maternal and child health services for the poorer segments of the population, a younger maternal age, and less abuse of psychotropic drugs and alcohol among mothers in Hong Kong.

Although the greatest reduction in infant and maternal mortality came from environmental improvements in the early 1950s, the decreases in recent decades have been promoted by the work of the government's Family Health Service. This service was established in 1973 by the Hong Kong government through integration and expansion of the existing maternal and child health clinics for wider coverage of the population. The service currently provides comprehensive health care to women of child-bearing age and children from birth to the age of five. The forty-five or so centres are widely dispersed throughout the territory and provide mothers with health education and examinations as well as treatment for contraception, ante-natal, and post-natal care. For children, there are developmental and medical screening, immunizations, and medical treatment all at minimal cost to patients. The coverage for childhood immunization and examination of newborns exceeds 90 per cent, with home visits by nursing staff to ensure broader coverage and education of mothers on infant care.

In terms of women's health, it is apparent from Figure 8.1 that the three rates shown, i.e. general fertility, maternal mortality, and infant mortality, are interrelated. The general fertility rate, defined as the total number of births per thousand women aged 15 to 49, declined from 174 in 1956 to 44 in 1990. The high fertility rates in the past implied that mothers had short interbirth intervals and were likely to suffer from maternal depletion, i.e. the mother through successive pregnancies and breastfeeding is unable to replete her nutritional status. As a result, she is likely to suffer from osteomalacia, goiter, anaemia, edema, and give birth to infants with low birth weights (Winkvist, Rasmussen, and Habicht, 1992).

The deleterious effects of high fertility on maternal health are evident in Figure 8.1 where 117 mothers died for every 100,000 live births in 1955, compared to only four in 1990 when the fertility rate had dropped by 75 per cent. It should also be noted that infant mortality and maternal mortality rates were likely to have been much higher, although undocumented, in the years before 1955. The trends in Figure 8.1 indicate that given a stable environmental situation, when women have fewer children and have the means to do so through birth control, their mortality and morbidity from childbirth is reduced, and the health of their infants is improved.

However, it should be noted that birth control was not simply an import from the West. Traditional Chinese medicine also had methods to reduce fertility or induce abortions. In the ancient classic, *Shan Hai Ching* (Classic of the Mountains and Rivers) that can be traced back to 400 BC, some ninety-one different methods of preventive medicine are described (Needham and Lu, 1970). Among them are two external (to use on the body), and one internal (an ingestant) method of preventing conception. Around 2,000 years later, the classical pharmacopoeia text, *Pen Ts'ao Gan Mu*, provided a comprehensive description of the extant knowledge of preparing and utilizing herbs for medicinal use. For example, the fruit of the water plantain is described as causing sterility, a particular mixture of distiller's leaven was used to induce abortions, and a powder made from the kernels of the strychnos nux-vomica plant was 'introduced into the vagina to produce abortion' (Porter Smith and Stuart, 1973: 426).

The extent of usage and efficacy of such traditional treatments is unknown. However, given the fact that women in all societies have always wanted to limit their fecundity, the use of such birth-control methods as withdrawal, barriers, and indigenous herbal abortifacients is not unusual in traditional societies. If we recall the aforementioned zig-zag pattern of Singapore's infant mortality between 1928 and 1950, and note that fertility rates tend to coincide with infant mortality rates, then this is an indirect indication that even before the introduction of modern contraceptives, Chinese women were able to exercise birth control. It is in periods of political and economic instability, especially during wartime when the social fabric breaks down, that fertility and mortality increase due to lack of social ties and access to health care and knowledge.

In addition to traditional Chinese methods of fertility control, Western contraception services have been provided by the Family Planning Association of Hong Kong since 1950. Their birth control clinics expanded from an initial three in 1950 to twelve in 1990. Over the years, they have added other services at minimal cost to women, such as venereal disease screening, Papanicolaou smears for early detection of cervical cancer, testing for Rh and other blood groups, rubella testing and immunization, sub-fertility treatment, medical check ups, pregnancy tests, etc. (FPA, 1991). Thus, with the specific health services provided by government aimed at infants and mothers, mortality for both of these groups has been greatly reduced in the post-war period.

## Life Expectancy at Birth

Another indicator of health is the years of life expected at birth, as shown in Figure 8.2. Government statistics are available from 1971 only, and they show that female life expectancy at birth increased from 75 in 1971 to 80.5 in 1991. The comparable data for males in the same periods was 67 and 75. Females in Hong Kong therefore have a relatively high life expectancy, averaging some six years longer than males, and these figures are similar to those found among the wealthy developed countries shown in Table 8.1. It is also apparent from Table 8.1 that life expectancy for women in China at 75 years for urban women and 73 for rural women, is not much lower than for women in Hong Kong. This suggests that even in a predominantly agricultural and poorer country like China, life expectancy can be increased with moderate levels of sanitation and health care. Since most deaths in poorer countries occur among infants, most of the improvements in life expectancy are due to a reduction in infant rather than adult mortality.

However, Figure 8.2 does not show the earlier historical situation with regard to women's health, which was not so

*Fig 8.2 Trends in life expectancy at birth in Hong Kong, 1971–1991*

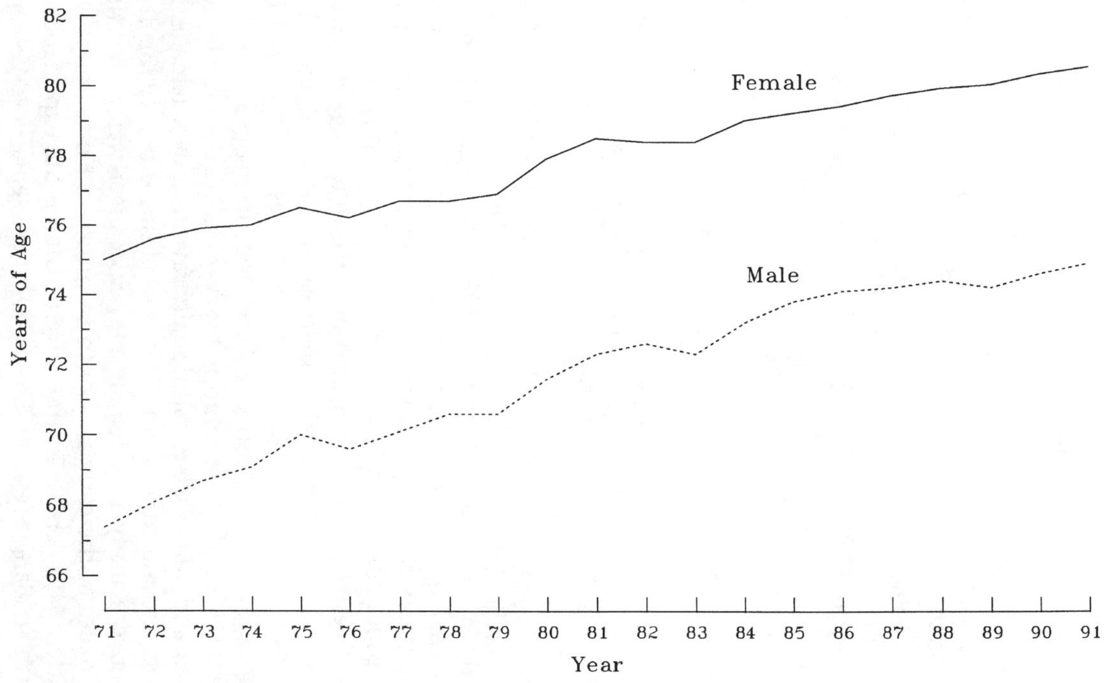

Source: Census and Statistics Department

## Table 8.1  Life expectancy at birth from selected countries

| Country (year estimated) | Female | Male |
|---|---|---|
| Japan (1989) | 82.5 | 76.2 |
| Hong Kong (1991) | 80.5 | 74.9 |
| Australia (1988) | 79.8 | 73.2 |
| USA (1988) | 78.6 | 71.6 |
| UK (1989) | 78.2 | 72.7 |
| Singapore (1987) | 76.5 | 71.3 |
| China, urban (1989) | 75.4 | 71.4 |
| China, rural (1989) | 72.8 | 68.5 |
| Sri Lanka (1985) | 71.9 | 66.2 |
| Bangladesh (1986) | 49.2 | 50.2 |

Source: WHO Annual Statistics, 1990 except: Hong Kong, Department of Health; Bangladesh, Population Reference Bureau.

rosy. It is apparent from Figure 8.1 that maternal mortality had already dropped by 88 per cent from 1955 to 1971. It is likely that maternal mortality rates were much higher in the first part of this century when the correlation between maternal and infant mortality is taken into account. If the Singapore data serves as a model, infant mortality rates prior to 1950 were likely to be two or three times higher than in 1955, with a comparable increase in maternal mortality. Moreover, when competition for resources is a matter of life and death, as happened among the poor or economically/politically displaced during the war-time periods, male children and adults were traditionally favoured over females for food and nurturance in Chinese culture (Koo, 1982). It is therefore likely that female life expectancy was below that of males in the early part of this century in Hong Kong. This pattern still persists in the current data on life expectancy at birth in Bangladesh in Table 8.1 where females have a life expectancy of 49 versus 50 for males.

International studies on gender differences in mortality indicate that when life expectancies are less than sixty, as is still currently true in many developing countries, female mortality is usually higher than that for males, whereas the reverse happens when life expectancies exceed 65 (Waldron, 1987). This author also stated that 'in all developed countries today males have higher mortality than females at all ages but in many developing countries the reverse is true for part or all of the age range one to forty-four years' (Waldron, 1987: 194). When female life expectancies are lower than those among males, this is due to the relative neglect of female infants and children (Population Crisis Committee, 1988), maternal mortality, and malnutrition (Winkvist, Rasmussen, and Habicht, 1992).

## Major Causes of Female Deaths

Figure 8.3 shows the changes in the ten major causes of female deaths over the past twenty-five years in Hong Kong. The data have been age standardized to the 1990 female population to eliminate the distortions of an ageing population over the period covered. It is apparent that with the exception of cancer, mortality rates for all the other specific causes of death have decreased from 1966 to 1990. The declines are most obvious for the two infectious diseases, pneumonia and tuberculosis. Mortality from pneumonia dropped from 632/100,000 in 1966 to 324/100,000 in 1990. Deaths from tuberculosis dropped even more sharply, from a high of 317/100,000 in 1966 to 32/100,000 in 1990. These two infectious diseases were among the top two killers in Hong Kong in the first half of this century, and some 85 per cent of the decline in the tuberculosis death rate already occurred from 1950 to 1965 (Phillips, 1988: 55–6). Thus Figure 8.3 only shows the tail end of the decline in mortality rates for these two diseases, and this is the general picture for most of the other specific causes of death with the exception of cancer.

Mortality trends for males, based on age-adjusted figures from the annual reports of the Medical and Health Department from 1960–1990, were similar to those of females over the same twenty-five-year period. With the exceptions that will be discussed later, male mortality from most causes of death is generally higher than that for females. Male death rates from cancer, injury and poisoning, bronchitis/emphysema/ asthma, tuberculosis, and cirrhosis of the liver are about twice

Fig 8.3  Trends in female mortality in Hong Kong, 1966–1990

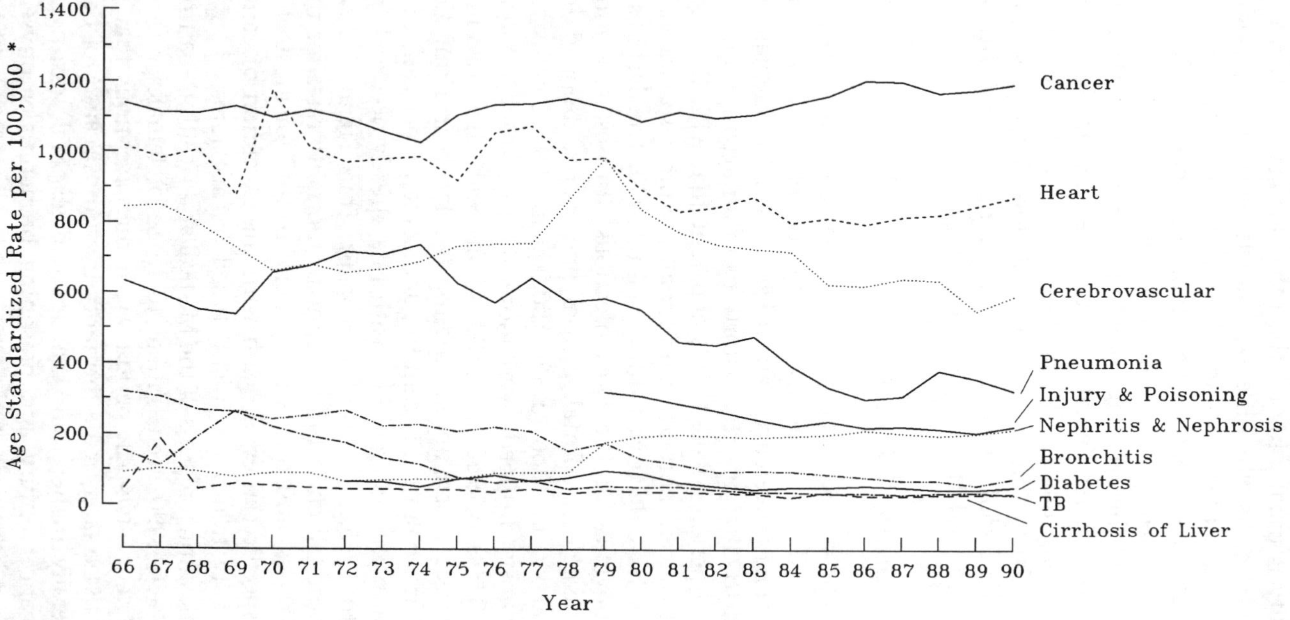

Sources: Department of Health,
Census and Statistics Department

* Standardized to 1990 female population age structure.

those of females, whereas those for heart disease, stroke, pneumonia, kidney diseases, and diabetes are about equivalent.

Since cancer is currently the foremost cause of death among Hong Kong women, and its total incidence seems to be increasing, Figure 8.4 shows the trends in female cancer incidence from 1974 to 1988 by the seven most common sites. For this entire fifteen-year period, breast cancer, with incidence rates hovering around 30/100,000, was the most frequent cancer among women. Breast cancer is also the most frequent cancer among women in North America, but their incidence rate is more than twice as high as that of women in Hong Kong. For example, the world age-adjusted incidence rate for breast cancer among white women in Los Angeles was 77/100,000 for 1978–82 (IARC, 1987).

Although mediated by hormonal factors, diet is the major suspect in breast cancer causation. Various epidemiological studies have indicated that women who consume more total fat and animal protein have the highest risk of developing this form of cancer (National Research Council, 1982). Given the current lifestyle trends in Hong Kong of shifting from a diet predominantly of rice, vegetables, and fish to refined carbohydrates, high protein, and processed fast-foods high in fat, it can be expected that the incidence of breast cancer will increase in the coming decades. This increase has already occurred for another cancer heavily influenced by similar dietary factors: colon cancer. Its incidence rose from 12/100,000 in 1974–7 to 18/100,000 in 1988, and is likely to increase even further.

The second most frequent cancer among Hong Kong women, lung cancer, is actually the predominant cause of cancer death because of its poor prognosis, whereas breast cancer is more treatable. The high incidence of lung cancer among Hong Kong Chinese women is unusual because some two-thirds of the cases that occur are not attributable to a history of active smoking (Koo, Ho, and Lee, 1985). This characteristic of high lung cancer incidence among non-smoking women is also found among Chinese women living in San Francisco, Hawaii, Singapore, and Shanghai (Koo and Ho, 1990a). Current research suggests that ingestants rather than inhalants seem to be related to its aetiology. Epidemiological studies in Hong Kong have found that more frequent consumption of meat, fish,

*Fig 8.4 Trends in female cancer incidence rates for seven sites, Hong Kong 1974–1988*

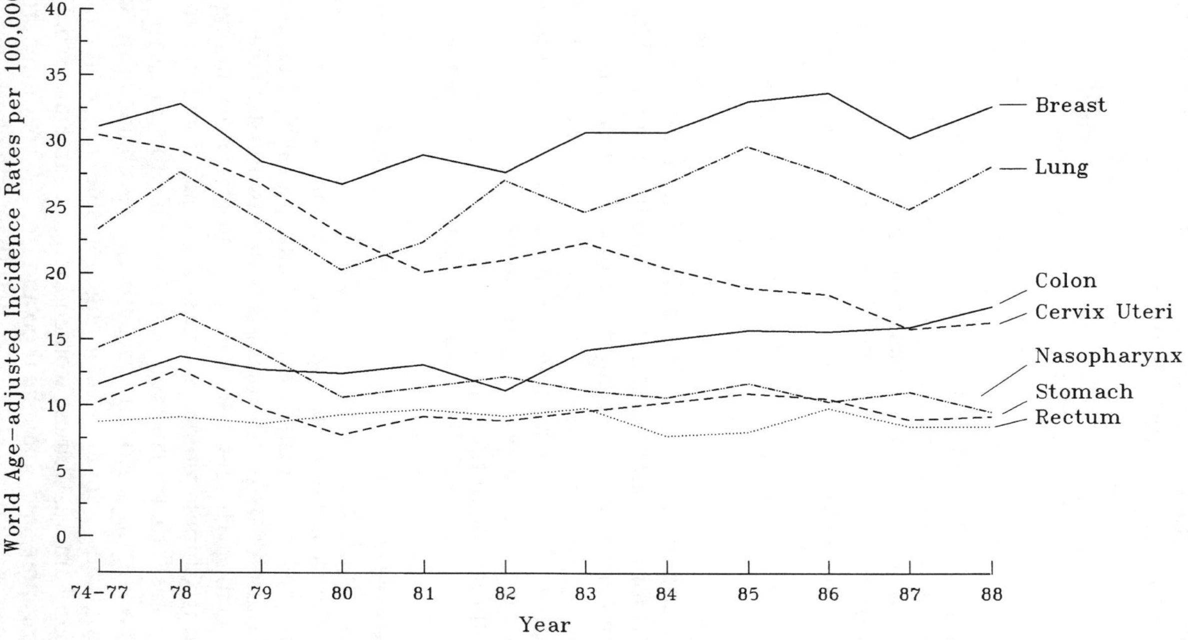

Source: Hong Kong Cancer Registry

or vegetables that have been salted, cured, or pickled increase the risk of lung cancer, whereas fresh fruit and vegetables are protective. These same dietary factors have also been associated with nasopharyngeal cancer and chronic bronchitis among non-smokers in Hong Kong (Koo and Ho, 1990b).

As the influential factors affecting the lifestyles of successive age cohorts of Hong Kong women changed from rural peasant to urban modern, their incidence of cancers typical of traditional society have also changed: Cancers of the cervix, nasopharynx, and stomach have decreased in recent decades. The incidence of cervical cancer dropped due to better hygiene, early detection by Papanicolaou smears and treatment, and possibly better nutrition. Nasopharyngeal cancer, associated with the traditional habit of feeding weaning children salted fish rice porridge, has been reduced as the weaning diet is replaced with cow's milk, orange juice, cereal, and conveniently prepared infant foods. Stomach cancer incidence has decreased in Hong Kong and worldwide, probably due to refrigeration which has allowed the consumption of preserved foods to be replaced by fresh food. The traditional methods of food preservation, i.e. by salt, smoking, or pickling tend to produce higher levels of polycyclic aromatic hydrocarbons and N-nitroso compounds, many of which are mutagenic or carcinogenic (National Research Council, 1982).

## Gender Differentials in Health Status

### Trends in Mortality from Heart Disease and Cerebrovascular Disease

The second and third major causes of death among women are heart disease and cerebrovascular disease. With the exception of rheumatic heart disease and congenital heart disease, which mainly afflict children and adolescents and contribute to a minor fraction of the total heart disease mortality, ischaemic heart disease and strokes are the main health problems in these two categories. Both are closely related to hypertension, 'a known chronic condition that is often undetected and, if persistent, must be treated in order to prevent further complications' (Lee, 1986: 193).

Figures 8.5 and 8.6 show the trends in mortality from heart disease and cerebrovascular disease by age group, gender, and time. Although the earliest available data are from 1966, it is apparent that male mortality for both disease categories consistently decreased from 1966 to 1990 in a step-down fashion. Such improvements were not consistently found among the female rates, although as a whole female mortality from both diseases was generally lower than that for males for any given year. Yet the general tendency for lower female mortality rates for most causes of death is not necessarily inevitable for cerebrovascular mortality. The male cerebrovascular mortality rates in 1990 were at their lowest, with the rates for men aged 65 and over even lower than those for females in the same age group.

One possible explanation for the smaller and less consistent improvements among women than men for these cardiovascular diseases is differential access to diagnosis and medical care. The age groups most at risk are those aged 45 and older. These women, beyond their child-bearing years, no longer attend the Family Health Service where blood pressure is normally screened as a standard procedure. When they do visit physicians, the general practitioner has been given the impression from the medical literature that pre-menopausal women are less at risk for heart disease. Women are therefore less likely to be screened for hypertension, and when diagnosed as hypertensive, their treatment is less aggressively pursued by the physician.

By contrast, the well known belief that men are at higher risk of heart disease and hypertension, especially if they are obese or smokers, leads to more aggressive diagnosis, treatment, and advice for them to change their high-risk behaviours. Men are also more likely to work outside the home and thus have employment medical screening which includes blood pressure screening. As a result the smaller improvements among women for cardiovascular mortality may be due to unequal attention paid to the types of preventive care necessary to reduce heart attacks and strokes, especially since the early detection and treatment of asymptomatic conditions like hypertension are essential in reducing its morbidity and mortality.

This finding of possible gender discrimination in care for

**Fig 8.5 Trends in mortality from heart disease\* by age group and gender, Hong Kong**

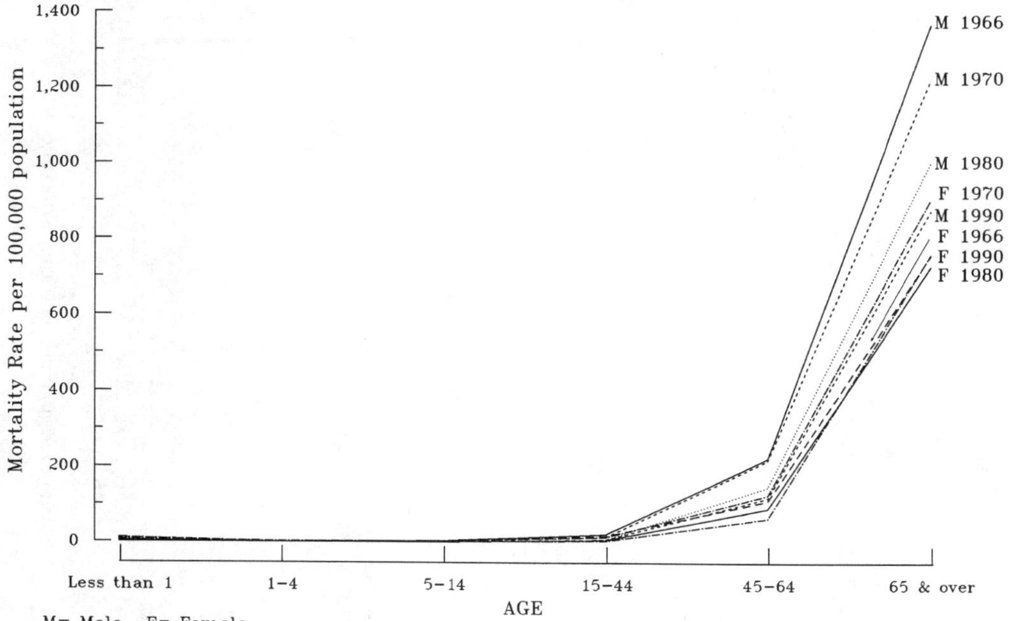

Mortality Rate per 100,000 population

M 1966
M 1970
M 1980
F 1970
M 1990
F 1966
F 1990
F 1980

AGE: Less than 1, 1–4, 5–14, 15–44, 45–64, 65 & over

M= Male, F= Female

\* Heart diseases, including hypertensive heart disease

Sources: Department Of Health,
Census and Statistics Department

Fig 8.6 Trends in mortality from cerebrovascular disease* by age group and gender, Hong Kong

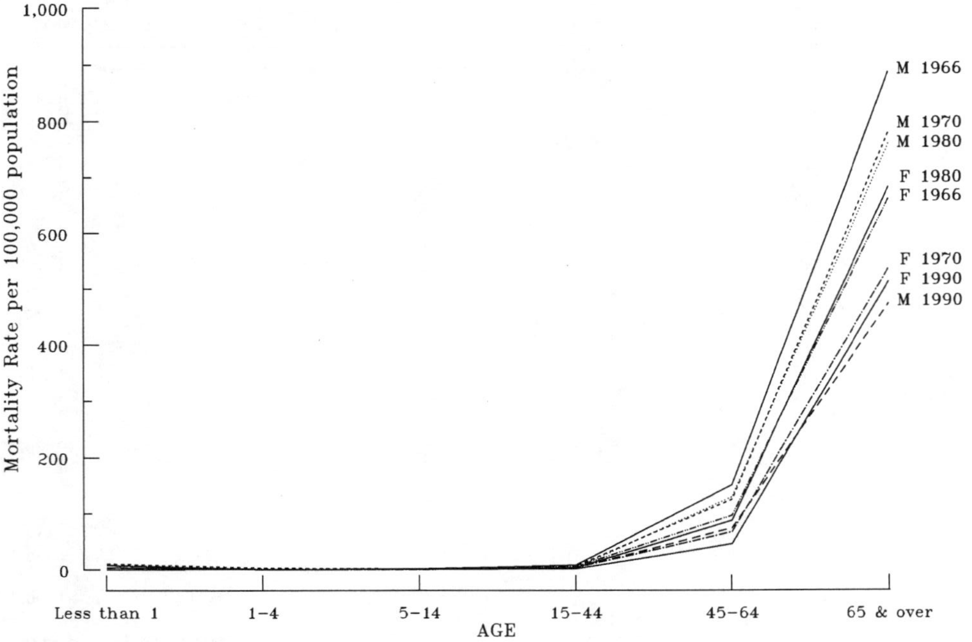

M= Male, F= Female
* Heart diseases, including hypertensive heart disease

Sources: Department Of Health,
Census and Statistics Department

women with coronary heart disease has been reported in a number of studies in the United States. For example, Ayanian and Epstein's (1991) retrospective study of all coronary heart disease patients hospitalized in the states of Massachusetts and Maryland in 1987 totalled over 80,000 subjects. They found that women were significantly less likely to undergo the diagnostic procedure of coronary angiography or the therapeutic treatment of revascularization (e.g. coronary-artery bypass surgery) than men, even after adjusting for age, race, insurance status, etc. In response to such findings, the writer Mantosh Singh commented 'if we are menopausal, we are not expected to have coronary artery disease, and our diagnosis and treatment is neglected. If we are post-menopausal, we are suffering from the "empty nest syndrome" and need an affliction to fill our emptiness. In either case, our illnesses are supposed to be mostly psychosomatic: of the mind, rather than physical' (Time, 1992). It is unfortunate that these comments typify society's and many physicians' reactions to women when they describe physical symptoms so that their symptoms are not taken seriously and therefore left untreated.

## Victims of Violence

The health consequences of women suffering from injury and poisoning, the fifth leading cause of death among women, are frequently due to their gender. Women are victimized in the home because of their inferior social status and physical strength. It has been estimated in the United States that 'assaults by husbands, ex-husbands, and lovers cause more injuries to women than motor vehicle accidents, rape, and muggings combined' (Rodriguez-Trias, 1992: 663). Moreover the health consequences are far reaching since 'spouse abuse, a major cause of injury to women, contributes to female alcoholism, rape, child abuse, and attempted suicide' (Rosenberg, Stark, and Zahn, 1986: 1399). Unfortunately, data from the hospital services in Hong Kong does not classify the accident and injury cases they treat by gender, place and source of injury, and perpetrator, so it is not possible to enumerate female morbidity from violence coming from various sources. This is an example where data on sensitive issues are simply not collected because of the institutional tendency to avoid obtaining embarassing data. Other examples are the dearth in statistics on the incidence of incest, prostitution, child abuse, attempted suicide, etc.

However, statistics on another type of violence, i.e. self-inflicted violence in the form of 'successful' suicide, indicate that suicide rates have generally declined for men and women from the period 1966 to 1990 (Table 8.2). The only age group where there has not been a noticeable decline is among children aged between five and fourteen. It is also clear from the table that suicide rates increase with age. With the exception of females in the five-to-fourteen age group during the three five-year periods from 1971–85, male rates were always higher for each age group and time period. Although the absolute numbers of deaths in the five-to fourteen age group for this twenty-five-year period only totalled twenty-eight males and thirty females, so that the gender differences may be minimal even if mortality was equivalent, this would still be remarkable since male mortality has always exceeded female rates for all the other age groups.

The finding that adolescent girls may have higher suicide rates than boys was also discussed in T. S. Chan's study of suicide among children and adolescents in Hong Kong (Chan, 1993). He noted that the suicide rate among females aged between 10 and 14 for the period 1981–90 was 0.62 per 100,000 versus 0.48 for males of the same age group and period. It is interesting to note that this female preponderance is also found among Singaporean Chinese aged between 10 and 19 and among females aged between 15 and 19 in Thailand. By contrast, male adolescents in Japan and the USA in the 10 to 14 or 15 to 19 age groups have suicide rates two or more times higher than females of the same age groups. This suggests that cultural influences on unfulfilled gender-associated personal and familial expectations may lead to tragic results. The irony is that for Chinese females, it may be due to the lack of attention and concern shown to them, whereas for Chinese males it may be due to excess pressure and expectations from their families and society.

## The Care of Infants

To explore whether at the vulnerable infancy stage, boys get better care than girls, Figures 8.7 and 8.8 depict the trends

Table 8.2  Male and female suicide statistics in Hong Kong, 1966–1990

| Age group | 1966–70 Male | 1966–70 Female | 1971–75 Male | 1971–75 Female | 1976–80 Male | 1976–80 Female | 1981–85 Male | 1981–85 Female | 1986–90 Male | 1986–90 Female |
|---|---|---|---|---|---|---|---|---|---|---|
| 5–14 | 8 | 6 | 5 | 6 | 3 | 5 | 5 | 9 | 7 | 4 |
| 15–44 | 590 | 410 | 677 | 422 | 760 | 536 | 769 | 435 | 852 | 592 |
| 45–64 | 524 | 257 | 519 | 282 | 613 | 347 | 497 | 294 | 475 | 328 |
| 65 and over | 138 | 224 | 190 | 265 | 294 | 395 | 281 | 344 | 456 | 447 |

*Rates per 100,000 population*

| Age group | 1966–70 Male | 1966–70 Female | 1971–75 Male | 1971–75 Female | 1976–80 Male | 1976–80 Female | 1981–85 Male | 1981–85 Female | 1986–90 Male | 1986–90 Female |
|---|---|---|---|---|---|---|---|---|---|---|
| 5–14 | 0.30 | 0.24 | 0.19 | 0.24 | 0.13 | 0.22 | 0.23 | 0.44 | 0.32 | 0.20 |
| 15–44 | 14.69 | 11.07 | 13.78 | 9.62 | 12.63 | 10.17 | 10.77 | 6.85 | 11.35 | 8.46 |
| 45–64 | 29.59 | 16.28 | 27.17 | 15.13 | 27.22 | 16.35 | 19.38 | 12.73 | 17.84 | 13.99 |
| 65 and over | 53.81 | 42.56 | 51.94 | 38.46 | 55.71 | 44.91 | 35.93 | 31.29 | 46.59 | 34.60 |

*Source*: Department of Health, Census and Statistics Department

Fig 8.7 Trends in death rates from pneumonia among infants by gender, Hong Kong 1966–1990

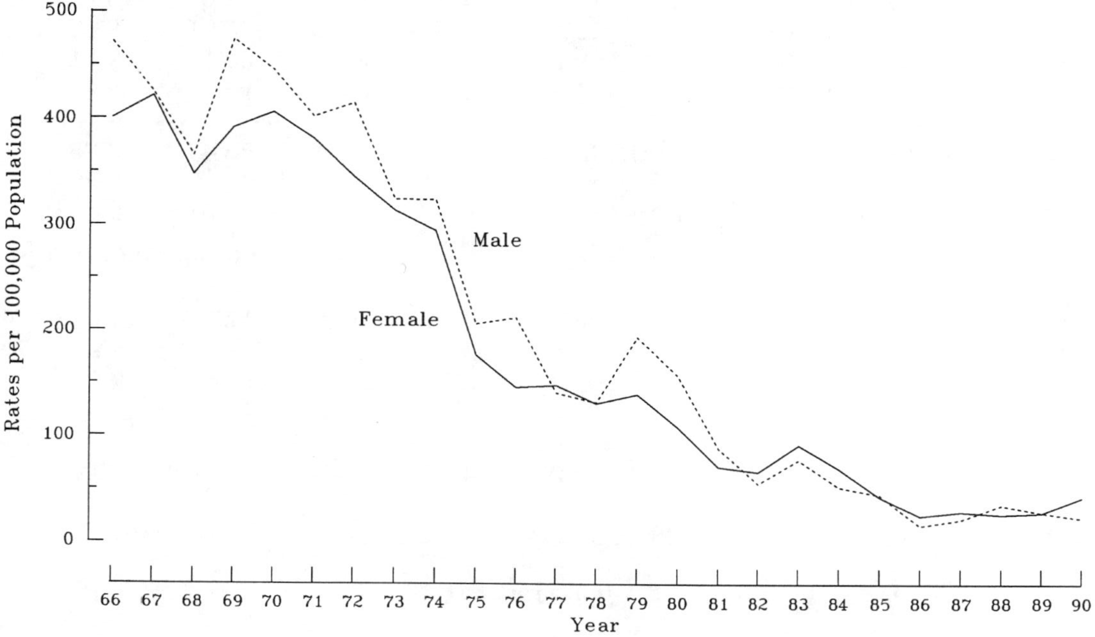

Sources: Department of Health,
Census and Statistics Department

Fig. 8.8 Trends in death rates from accidents among infants by gender, Hong Kong 1966–1990

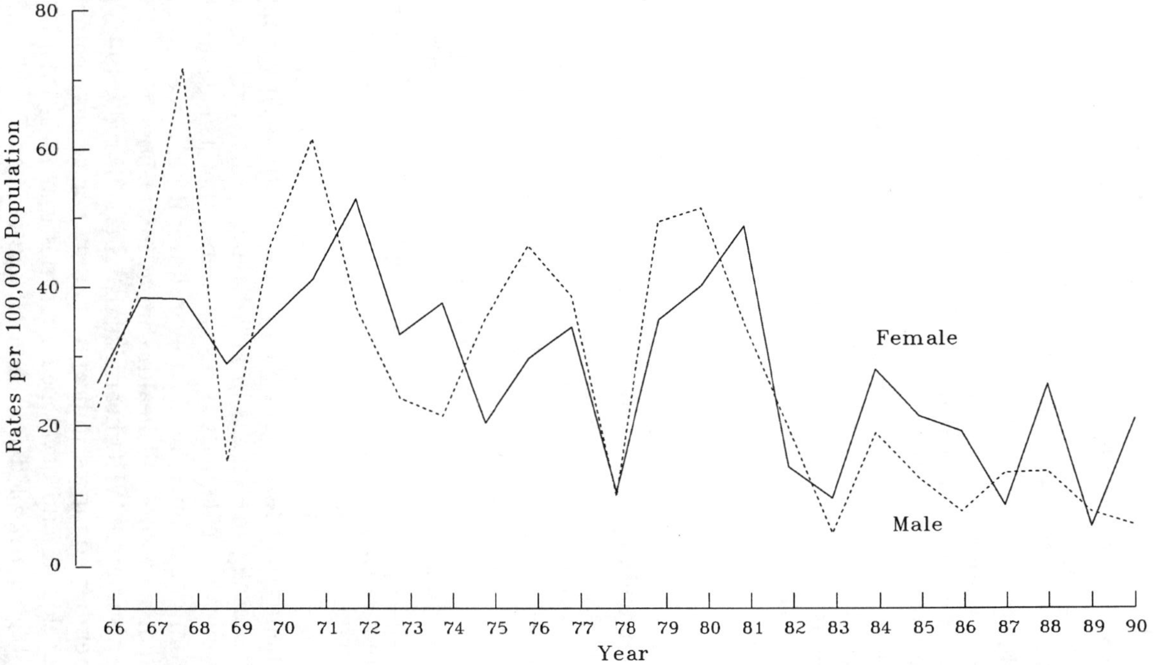

Sources: Department of Health
Census and Statistics Department

in mortality from pneumonia and accidents among male and female infants from 1966-90. Both causes of death are affected by care and nurturing by the mother or caretaker, and less by other biological factors like birth trauma, congenital defects, etc., which are currently the major contributors to infant deaths. Although there are annual fluctuations, it is apparent that for both causes, there was a decrease in mortality from 1966 to the early 1980s, and since then the decrease has levelled off. Male babies also tended to have higher mortality than females in the early years, and this is more noticeable for pneumonia. However, since the 1980s, female infants generally had higher death rates from accidents and about equivalent death rates from pneumonia when compared with male infants in the same year.

This reversal of the gender-specific death rates for accidents, and the lower reduction in pneumonia death rates among female than male infants, are difficult to explain. If one uses the argument that male babies are constitutionally weaker and tend to be more active (Waldron, 1987), this could explain the pre-1980 patterns in mortality. Yet this assumption does not explain the current trends, and if it is valid, then it accentuates the possible discrimination against female infants. For comparison with the Hong Kong pattern, the WHO statistics for Singapore 1987 (WHO, 1988) suggest that male infants were three times more likely to die from pneumonia and twice as likely to die from accidents as their female counterparts.

More research is thus needed to document the prevalent belief that, all other things being equal, Chinese mothers frequently pay less attention to female babies. This comparative negligence results in girls having a higher risk of dying from an accident. It is also possible that female mortality from pneumonia could be even lower if girls received equivalent nutrition and health care as infant boys.

A survey of WHO health statistics (1988, 1989, 1991) from member countries indicates that it is a general pattern in developing and developed countries that male infants have a higher risk of dying from all causes than female infants. In terms of pneumonia deaths in developed countries, male infant mortality rates always exceeded female rates in the USA, 1988; Denmark, 1988; France, 1988; UK, 1989; Australia,

1988; Japan, 1989; and Singapore, 1987. A survey of infant deaths by Waldron (1987) also indicated that death rates from pneumonia and accidents were higher among male infants in most developing countries. The notable exception was Bangladesh where female infants had higher mortality rates than males for pneumonia, intestinal infections, nutritional deficiencies, and accidents.

The infant mortality death patterns in Hong Kong, suggesting the possible neglect of female children resulting in higher mortality are also supported by the suicide statistics in Table 8.2. As commented previously, it is only in the youngest age group, i.e. those aged between 5 and 14, that female suicide rates were ever higher than males in the twenty-five-year period of 1966 to 1990. A possible explanation is that these figures reflect the traditional cultural belief of the inferior status of female children, which is instilled in a female child from birth. At the vulnerable ages of 5 to 14, she is still very much dependent on her family and may attempt suicide when she is given less emotional support or is told that she is a burden to her family. When she gets older, she is less dependent emotionally and financially on her natal family, and therefore suicide rates among females are less than males of comparable ages.

In the description of the health status of Hong Kong women, limitations were posed by the lack of historical data in government statistics. There were few reliable estimates in the first half of this century, when the health picture in Hong Kong was likely to be very poor. It was only in the 1950s that the population was stable enough and environmental conditions improved sufficiently for proper collection of vital statistics. This reflects the usual dilemma in public health, that by the time events can be accurately enumerated, the conditions have already improved considerably. This means that the historical improvements in public health are even greater than the rather late picture that has been portrayed.

Yet from the available, albeit limited statistics, it is apparent that women's health is inextricably intertwined with socialization, education, economic independence, empowerment, and women's rights. As these lifestyle factors improved in the post-war period, various indicators of women's health status also improved. The usual public health measures of community health, i.e. maternal and infant mortality, and life expectancies at birth, indicate that Hong Kong's vital statistics are among the best in the world. The major causes of death are cancer, heart disease, and cerebrovascular disease. Again, these are patterns typically found in wealthy developed societies.

Historically, the initial improvements to women's health were accomplished by better sanitation, nutrition, and education. Later, in more recent decades, specific medical interventions provided by the Hong Kong government through the maternal and child health centres, with the assistance of the services of the Family Planning Association, helped lower maternal and infant mortality.

Empowering women to control their fertility played a crucial role since it freed women to have more choice concerning their activities and aspirations, and reduced the burden of maternal depletion through numerous childbirths. International studies have clearly shown a direct correlation between contraceptive use among married couples and economic and human development (WHO, 1992). Moreover, it is almost a universal belief that women's economic worth in a society will be inversely associated with the preference for male children (WHO, 1992). Thus Hong Kong women's increasing participation in the labour force means that the traditional Confucian preferences for male children and patriarchal family life would have to give way to more equality. Consequently women in the family would have more access to resources, like food, education, and money for health care.

It has been suggested in the discussion on gender differences in health status that there are some hints that Hong Kong women may still suffer from gender discrimination in health status. This appears to occur at the two ends of the life cycle, as infants and older women. In the 1980s, the mortality rates among infants suggest that baby girls were likely to have higher mortality from accidents than boys. The decline in pneumonia deaths among female infants was also less than that among males. Since both accidents and pneumonia involve maternal care, it is possible that these statistics exemplify the traditional Chinese preference for male children, so that female babies tend to be neglected.

When resources are scarce, it is generally true in developing countries with cultural preferences for male children, that female children will get less nutrition and health care than their male siblings. Some proverbs which typify this attitude are: 'One son is worth more than three daughters' and 'Having a son is like having two eyes. Having a daughter is like having only one eye' (WHO, 1992: 17). Community surveys have also borne out the fact that hospitalization rates were higher for male children than female children in many developing countries (WHO, 1992). The effects of this traditional cultural preference in Hong Kong may also explain why female suicide rates exceed those among males only in the 5 to 14 age group.

For older women, the decline in cardiovascular mortality was more marked in men than women in the last twenty-five years. A possible explanation is that physicians have been less aggressive in screening and treating women for hypertension — which underlies most cardiovascular mortality. Studies in the United States have supported this contention by showing that men have more medical diagnostic and therapeutic procedures done for their coronary heart disease symptoms than women with similar presenting symptoms.

This differential access to health care because women are not seen to be as important as men, is probably accentuated among older women, especially those who are poor and illiterate. Health statistics indicate that these older women are unlikely to get comprehensive health care and screening. Cancer of the cervix uteri, with a world age-adjusted incidence rate of 16/100,000 in 1988, is the fourth most common cancer among Hong Kong women. This incidence could be reduced, perhaps even halved, if older post-menopausal women who are most at risk for developing this cancer, were screened and treated for early pre-cancerous changes. After all, the world age-adjusted incidence for cervical cancer among Japanese women living in Los Angeles 1978–82 was 7/100,000 (IARC, 1987). Another female cancer, breast cancer, which is amenable to secondary prevention by screening with mammograms, is increasing in incidence. It is noteworthy that this gap in health care provision is beginning to be recognized by the government so that a Well-Woman Clinic was established in 1990 at the Kwong Wah Hospital to meet these needs on an experimental basis.

Nonetheless, it seems justifiable to conclude that concern about women's health has largely reflected an emphasis on the 'breeder-feeder' role. Some of the most frequently used public health indicators are those for infant and maternal mortality and, as already pointed out, Hong Kong can be justly proud of the low rates of both. But because these are the most frequently used indicators, resources are most likely to go into these areas. Once women's child-bearing and rearing days are over, their health needs tend to be overlooked. Thus it can be argued that Hong Kong's health model is essentially male-oriented which gives little attention to the differing health needs of women beyond their maternal role in society.

It has been said that 'a male-dominated society is a threat to public health' (Mann, 1991). Nowhere is this more poignant than the problem of women being the victims of violence, mostly in the form of wife battering, which is a major cause of injury to women worldwide (WHO, 1992). Unfortunately, it has not been possible to gather morbidity statistics on the extent of this problem. Because of its sensitivity, accurate statistics are always difficult to obtain. However, with the decrease in gender inequality in the home and workplace, this cause of morbidity and mortality among women may improve with their empowerment by education and financial independence.

## Conclusions

Much progress has been made in recent decades in women's health status in Hong Kong, but more can be done. Residual areas of discrimination, in the care of children, and access to health screening and treatment among older females have been identified, and these need amelioration. Many of the improvements to women's health in the future will come from education. Education can help change traditional attitudes that baby boys are more valuable than baby girls. Women need to be educated about healthy living habits, especially their diets, to reduce their risk from cancer and cardiovascular diseases. Currently, too much emphasis is placed on protein consumption, and women as well as men are eating too much salt, fat, and refined mineral- and vitamin-depleted processed foods. Women also need to be educated on the necessity for Papanicolaou smears and blood pressure screening. And finally, it is through a general uplifting of women's education and training that their social and economic status will truly be equivalent to men's. This can reduce wife battering, negligence of female children, and enhance knowledge to identify and pose solutions for the health problems that cause premature death and disability among women. Only then will further improvements be achieved in the future.

## Acknowledgements

The author is grateful to the following Hong Kong government departments for providing statistical data for this chapter: Department of Health, Hospital Services Department, Cancer Registry, and Census and Statistics Department. The Family Planning Association and Well-Woman Clinic at Kwong Wah Hospital were also helpful, and the financial assistance of the Hong Kong Anti-Cancer Society is much appreciated.

## References

Ayanian, J. Z. and Epstein, A. M. (1991), 'Differences in the Use of Procedures Between Women and Men Hospitalized for Coronary Heart Disease', *New England Journal of Medicine*, 325(4): 221–5.

Chan, Ting Sam (1993), 'Suicide Among Children and Adolescents in Hong Kong', *Journal of the Hong Kong College of Psychiatry*, 3: 19–27.

Colbourne, M. J. (1976), 'The Pattern of Disease in Hong Kong', *The Bulletin*, Journal of the Society of Community Medicine, Hong Kong, Vol.7, 1: 7–26.

Economic and Social Commission for Asia and the Pacific (ESCAP) (1986), *United Nations, Population Division of ESCAP, 1986 Demographic Estimates*.

Family Planning Association of Hong Kong (FPA) (1991), *Annual Report, 1990–91*, Hong Kong: Family Planning Association.

International Agency for Reseach on Cancer (IARC) (1987), *Cancer Incidence in Five Continents*, Volume V, IARC Scientific Publication No. 88 Lyon: France, International Agency for Research on Cancer.

Koo, L. C. (1982), *Nourishment of Life: Health in Chinese Society*, Hong Kong: Commercial Press.

Koo, L. C. and Ho, J. H-C. (1990a), 'Worldwide Epidemiological Patterns of Lung Cancer in Nonsmokers', *International Journal of Epidemiology*, 19: 14–23.

Koo, L. C., and Ho, J. H-C. (1990b), 'Chronic Bronchitis, Lung Cancer, and Nasopharyngeal Cancer in Hong Kong', in R. Sasaki and K. Aoki (eds.), *Epidemiology and Prevention of Cancer*, Japan: University of Nagoya Press, pp. 131–6.

Koo, L. C., Ho, J. H-C., and Lee, N. (1985), 'An Analysis of Some Risk Factors for Lung Cancer in Hong Kong', *International Journal of Cancer*, 35: 149–55.

Lee, H. P. (1986), 'Cardiovascular diseases' in W. O. Phoon and P. C. Y. Chen (eds.), *Textbook of Community Medicine in South-East Asia*, Singapore: John Wiley & Sons, pp. 192–200.

Mann, J. (1991), Remarks made during a presentation at the Fenway Center's Women and AIDS Conference, 19–20 April, 1991, in Boston, Mass. Quoted from H. Rodriguez-Trias (1992), 'Women's Health, Women's Lives, Women's Rights' *American Journal of Public Health*, 82: 663–4.

National Research Council (1982), *Diet, Nutrition, and Cancer*, Washington, D.C.: National Academy Press.

Needham, J. and Lu G-D. (1970), 'Hygiene and Preventive Medicine in Ancient China', in J. Needham, *Clerks and Craftsmen in China and the West*, Cambridge: Cambridge University Press, pp. 340–78.

Phillips, D. R. (1988), *The Epidemiological Transition in Hong Kong*, Centre of Asian Studies Occasional Papers and Monographs No. 75. Hong Kong: The University of Hong Kong.

Population Crisis Committee (1988), 'Country Rankings of the Status of Women: Poor, Powerless and Pregnant', *Population Briefing Paper*, 20: 1–10.

Porter Smith, E. and Stuart, G. A. (1973), *Chinese Medicinal Herbs*, San Francisco: Georgetown Press.

Rosenberg, M. L., Stark, E., and Zahn, M. A. (1986), 'Spouse Abuse' in J. M. Last (ed.), *Public Health and Preventive Medicine*, Connecticutt: Appleton-Century-Crofts, pp. 1,399–1,424.

Rodriguez-Trias, H. (1992), 'Women's Health, Women's Lives, Women's Rights', *American Journal of Public Health*, 82: 663–4.

Time (1992), 'The Biggest Killer of Women: Heart Attack', *Time Magazine*, 9 November 1992, pp. 50–1.

Williams, C. D. and Jelliffe, D. B. (1972), *Mother and Child Health*, London: Oxford University Press.

Winkvist, A., Rasmussen, K. M., and Habicht, J. P. (1992), 'A New Definition of Maternal Depletion Syndrome', *American Journal of Public Health*, 82: 691–4.

Waldron, I. (1987), 'Patterns and Causes of Excess Female Mortality Among Children in Developing Countries', *World Health Statistics Quarterly*, 40(1): 194–210.

World Health Organization (WHO) (1988), *World Health Statistics Annual, 1988*, Geneva: World Health Organization.

―――― (1989), *World Health Statistics Annual, 1989*, Geneva: World Health Organization.

―――― (1991), *World Health Statistics Annual, 1990*, Geneva: World Health Organization.

―――― (1992), *Women's Health: Across Age and Frontier*, Geneva: World Health Organization.

# 9 Business and Pleasure: Aspects of the Commercial Sex Industry

*Veronica Pearson and Rose Y. M. Yu*

The core of this chapter is based on extensive interviews with eight women who provide sex for money, seeking their customers on the streets of a working class area in Kowloon (Shamshuipo). There is little empirical work carried out in this area in Hong Kong (Tang, 1977, Tang and Lam, 1986, and Chau, 1994). None of these examined the life experience of these women from their own perspective. Women who provide sexual services are generally denigrated within society; their contribution to the economy is overlooked, and their moral status despised. What follows is an attempt to rectify this current ignorance, although much work remains to be done. The respondents' experience cannot be fully grasped without some understanding of the social, historical, and geographical context in which their work is embedded. So before presenting this material we will discuss some of the wider issues as they pertain to Hong Kong.

Any study of commercial sex workers[1] has to begin with a definition of what is meant by the term. It is used here to mean 'a transaction by which a woman engages in sexual interaction with a transient partner for monetary gain. Cash is the primary motivation and focal point in the interaction' (Economic and Social Commission for Asia and the Pacific, 1983: 26).

Obviously, this avoids some of the issues about those who are marginal sex workers, part-time, or do not necessarily see themselves as commercial sex workers. A young starlet with a supplementary gold American Express card, a flat, and a Mercedes provided by a rich admirer will undoubtedly look upon herself, and be regarded by others, somewhat differently than a woman standing in a doorway in Shamshuipo soliciting customers. However, the main focus of this chapter is on transactions where money changes hands.

Explanations for the existence of commercial sex have frequently been sought in the pathology of individual women.

As an explanation, this is grossly inadequate, not to say misleading. Such moralistic attitudes do not adequately account for the more or less universal existence of commercial sex. Furthermore, they serve to deflect attention from the more important ideological, social, economic, and political structures which serve to justify, support and encourage the trade. It is not the main purpose of this chapter to examine these structures. However, some theoretical context is necessary to put the research into perspective.

The organization of the commercial sex industry reflects the patriarchal pattern generally obvious in Hong Kong society. As Jones (Chapter 6) points out, when Hong Kong was ceded to the British in 1842, the British and Chinese élites (inevitably male) shared an unassailable acceptance of male supremacy and thus found that they had much in common regarding their attitudes towards women. Both Chinese and English societies trained women to see themselves as inferior to men and destined to serve them, thus preparing the ground, at least for some, for entry into commercial sex work. They were also as one in their perception of men as essentially sexual creatures for whom easily available physical release must be provided via commercial sex outlets of various sorts to cater to different races and classes (Hyam, 1990; Miners, 1987; Lethbridge, 1978a).

Attitudes towards women have changed since that time, but patriarchal structures remain in place. The industry is run by men, with significant input by triad societies for whom it represents a comparatively more legal side of their business; the trade is extraordinarily lucrative, generating huge, tax-free profits. These profits are, of course, earned largely by the labour of women. The position of the female workers in the industry is very variable. The highest position in the organization of the industry women can generally occupy is the 'middle-management' level of *'mamasan'* in a bar or club. Some are able to make large sums of money, whilst others are treated as debt-slaves. All are vulnerable to exploitation and mistreatment, either at the hands of customers or pimps.

In the light of these circumstances, why do women enter the trade? This is a question we will return to. We cannot ignore the fact that there may be what Heyzer (1986) calls internal pre-disposing factors, resulting in a self-concept that allows the choosing of the commercial sex industry as a career. After all, only some women in very similar socio-economic circumstances make this choice. In our view this is not the predominant reason. There are also attracting and precipitating factors. The attracting factors involved are the perceived comparative advantages of the commercial sex industry in terms of income, an exciting life, approval or tolerance of prostitution, and the working environment. Precipitating factors may include limitation on alternative courses of action, lack of opportunity for marriage, unemployment, lack of education, persuasion or coercion by a pimp or acquaintances, and severe economic pressure.

Lethbridge (1978b) has argued that the reasons why women enter the commercial sex industry are predominantly economic. It is a career that demands no educational qualifications, few special aptitudes, no specialist or technical skills, and hardly any apprenticeship. As such, it is not surprising that it tends to attract women from poor families who, perhaps, have relatively less to lose in the way of social standing and relatively more to gain from monetary rewards. They are making a predominantly rational choice given the available alternatives (Murray, 1991; Heyzer, 1986). As far as can be judged, coercion through rape or bonded labour is not currently a major factor explaining why Hong Kong women enter the sex trade (Lethbridge, 1978b; Tang and Lam, 1986). Women today are more willing recruits who succumb to trickery rather than require outright coercion. Many of the young ones become involved with a triad 'boyfriend' who deliberately uses the young women's devotion as a lever to persuade her into commercial sex. The usual pretext is to help him to pay his debts and avoid assault at the hands of triad 'big brothers'. This subterfuge remains popular because of its success rate.

## Attraction and Precipitation Factors in Hong Kong's Commercial Sex Industry

If we assume that women are predominantly making a rational choice, then we have to ask, what are the alternatives? The major alternatives for working-class women are factory work or the service industry. There has been a noticeable drop in the number of factories, workers employed in them, and the sector's share of the GDP. In 1984, manufacturing was the largest employment sector with 41.7 per cent of all employees contributing 24.1 per cent to the GDP. By 1993, this had fallen to 21.1 per cent of the workforce and 13 per cent of GDP (Hong Kong Government, 1994). About 90 per cent of manufacturing establishments in Hong Kong employ less than twenty workers and are essentially small family-run concerns (Hong Kong Government, 1990). It is generally accepted that the main reason for the contraction in the size of the industry is due to the relocation of factories to Southern China, where wages are lower and the enforcement of safety regulations considerably less stringent. Women are most affected by this relocation as they provide the bulk of factory operatives (Levin, 1991).

The Monthly Digest of Statistics (Hong Kong Government, December 1992) reports that, on average, male operatives in the manufacturing sector received HK$266 per day, while women received HK$186. A similar differential was maintained at a supervisory level. Levin (1991) contends on the basis of his research that if figures are analysed holding the job constant, then some, but not all, of the disparity is reduced. Nonetheless, women have fewer choices in the area of manufacturing work at the technician and craftsman levels, and therefore restricted opportunities for job improvement or promotion.

Young women's chances of receiving the necessary training are less than those of young men. The Vocational Training Council does not routinely publish figures showing the differential registration of males and females in their courses. The information in Table 9.1 was supplied at our request.

All courses are open to both young men and women, but overall, men outnumber women in a ratio of 2.5:1. However, the table makes it quite clear that women predominate in the non-technical courses and that men vastly outnumber women in the technical courses. It also seems that employers are more willing to invest in the training of young men if the numbers attending day-release courses are taken as an indicator. Thus it may be argued that young men have more vocational training opportunities than women. Furthermore,

## Table 9.1 Enrolment in Vocational Training Council courses, 1993, analysed by gender

|  | Technical | | Non-technical | |
| --- | --- | --- | --- | --- |
|  | Male | Female | Male | Female |
| Full-time | 3,695 | 715 | 1,545 | 3,161 |
| ratio | 5.5 | 1 | 1 | 2 |
| Part-time day-release | 12,569 | 744 | 113 | 441 |
| ratio | 16.8 | 1 | 1 | 3.9 |
| Part-time evening | 11,271 | 1,702 | 5,447 | 7,176 |
| ratio | 6.6 | 1 | 1 | 1.3 |

*Source*: Vocational Training Council, 1993.

the type of courses they attend lead to better career prospects, particularly in the manufacturing industry. Even when men and women receive similar training, the men are likely to rise higher up the career ladder than women, and men rise higher with fewer formal qualifications (Choi, Chapter 4).

The nature of factory work is neither intrinsically satisfying nor physically comfortable. Lam's study (1990) of female factory workers' view of their working and personal lives reported that the women complained about their working conditions — noise, ventilation, lighting, and space. The small, family-owned nature of the factories also meant that there were scarce promotion opportunities and few extra benefits or facilities that one might have expected with larger firms. Many of them were on piece or daily rates, (meaning less job security). Talking was not encouraged and time strictly controlled.

As the manufacturing sector has declined, the service sector has expanded, marginally outstripping manufacturing, for the first time in 1991, as the sector employing the largest number of people (Hong Kong Government, 1992). This trend has continued. Jobs are available in the service industry but it means working shift hours, often inconvenient for mothers, and the kind of jobs that poorly educated women could hope for would involve very menial work. In addition, there is often a premium on looks. Employers prefer young attractive women, meaning limited opportunities for older women (Choi, 1993).

Despite all this, it is wise to bear in mind Hoigard and Finstad's (1992) caution against what they consider to be the over-emphasis on the lack of suitable jobs as an explanation for women choosing the commercial sex industry. After all, many women do work in the service industry and factories despite poor pay, conditions, and inconvenient hours.

We must not lose sight of the fact that women have a right to choose to sell sex that goes beyond the usual liberal justification based on lack of alternatives — as if this was the only acceptable reason. Seen from this point of view, the chance to earn much more money, flexible working hours, dressing attractively, possibly having a more pleasant working environment than a factory, the dream of catching a rich man's eye and retaining a greater degree of control over one's own life are attractive features of the job. They may not all be realistic but that is often not apparent to the women at the beginning.

The commercial sex industry is divided into many sectors. At the top end of the pyramid the women may well be highly educated, possibly working part-time for material gains at a level unavailable to them as students or in their day-time jobs. The young women based in the East Tsimshatsui clubs (a wealthy hotel and shopping area) can command very large sums of money indeed[2] and a sufficient number of them end up marrying their patron to encourage the others to believe that this could be a possibility for them also.

Women in Hong Kong are frequently in a very much better position economically and socially than their sisters in Thailand, the Philippines, and Malaysia. But they are not the relevant reference group for Hong Kong women, who look within their own society to a materialistic culture that puts a high value on appearances, brand names and designer labels, and they want some of the 'goodies' for themselves. Such goals are held by the majority of Hong Kong people. It is the path they choose to achieve them that raises eyebrows.

But should it? Virtually any book or article written about

the commercial sex industry has to mention the 'double standard'; that men are allowed the more or less free expression of their sexual needs, while women are expected to suppress theirs in the interests of maintaining hearth and home and reassuring men that their children are indeed the fruit of their loins and not cuckoos laid in another nest (Gagnon and Simon, 1973; Heyzer, 1986; Murray, 1991; Truong, 1990). The ideology of the irresistibility of the male sex-drive, combined with the need to maintain 'purity' in women, has created two classes; the virtuous woman whom you may marry and the 'bad girls' whom you may bed. Choi (Chapter 4) cites research carried out at the Chinese University of Hong Kong which found that different attitudes towards chastity for men and women are still prevalent.

A study by Luis and Chan (1991) analysed data collected as part of the Family Planning Association's 1986 survey on adolescent sexuality of 1,544 subjects aged between 13 and 27. The cumulative proportion of women respondents admitting to having had pre-marital sex rises from 2 per cent at the age of 17, to 24 per cent at the age of 24 and then levels off.[3] They found that the strongest factor influencing whether the women remained virgins was severe parental disapproval of sexual behaviour.

In contrast, the AIDS foundation completed a survey of Hong Kong men in 1993, attempting to establish how many of them had experience of paying for sex or casual sex. The sample was over 1,000 and based on the responses they estimate that a very conservative figure would be 100,000. This double standard has always pertained to Chinese societies. Men were permitted to have numerous wives and concubines and for those who could not afford the expense, brothels were available. Wang Shu-nu (quoted in Tang, 1977) reports that the first government brothel was established in China in 645 BC! Commercial sex was a fact of life (van Gulik, 1961; Gronewald, 1985; Hershatter, 1989). It was even considered better for a man's health, if he did not have a wife, to pay for sex rather than to masturbate or risk nocturnal emissions (Koo, 1982). But needless to say, this relaxed attitude towards sex for men did not extend to women.

Naturally enough, when the colony of Hong Kong was established, brothels quickly followed (Lethbridge, 1978a).

Miners (1987) charts the history of brothels in Hong Kong up until the Second World War. The Korean and Vietnam wars changed the character of prostitution in South-East Asia and created what Hyam (1990) calls 'an unexpected sexual explosion'. Facilities built around providing rest and recreation (R and R) for US troops placed a premium on servicing their sexual needs because that was what the customer demanded. Previously, the commercial sex industry in Asia had catered for local and overseas residents, as was the case in Hong Kong.

Much has been written about the link between the development of tourism and the provision of commercial sexual services in South-East Asia (Heyzer, 1986; Odzer, 1992; Truong, 1983 and 1990; Pongpaichit, 1982), and the consequent gross exploitation of women. However, Hong Kong women have never been so ruthlessly marketed as sexual assets as have been women from Thailand and the Philippines. Although reliant on 'R and R' during the Vietnam war, the area mostly involved in providing sex for foreigners, Wanchai, has been developed as an extension of the Central business district. To an extent it has lost its raunchy image, although it continues to be the location of commercial sex activities on Hong Kong island. Of course, the Hong Kong government has, like most others in the region, tried to encourage tourism. To be successful at this, tourists have to be provided with what they want, including sex. But the character of the business is very different from Bangkok and Manila — it is all a good deal more discreet.

## Attitudes Towards Commercial Sex in Hong Kong

It seems safe to conclude that if ancient and modern history are any guide, the provision of commercial sex for men has a long and continuous history in China and Hong Kong. It has been a source of employment for poor women since time immemorial. So to that extent, it is accepted as a business, as a normal part of society. But if the industry itself is accepted, that does not mean that commercial sex workers enjoy the same privilege. The class of virtuous women are unlikely to accept those they see as moral inferiors as well as, on occasion, potential threats to their marriage. Men are frequently hypocrites, particularly those in positions of power and influence, condemning in public what they enjoy in private.

The reality of commercial sex confronts both the ethic of labour and the ethic of public morality (Truong, 1990). Murray (1991) links the attitudes towards commercial sex in Jakarta with those in Victorian times — particularly one study from that era that dealt with commercial sex workers under the chapter title 'Those Who Will Not Work'. There are echoes here of current Hong Kong themes: anyone who knows Hong Kong will appreciate that the need to work hard is a moral imperative. Having sex for money does not necessarily strike people as 'work' because it is something they may do themselves, but as a recreational activity. It is not a 'proper' job. Indeed, it is a most improper job. This attitude is neatly captured in an exchange in the Legislative Council when the Secretary for Security was asked why female illegal immigrants from China working as commercial sex workers were not prosecuted (and given the mandatory sentence of fifteen months imprisonment), in the same way as other women found illegally working in Hong Kong (*South China Morning Post*, 17 March 1994). His answer was that the government did not regard them as doing a job! Following an outcry from legislators and others, this policy was reversed some two months later. It is this combination of the supposed rejection of both the work ethic and moral standards within the same activity that makes the issue of commercial sex workers so potent in Hong Kong. This is in the face of evidence that suggests that their labour creates vast surpluses that are extracted by various agents, even if the government sees no direct benefit in the form of taxes. It is impossible to estimate the amount of profit the sex industry generates each year, but it is likely to be in the hundreds of millions.

Vagg (1991) comments on local tolerance for the commercial sex industry (as opposed to commercial sex workers), saying that objections tend to centre on peripheral issues of decorum like the signature yellow signboards advertising various sex establishments.[4] The most vociferous objection to the commercial sex industry comes from residents of Mongkok, an area of Kowloon famous for its sex outlets. They find it deeply offensive that the trade is conducted in residential buildings, causing noise and disturbance in the night and exposing their children to activities of which they would prefer they remained innocent (Mongkok District Board, 1986).

## The Current Scene

Vagg's study (1991) contains a comprehensive description of the various outlets for commercial sex which it is not intended to repeat here. Possibly the only necessary up date to his information is the continued decline in popularity of 'fishball stalls',[5] now staffed by aging commercial sex workers as opposed to the under-age girls of yore, and the rise of 'blue' karaoke bars. Karaoke has become exceedingly popular and Hong Kong entrepreneurs, never slow to exploit an opportunity, have introduced 'PR girls' into many of them. They are paid to be singing partners of the customers, generally permit fondling and kissing and may be 'bought out' after which the customer must negotiate a fee for the woman's services.

Prostitution in Hong Kong is not illegal, but almost everything associated with it is, including public soliciting, trafficking in women, harbouring or exercising control over a woman for the purposes of prostitution, procuring, living on the earnings of a prostitute and keeping a vice establishment or permitting premises that one owns to be used as such (Vagg, 1991). It is not the purpose of this chapter to discuss the role of the police. Suffice to say they are never going to eradicate commercial sexual activities, nor do they intend to. The most they can hope to do is to contain it and to stamp on what are considered to be the worst abuses, particularly the use of under-age girls and forced participation.

The commercial sex industry is enormously lucrative and, predictably, is dominated by triads, who perceive it as a legitimate side of their various activities. It is impossible to estimate accurately the sums involved, and the outlets vary from the opulent, Japanese-style hostess clubs in East Tsimshatsui, like China City and Club Bboss, to running a 'stable'[6] of commercial sex workers servicing various hotels. *Next* magazine (Vol. 126, 7 August 1992) estimates that there are about one thousand commercial sex workers (a figure the police confirm) operating in and around Portland Street, in the centre of Mongkok's 'red light' area. If we assume that the women turn fifteen tricks a day, work twenty days a month, and are paid at the lower end of the scale (HK$200 a time), then the women in Portland Street alone generate HK$60 million a month gross. If one extends the arithmetic to the more upmarket Tsimshatsui area where, for instance, one club (Bboss) is reputed to employ about a thousand hostesses, the figures are staggering.[7]

Probably the women who are most vulnerable in the trade are those imported from overseas, usually Thailand, the Philippines, and Malaysia. Of these, the police consider that the Filipinas are the most vulnerable. They often believe that they have been recruited to work in the entertainment industry as dancers or singers and then find that they are expected to provide sex. They are imported by the triads and have to work off their 'debt' for the expenses incurred in bringing them over. They do not speak Cantonese and their English may not be very good either. They may well need to receive 1,000 customers before they are able to keep any of the money they earn.

On the other hand, the Malaysian women, always of Chinese extraction and Cantonese speakers, enjoy considerable local popularity and can command quite a high price, leaving them with a reasonable amount of money after the various 'cuts' have been paid. It is said that a Malaysian woman who works reasonably hard for a year can return to her country with one million dollars and her reputation relatively intact, as she can claim to have been working in the entertainment industry.[8]

In order that the women are able to stay in Hong Kong without fear of deportation they need visas or Hong Kong identity cards. This has generated a market in false bridegrooms who enter into marriages of convenience for a price, usually around HK$25,000. The triads usually prefer men in respectable jobs, because there is less trouble with the Immigration Department. Often, the 'bridegrooms' are in debt to loansharks and the triads pay off their debt in return for the marriage. Every time his 'wife's' visa needs to be renewed, the 'bridegroom' receives another substantial additional payment.

If they do not enter into such an arrangement, the women are vulnerable as illegal immigrants, although the women from Malaysia are in a slightly better position because it is a Commonwealth country. The foreign women are seen as a potential source of AIDS, particularly those from Thailand and the Philippines. One of the reasons said to account for the increase in raids on commercial sex premises in Mongkok in the latter part of 1992 and early 1993 was the discovery of Thai sex workers who were HIV positive.

## The Shamshuipo Streetwalkers

There are essentially three levels of independence for individual commercial sex workers. They work for themselves; they work through contacts and structures like bars and hotels; or they are owned by criminal organizations. All women engaged in the trade are wary of outsiders, certainly people claiming they want to do research. We found that it was impossible to make contact with women in the third category because of the difficulty of breaking through the barrier of their 'protection'. Women in the second category are hard to reach except when they are at work and the owners of the clubs rarely permit the young women to talk for extended periods of time as a charitable exercise. Because of these circumstances we decided to concentrate on the individual entrepreneurs, which means streetwalkers and women in the 'one phoenix, one apartment' brothels. Again, circumstances dictated our choice in that the latter category proved unwilling to talk to us, while the former were more amenable.[9] What follows is based on the information about their lives that they were willing to share.

### A Profile of a Working Life

Shamshuipo is an old working-class residential area in Kowloon, close to Mongkok and has one of the highest population densities in Hong Kong. It is likely to be familiar to foreign residents because it is where the Golden Arcade computer centre (famous for its bargain priced computer wares) is located, but other than that it is rare to see a non-Chinese face. The commercial sex workers cluster at the bottom of stairways or walk casually up and down the street. Some are dressed to advertise their intentions, others look like housewives chatting with friends. The women tend to form small groups of friends who 'look out for' each other. As a means to protect their identity they are generally known by nicknames or adopt another name for business purposes.

Business has been bad for a while and mostly the women average four tricks a day. They are older and cannot charge very much money, usually about HK$130–170 for fifteen minutes, although they will also receive tips if the customer is particularly pleased with their service. If the customer takes longer than that he has to pay the same sum again. The room costs HK$20 and the remainder the woman keeps. Oral sex will cost more (about HK$250) as will anything other than the missionary position. If a woman receives twenty-four customers a week, she will earn approximately HK$12,000 per month, much more than is possible in any other job available to her. Even though they cannot charge as much as the younger women, they say there are some advantages to being an older sex worker because men think that you will receive fewer customers and are less likely to be infected.

We initially assumed that the women would be under triad protection, but they went to some lengths to reassure us that this was not the case. Indeed, that was one of the good things about being a streetwalker, that they were much more independent and could keep their own money. One of them had undergone a triad initiation ceremony. Another followed a 'big brother' but largely because he enjoyed having many followers. She did not pay him anything and she appreciated the help she could ask for if she ever needed it. It would be impossible for the women not to have triad contacts, doing the job they do, where they do it. But whatever was involved seemed to be on a largely informal basis. We could observe the triad *mafoos* in vans escorting and guarding some of the Thai women. But in all the hours we spent down there, we were never aware of triads actively taking an interest in the local streetwalkers.

The 'golden' times of the day, at least as far as earning money is concerned, are after about 9 p.m., when men come out of restaurants and are looking for some action, or finish work in restaurants. Later on in the night there are customers who come off evening shift work. Racing days tend to be dead and the weather also has an effect on customer flow. While some of the women live locally, others prefer to put distance between their domestic selves and their work selves, especially those who live with families.

Nearly all the women are aware of the importance of using a condom but only one of those whom we interviewed insisted on it. The others took the attitude that they would ask but if the customer refused, what could you do? Only Lam charged more, HK$30, if they would not wear one. Yang considers that it is the more unbridled ones, the ones looking for 'feelings' who do not like using a condom. Generally, these women are conscious about their health, particularly catching venereal diseases. Many of them claim to go to the Yaumatei social hygiene clinic regularly for a check-up and speak highly of the service they receive there. Leng Mui says that sometimes the nurses will come and look for them if they have not attended for some time. They are quite strict with each other and if they know that one of the women is infected they force her to go to the clinic for treatment. Customers move from one to the other and they are afraid of catching it themselves.

## Why Did the Women Enter the Trade?

With the exception of Leng Mui, Hon, and Yang, all of the women entered the trade in their teens. Hon is forty-eight and used to be a *dim sum* hawker. She has been doing the job for about three years since she took up playing mahjong: she frequently loses the housekeeping money at the mahjong table and has to come down to Shamshuipo to earn it back. She works three or four evenings a week and tells her husband that she is going to play mahjong. A woman she knew who also sold *dim sum* worked part-time in Shamshuipo, and Hon got the idea from her.

Leng Mui's husband died suddenly when she was 23, leaving her with a baby son to support. She knew a woman from the same home town as hers who was already working in Shamshuipo and asked the friend to bring her along. The friend agreed to do this, as long as she gave her HK$10 from every customer for her trouble. Leng Mui had previously worked in cigarette, garment, and electronics factories, but streetwalking was more profitable and 'part of it is my own vanity. Seeing people wearing high-heeled shoes and a pretty dress when I was young, I envied them'.

Yang has almost no education and started factory work at 12, in addition to looking after the pigs and collecting and breaking up wood to burn. She spoke fondly of her mother but said her father was a 'no-use gambler'. Eventually, she ran away, got in with bad friends and started trafficking in heroin. By 18 she was taking it herself and had spent a period in a correctional institution. However, she did not enter the world of commercial sex until she was a little over 30, when she started to work in nightclubs in order to pay off gambling debts. Before that she worked as a cashier and washed dishes.

For the others, the tale is a familiar one. All of them come from impoverished and disturbed family backgrounds, and have little education. Lam describes herself as having a greed for money and being curious so that when a group of friends went to work in a nightclub she joined them. Like some of the others, she sees herself as being bad in character 'otherwise you wouldn't go to work in a nightclub, because you know what is expected of you'.

Only Fok started receiving customers for money to pay off her future husband's debts, considered to be a common way young women are persuaded to become commercial sex workers. (He was a triad member and a drug addict.) As she said, 'When you are young, you will do what your loved one asks you'. Nowadays, 'street sisters are a good deal more pragmatic. They see the importance of money and won't use it to keep a boyfriend' (Lam).

Sometimes the women are able to leave the trade for a while but are then sucked back into it. In Siu Ling's case it was because of her husband's gambling debts and for Yang, her own. Only Fok and Yang currently have a drug habit to support, although Siu Ling and Lam report using soft drugs in the past.

## *The Ties That Bind*

There are primarily two reasons which keep women in the trade; money and lifestyle. With the exception of Leng Mui, the others were all in debt, mostly to loansharks. Leng Mui has three children still at school and hers is the sole income. She does not consider that they could manage financially if she took a lower paying but 'respectable' job. She already thinks she is fortunate to have stayed out of debt and the clutches of the sharks.

Not only do the women get into debt on their own account. Two of them, Fok and Chui, were persuaded by friends, who had reached their credit limit with the sharks, to borrow on the friends' behalf. They promised faithfully to pay back but, of course, did not, leaving Chui and Fok with an even more unmanageable burden. Listening to the woman's predicaments it is very difficult sometimes to see why they permitted themselves to get into such a position. The initial sums of money are not necessarily very large. The biggest debt that was mentioned was HK$60,000, but others could have been paid off within a fortnight with a few extra customers a day. Yang described one debt where she was loaned HK$10,000, and for every day she did not pay it back the interest was HK$2,000. Sometimes the loan was to pay gambling losses. The largest sum was HK$30,000 in Macau where there seems to be a particularly usurious rate of interest. But often it did not seem to be for any very pressing reason, new clothes or rent on a new apartment.

What was obvious from these stories was that this was a deliberate strategy to gain control over the women, used by the nightclub owners and the triad 'big brothers'. They encouraged the women to borrow money, until the debt was sufficient to give them control. Particularly at the beginning of their careers, this gave them leverage over the women to make them go with men or do things against their will. Fear of loansharks was very real for the women. Siu Ling said that she was afraid to stand on the street too long in case the loanshark spotted her. Doubtless, if he had a mind to find her, he could have done so anyway. And as another one said 'they can't actually beat us to death, or how would they get paid back?'

The lifestyle factor is also a powerful one. They like being their own bosses, having money to spend, being shown respect in shops because they have money, working hours that suit them. Siu Ling says that she gets bored too quickly and could never settle down to sitting still for eight hours in a factory.

They simply could not afford to maintain their current lifestyles in other employment and like most of us are unwilling to give up material comfort, certainly not for the intangible gain of improving their moral status. Indeed, they may not believe that this is possible anyway. They frequently described themselves as 'bad' and said that once you have been a prostitute for one day, you are one for the rest of your life. There is this sense of being 'spoilt', 'damaged goods'; that others will be able to tell what sort of women they are.

## Attitudes Towards Themselves and Their Job

> Doing our kind of job is the worst, the worst, the worst. When people say that you are a prostitute it makes you feel very uncomfortable and you have to stand and face so many people. We are hopeless and good for nothing. (Lam)

> When I started to work at the beginning, although I had been married and had children, it was very different facing different men. It gets very hot 'down there', like having a fever. Even after just three or four, I had to spread my legs and cool myself down with a fan. Not used to it, you see. Couldn't do so many. (Leng Mui)

Some of the women take a matter-of-fact view of what they do, that after the first few times it is a job like any other. But some of them, as the interviews progress, express much more negative feelings.

> Having someone you don't like and don't know on top of your body . . . (sigh) just close your eyes and take it as nothing. You feel numb more than getting used to it. You close your eyes and say to hell with it. I just do it for the money. All for the sake of the money. (Lam)

Yang says much the same: 'Close your eyes and think, money, money, money'. Hon treats it in the same way as a ghost 'squashing' her while she is asleep — you feel awake but are paralysed and cannot move or speak.

With the exception of Leng Mui and Hon, the women had all entered the commercial sex industry higher up the ladder, in nightclubs, massage parlours, as call girls, dance hostesses, and 'fishball' girls. Lam actually spoke about the 'drift downwards' that she had experienced and Fok 'used to pass streetwalkers when I was a dance hostess and a call girl and think, "how can they make money from that?" Now I am one'.

Chui considered that the work on the street was more difficult and that being called a massage girl sounded a good deal better than a streetwalker. However, there were advantages. Lam spoke about the greater freedom, shorter hours and flexibility of being on the street. Although the conditions in a nightclub were more comfortable, you were under other people's control. On the street, you kept most of the money you earned and could refuse customers whose look you did not like. Nor did you have to receive so many customers that it hurt, according to Leng Mui, who was comparing her position favourably with that of the women working in villas in Temple Street (a notorious area of the commercial sex industry in Kowloon).

Some of the women greatly disliked having to approach customers and all of them spoke of how common it was for the women to use alcohol or soft drugs to numb their feelings before going to work. Yang sometimes has to drink three cans of beer to give herself the courage to ask 'sir, are you waiting for someone?' Siu Ling just refuses to do it, finding it preferable to wait to be asked. Lam will ask but is highly embarrassed. One of the reasons why she prefers nightclubs is because 'clients come for you, not you who beg others'. Women are brought up to believe that men should be the assertive ones, the ones who do the chasing. Even in their situation of probable enforced intimacy, this role reversal is potentially deeply uncomfortable.

## Attitudes Towards Foreign Prostitutes

Our informants viewed the Thai and Philippine women as unwelcome competition. First, they were younger and secondly, they undercut prices charging less than local women in the same age bracket. In addition they were a likely source of AIDS. Yang considered that there were some things that the local women would not allow but:

> Thai girls are different. Thai girls will do oral sex and allow men to do it at the back. Honestly speaking, women in Hong Kong won't do things like this. If they do it in the front and want different positions, that's OK. If you are talking about oral sex . . . I am not that cheap.

Not all of our informants shared Yang's views about oral sex but they did tend to hold negative views about the foreign women, and perhaps by comparing themselves with the outsiders were able to maintain a sense of greater integrity.

## Who Are the Clients?

At this end of the trade, the customers are predominantly older men (50 plus) and manual workers, often from construction sites and restaurants. Siu Ling reckons that they will never be short of clients because they can always lower their prices and 'there are always *haam sap* (lecherous) men around'. The younger clients tend to be more generous with their tips, but there is a moral reaction against men who are thought to be too young.

> Occasionally, there is a very young man. Many sisters in our street know him. We scold him for not being a good boy. He is supposed to be at school but instead goes shoplifting in the supermarket. Then he sells the goods he has stolen and uses the money to 'call a lady'. He has already had many of our 'sisters'. He asks whether you are willing to take off your clothes, whether you will agree to do this or that, do it in different positions. But he is too young! (Leng Mui)

## Relationships with Clients

All of the women have regular customers who form the bread and butter of their work and on whom they rely for work when times are hard. But when it comes to forming relationships with customers, they are ambivalent although they realize that men do become attached to them.

Siu Ling says that her work has given her a bad impression of men generally and thinks that if she were to marry in the future 'I definitely won't find one in this circle. They are definitely no good. If you find a man in this circle your marriage certainly won't last for long'. The women have their suspicions about men who offer to pay monthly.

> Oh, it is just because they like you, or for your beauty which has turned their head. It is not that they want to help you — give you money, ask you to quit the job and go home — nothing like this will happen. It is because they like you and want to pay you monthly, so they ask

you to quit the job. They want to possess you. It's not help, it is mutual benefit. (Lam)

Even new customers can be quite naive. They ask me to stay with them and offer to pay my debts. I've met three like that since I've been in Shamshuipo. One of them, I thought he was only joking but he really transferred HK$5,000 into my bank account. If they really mean what they say, it would be better to have one monthly customer rather than so many. But if they don't give you money, what protection do you have when you have stayed with them for one month like a fool? There's no contract, there's no obligation to do so. They may give you some money if they feel in a good mood or they have good winnings. After several times, they just disappear. (Siu Ling)

Two women established longer-lasting relationships with customers. Fok met a man who was a night watchman at a hospital. He had a key to her apartment and thought of himself as her second husband. He visited her while she was in prison on drugs charges (for the third time) and paid the rent on her apartment during that time so that her young daughter would still have somewhere to live. But eventually, he seemed to give up on her when it became apparent that she was not going to be able to beat her drug addiction.

Yang became attached to an old man of 70 who used to see her frequently (as well as others), and paid her HK$400 each time. She was touched by the fact that he wanted her to visit him at home and not use an hotel. His wife was in Singapore looking after a grandchild. Over a period of time, he paid her over HK$100,000. He asked her to invest it in a small business 'but I was such a bitch and said no. I wanted to find a small shop to sell underwear and clothes, but I just didn't go to look'.

Then her friend became ill and she accompanied him to the doctor. After he got home she told him that he was to call her if he wanted anything. But then when he did call over ten times (at least she thought it was him) she refused to answer the phone.

> I thought, I don't want to keep you company. I don't want to know what is happening to you. The next day, there was no phone call. He was not like this before. If he couldn't find me one night, he would call me the next morning. He was always worried about me, being caught by loan-

sharks . . . then I called the hospital and found that he had been admitted. When I heard this I was unhappy and guilty. Although he was my customer, after these months I had feelings for him. (Yang)

She went to visit him in hospital but then did not go to see him for five days. When she went back, she found he had died. 'I had a real lump in my throat and felt unhappy. First of all, it has been a long time and I have feelings towards him. I considered him as a friend. Secondly, I have lost this line to get money. I was really upset . . . I lost him and had to go to work again.'

## What Do Clients Want?

Clients, on the whole, tend not to be very adventurous in their tastes. Mostly they are satisfied with straight intercourse in the missionary position and it is over very quickly.[10] They negotiate their wants with the women before going upstairs to the villa and a price is agreed. The women say that they are able to refuse both a particular customer and a particular act if they wish. If the client changes his mind once upstairs and wants something not included in the original agreement, the women can still refuse. They say that there is rarely any trouble and if there is, then the staff in the villa will intervene to protect them. As Siu Ling commented, 'they are always on the women's side because we are the ones who bring them business'.

Sometimes the man will request 'an overnight' for which the woman will be paid between HK$500–700. In their experience this is not because the customer wants to have sex all night (maybe only twice) but is more for the companionship of sharing a bed. 'Perverted' requests are rare. One man wore the worker's underpants over his head while masturbating, another liked to lick toes and smell feet. A third would ask to have a rod inserted into his anus. None of the women would permit buggary. Most of them would perform oral sex but gave the impression that they found it disgusting and unhygienic. Yang thought it was the last resort of the old women on the game who were good for nothing else. This contrasts somewhat with Freund, Leonard, and Lee's study (1989) of commercial sex workers working the streets in New

Jersey. They found that the predominate sexual contact was oral sex (62.1 per cent) as opposed to vaginal sex (23.2 per cent). There was a tendency in their sample for vaginal sex to be performed with their regular clients rather than the casual 'tricks'.

## Managing an Identity Within the Family

All our respondents are mothers. Three are currently married and living with their husbands, one is widowed and the other four are divorced. Chui claims that her husband knows about her work and does not mind but her position will not be discussed in detail here as this was the respondent whom we felt was unreliable.

Hon and her pretence of playing mahjong have already been mentioned. Her husband is a hawker and she thinks he is in a state 'between knowing and not knowing' as far as her job is concerned. 'I don't know whether he could guess or not. He has never said anything and he has never seen me on the street. He might suspect where I go, even though I tell him it is to play mahjong.'

Hon also said that her children do not know. But on the night we interviewed her, she had arranged to meet her 17-year-old daughter in the area for an evening snack. A willing suspension of disbelief seems to be the defence mechanism in Hon's family.

The third married woman is Lam. She has told her husband that she works in a nightclub, just sitting with the customers, not 'going out' with them. He more or less accepts this but they have arguments over her work and her gambling debts. Her husband is unemployed, making her the major breadwinner. However, if it was not for her gambling debts, they would not need such a large monthly income. When they married, his financial condition was quite good and he was generous to her. Now she feels it is her turn to support him. Lam works in the evening so that she can look after her young daughter during the day.

Leng Mui's problem is different. She is widowed but has three sons, the eldest of whom is 17 and old enough to put two and two together. She spoke very freely on this subject and it is worth quoting her at length.

> Putting myself in my children's shoes, do I want my mother to be a prostitute? Of course not! I would not want my mother to pull down her trousers and do it with this man and that man. For about HK$100, people could see what your mother looks like without trousers. People will say to them, 'the clothes you wear are bought by money your mother earned as a prostitute'. Of course I don't want people to say these things to my sons. I also want my sons to have a happy family. But I feel that since they are my sons they have to comply with Fate, as I did. (Leng Mui)

Towards the end of the interview, when asked whether her neighbours know what her job is, she answers that she tells them she works as an *amah* (a maid) in a mahjong parlour. This is also the story she tells her children. What her sons really think they keep to themselves.

> My eldest son understands quite well. At his age he has considerable understanding of sex. He realizes that men have this need and go to massage parlours and so on.... In front of him I still wish to be a good mother. I won't swear, talk about the daily stresses and I won't complain about having no money to pay the rent. I try my best to be friends with him. (Leng Mui)

Siu Ling is now divorced and describes her second husband and marriage with some bitterness.

> My husband was a gambler. We were married for nine years and during that time there was not one good year, not even one good day. Nearly everyday I sold *dim sum* at HK$12 an hour, even when pregnant. I worked hard for him. And what do you get for struggling and working hard? Nothing! He continued to gamble, even when he lost heavily. Men are really no good. It is better to be on your own. (Siu Ling)

Her husband gambled away all his earnings and Siu Ling could not manage to support the family on the money she earned selling *dim sum*. So she went to work in a massage parlour in the evening so that she could look after her small son during the day. But she told her husband that she was working as a waitress in a karaoke bar, which she considered to be sufficiently believable. Now she lives in a small room and her son is cared for by her mother-in-law, much to her regret.

## The Future

When we asked Yang about what she thought the future held for her, she began to cry. She knew that she should stop taking it (heroin) and stop doing it (commercial sex) but:

> It's very difficult to do. Is there anyone who would want you, accept you? A man might accept you initially, promise you everything but in the future, when you quarrel, this would come up. It is inevitable. I want to save some money and have a stable life, settle down. I've also thought about needing a companion, everyone needs a companion. But could they accept you? That is the problem. (Yang)

Leng Mui, who has a serious kidney problem, realized how much she would like a companion when she was in hospital. Visiting hours were particularly painful when she could see others receiving visits from their families.

> I really wish there is someone to care for me. But if you have done this job and have this illness it is not easy to find someone whom you care for and who feels the same way about you. To love and be loved is the most happy experience. But to find it — that's the problem. (Leng Mui)

She was quite sure that it would be better to tell your history to any man you were serious about, even at the risk of driving him away. The consequences of not telling him would be worse and lay her open to threats from others. The most she feels she can realistically hope for is to live long enough to be able to support her three sons until they have finished school and established their own lives.

Siu Ling does not want to be like the really old workers in Shamshuipo who will do it for HK$30. She commented that if you don't know how to save money when you are young then old age is going to be really sad — yet none of them can save money. Lam knows that the only way to a secure future is to give up gambling and pay off her debt. But she also knows that this is not very likely, so she 'doesn't think about long-term things'.

Generally, the view of the future, when there was one, was pessimistic which in itself is probably realistic. Mostly they coped by not thinking about it. About the only person who could be said to have attempted to deal constructively with the question was Lui. She was in her forties and had been involved in the trade since she was 16. She had so far managed to buy five 'one phoenix, one apartment' units and a small, simple restaurant. She acted as an agent for the women in the units, finding customers on the street for them and taking a sizeable cut from their earnings.

## Conclusions

Only a very small segment of Hong Kong's commercial sex industry has been examined in this chapter. The specific focus of interest has been to explore this world from the point of view of the women who provide sexual services in one particular sector. It would be inadvisable to make sweeping generalizations from this data, although it has considerable intrinsic interest.

The women get into the trade through one of two routes. Either they have been in it since their youth, and have slipped down the career ladder as a result of the premium on looks and young flesh, or they have entered the trade at their current level as a result of unexpected necessity, for instance sudden widowhood or gambling debts. By the time they reach the level of streetwalker, they appear to be more independent and primarily working for themselves. They readily admit that they are not as soft-hearted as in their youth, when they were willing to work to pay off a boyfriend's supposed debts. Although working on the streets has its own embarrassments and hazards (for instance having to approach men, and little physical protection), it also has advantages. The women are much more in control of their working environment, being able to accept or reject customers and choose their own working hours. However, an indirect form of control is exerted through the process of loansharking. All of our sample, with one exception, had significant debts. It seemed to the authors that many of them were enticed deliberately into debt by the loansharks, presumably as an alternative means of getting their hands on the women's money without the labour of pimping. At this level of the trade, the percentage cut from HK$180 per trick would be unlikely to make formal pimping worthwhile.

The women are clearly motivated by the fact that they can earn more money this way than by any other. At the same time they do not report a high level of self-esteem or claim any enjoyment from their work. Indeed, some use soft drugs or alcohol to give them courage before going out on the streets. Furthermore, there is a clear sense that, unlike other jobs, commercial sex cannot be walked in and out of with little effect on the person. The women talk of themselves in a way that clearly implies that they see themselves as polluted for ever; that even if they tried to become 'respectable', they would always be different and discernible as such to others.

The relationships that the women have with their clients raise interesting questions about power. The women do not trust men. They are constantly suspicious about being taken advantage of in their working lives. At the same time, there is also evidence that some of their customers develop genuine affection for the women. These liaisons may be quite long-lasting or brief, but during them men will offer not only money but affection, support, and in one case, child care while the woman was serving a prison sentence for drug offences. As Cohen (1988) notes, it can be to the advantage of the woman to underplay the commercial side of the transaction and to keep the boundaries between affection and commerce 'fuzzy', both in terms of improved self-image and also eventual financial gains.

Although the authors accept that women in the commercial sex industry are frequently victims of the males who organize it and the customers who use it, this is not the end of the story. Within this context, women are making choices, exploring alternatives, and have a variety of complex motivations. Some play the cards that Fate has dealt them better than others. As Ng points out in his chapter on the family, to class women as 'victims', as helpless sufferers, fails to take account of their individuality, achievements, motivations and their sense of sisterhood. Indeed, such a view would obscure what is most interesting, for instance how they negotiate their dual identities of commercial sex workers and family women.

If one sees women in the trade as victims then the answer to the most frequently asked question 'why do they do it?' seems easier; because they are victims of the men who entrap and enforce. There is a partial truth in this but it obscures another important question. Why ask the question at all? To illustrate the point, let us ask another question; why do men indulge in indiscriminate sex, with unknown partners on a financial basis? At best, the question seems redundant and, at worst, faintly ludicrous because the answer seems so obvious. It is in the nature of men, they require variety and must have easily available outlets for their sex drives; or so we are encouraged to believe. The first question masks the double standard that is applied to men and women.

A more legitimate question, raised at the beginning of this chapter, is why some women but not others? After all, if earning more money, choosing one's working hours, avoiding the monotony of factory labour are such attractive prospects, why are more women in a similar socio-economic category not on the streets?

Vagg (Chapter 7) asks a similar question about why there are more male than female delinquents. He suggests that the answer lies in the susceptibility of some over others to the processes of socialization. This assumes that society speaks with one voice and has only one message. But in the case of vulnerability to commercial sex, we have to concede that there are several messages that are being given to young women, not only the 'respectable' message of the necessity for sexual continence before marriage for females. The general sense that women are less important than men, that wives and daughters should serve husbands and brothers within the family is a message that most girls will have received, and may well dispose them to accept the male dominant relationships that characterize the sex industry.

But there is another socialization path based on material success as a goal, without too much concern at the price to be paid. The continuing popularity of beauty pageants, and the desire to become a film or television starlet are both ways of achieving this goal, despite the common belief that loss of virginity will be one of the first prices to be paid. Not all women are attractive enough to pursue this particular path, but that it is there at all legitimizes the belief that a woman may use her body to improve her, and her family's, material position. So presumably the answer to 'why some and not others?' lies in looking at what forces have been most influential on an individual and what the available alternatives and choices are. Such forces and choices are not uniform within a particular socio-economic category and sometimes not even within the same household. Ultimately, we should not lose sight of the fact that the culturally validated acceptance of the double standard in sexuality between men and women requires that there is a class of women who are available for cash.

## Notes

1. We have decided not to use the words prostitution and prostitutes in this chapter, preferring instead the terms commercial sex industry and commercial sex workers. These latter terms are less pejorative and recognize the fact that commercial sex is big business and that the women involved in it work hard to generate considerable profit, most of which they do not see.
2. In May 1993, the High Court heard a civil case brought by Club de Luxe against the Club Metropole (both located in the Tsimshatsui area), which it claimed had 'poached' two of its most successful staff, a *'mamasan'* and a public relations manager. It was alleged that the Club Metropole had paid them HK$750,000 and HK$150,000 respectively to move over and bring their client lists and some of their hostesses with them (*South China Morning Post*, 12 May 1993). As is the government's practice with its very senior staff who leave/retire and wish to go into the private sector, senior club staff have a restrictive contract clause that prevents *mamasans* from both enticing away clientele when they leave, and taking a similar job within the Tsimshatsui area for a year.
3. The 1986 Family Planning Survey found that 26.8 per cent of their male sample aged between 18 and 27 admitted experiencing sexual intercourse. The present authors consider it significant that it was only the women who were considered for further analysis in Luis and Chan's study (1991). Presumably this was because pre-marital sex is considered more worrying when it occurs amongst women than men.
4. The yellow signboards are becoming increasingly hard to find as the police have brought several successful actions against those who erect them. At the time of writing (Spring, 1994), long, plain white fluorescent tubes have taken their place, at least in Wanchai on Hong Kong island.
5. 'Fishball stalls' were popular at the beginning of the 1980s (Yang

Memorial Social Service Centre, 1982). They tended to be inexpensive and their predominant physical feature was that they were in total darkness, and customers were led to a high-sided stall by the light of a small torch pointed at the floor. Thus customers and hostesses never saw each other clearly. They were usually staffed by young girls, many under-age students 'moonlighting' for a few hours after school. The attraction of fishball stalls for the customers was the price and the youth of the workers. Generally, sexual intercourse did not take place on the premises, although oral sex might be provided. Usually the girls permitted themselves to be fondled. Fishball stalls are so named because of the similarity in the actions of fondling nipples and rolling fishballs.

6. A number of common terms from horse racing are used in the commercial sex industry including 'stable' for the place from which the women are organized and run; 'mafoo' for the men who protect and escort them to jobs; 'placing horsebets' for one of the forms of commercial sex.

7. In May 1993 the cost of buying a hostess out of Club Bboss ('bar-fining') was HK$1,700. In addition, the customer would pay the woman HK$1,500 for sexual services. On top of that, he would also have to pay for a decent hotel room (and probably dinner). This does not take into account the cost of drinks, plates of fruit and so on in the club earlier in the evening. Dreams of Eros do not come cheaply in such places. Hostesses at this level would be unlikely to receive more than two customers in an evening. The karaoke lounges are providing tough competition for these clubs and business apparently fell quite dramatically in 1992. In early 1995 the 'bar-fine' at Bboss was said to be HK$2,500.

8. The Malaysian women's earnings are very exceptional and not all of them earn at this level. The income of the majority of commercial sex workers is much more modest.

9. The authors are deeply grateful to Mr. M. C. Li who helped the second author carry out the interviews. Mr. Li is President of the Hong Kong Sex Education Association and a lecturer in the Department of Applied Social Studies at the Hong Kong Polytechnic. Initially, attempts by a single woman to contact women in the street were not successful. They appeared very nervous, possibly thinking that a lesbian approach was being made. Mr. Li's presence, combined with his knowledge of the topic, was very beneficial. The interviewers approached the women, explained the purpose of the research and asked them if they would be willing to participate. They were offered HK$200 to recompense them for their time. Finding respondents became

easier as the women recommended us to their friends. Most of the interviews took place in local parks or restaurants and lasted for up to an hour. The authors are aware that many people think that women in this trade are unlikely to tell the truth. All we can say is that both interviewers are social workers of long standing and seniority, and it seemed to them that the women were not being devious. Furthermore, the participants seemed to make little effort to portray themselves in a good light. The only person about whom there were doubts was Chui, who was clearly emotionally disturbed and seemed to be showing side-effects of prescription drugs. The interviewers had a semi-structured questionnaire but felt free to explore other aspects as raised by the women. All the interviews were recorded in Cantonese and the tapes transcribed into English by the second author. This generated 103 pages of single-spaced typed manuscript. Categories were then identified based on the content of the manuscripts which formed the basis of the material presented in this chapter. In order to gain a wider understanding of the commercial sex scene in Hong Kong, the first author accompanied both the Mongkok and Wanchai vice squads on raids in their respective districts. She also benefited greatly from lengthy informal discussions with various members of the Royal Hong Kong Police. Prices quoted reflect 1993–94 levels.
10. But it must be remembered that the customer has probably been anticipating the encounter for some time and may be quite aroused by the time he accompanies the women to the hotel.

## References

Chau, Fung-mui (1994) *An Exploratory Study of Adolescent Girls' Entry to the Karaoke Business*, Unpublished Master of Social Work Dissertation, The University of Hong Kong.

Choi, Po-king (1993), 'Women', in P. K. Choi and L. S. Ho (eds.), *The Other Hong Kong Report*, Hong Kong: Chinese University Press, pp. 369–400.

Cohen, Erik (1988), 'Open-ended Prostitution as a Game of Luck; Opportunity, Risk and Security Among Tourist Oriented Prostitutes in a Bangkok *soi*', in Michael Hitchcock, Victor T. King, and Michael J. G. Parnwell (eds.), *Tourism in South-East Asia*, London: Routledge pp. 154–78.

Economic and Social Commission for Asia and the Pacific (1983), *The Situation of Young Women in the Service and Entertainment*

Industries in the ESCAP Region, Geneva: United Nations Committee on Social Development.

Freund, Matthew; Leonard, Terri L., Lee, Nancy (1989), 'Sexual Behaviour of Resident Street Prostitutes with their Clients in Camden, New Jersey', *Journal of Sex Research*, 26(4): 460–76.

Gagnon, John and Simon, William (1973), *Sexual Conduct: The Social Sources of Human Sexuality*, Chicago: Aldine Publishing Co.

Gronewald, S. (1985), *Beautiful Merchandise: Prostitution In China 1860–1937*, New York: Harrington Park Press.

Heyzer, Noeleen (1986), *Working Women In South East Asia: Development, Subordination and Emancipation*, Milton Keynes: Open University Press.

Hoigard, Cecilie and Finstad, Liv (1992), *Backstreets: Prostitution, Money and Love*, Cambridge: Polity Press.

Hong Kong Government (1990), *Hong Kong 1990; A Review of 1989*, Hong Kong: Government Printer.

—— (1992), *Hong Kong 1992; A Review of 1991*, Hong Kong: Government Printer.

—— (1994), *Hong Kong 1994; A Review of 1993*, Hong Kong: Government Printer.

Hyam, Ronald (1990), *Empire and Sexuality: The British Experience* Manchester: Manchester University Press.

Koo, Linda (1982), *Nourishment of Life: Health In Chinese Society*, Hong Kong: The Commercial Press.

Lam, Michelle W. Y. (1990), *A Study of the Problems and Welfare Needs of Female Manufacturing Workers in the Wong Chuk Hang Area*, Unpublished Master of Social Work Dissertation, The University of Hong Kong.

Lethbridge, Henry (1978a), 'Prostitution in Hong Kong: A Legal and Moral Dilemma', *Hong Kong Law Journal* 8(2): 149–73.

Lethbridge, Henry (1978b), 'The Evolution of a Chinese Voluntary Association in Hong Kong: The Po Leung Kuk', in Henry Lethbridge, *Hong Kong: Stability and Change: A Collection of Essays*, Hong Kong: Oxford University Press, pp. 71–103.

Levin, David (1991), 'Women and the Industrial Labour Market in Hong Kong: Participation and Perspectives', in J. G. Scoville (ed.), *Status Influences in Third World Labour Markets*, New York: De Gruyter.

Luis, B. P. K. and Chan, Kwok Leung (1991), 'Determinants of Premarital Sex: The Case of Young Hong Kong Women', *Hong Kong Journal of Social Work* xxv: 11–10.

MacNamara, Donal E. J. and Sagarin, Edward (1977), *Sex, Crime and the Law*, New York: Free Press.

Miners, Norman (1987), 'The State Regulation of Prostitution

1857–1941', in Norman Miners, *Hong Kong Under Imperial Rule*, Hong Kong: Oxford University Press, pp. 191–206.

Mongkok District Board (1986), *Working Group on Vice Associated Establishments*, Hong Kong: Mongkok Working Group on Vice Associated Establishments.

Murray, Alison (1991), *No Money, No Honey: A Study of Street Trading and Prostitutes in Jakarta*, Singapore: Oxford University Press.

Odzer, Cleo (1992), *Patpong Prostitution; Its Relationship to and Effect on the Position of Women in Thai Society*, Ann Arbor: University Microfilms International.

Pongpaichit, Pasuk (1982), *From Peasant Girls To Bangkok Masseuses*, Geneva: International Labour Office.

Tang, Alex Yee Man (1977), *The Self Image of Young Women Involved in Prostitution*, Unpublished Master of Social Work Dissertation, The University of Hong Kong.

Tang, Alex Yee Man and Lam, Man Ping (1986), *Teenage Prostitution in Hong Kong*, Hong Kong: Centre for Hong Kong Studies, The Chinese University of Hong Kong.

Truong, Thanh-dam (1983), 'The Dynamics of Sex Tourism: The Case of South East Asia', *Development and Change*, 14: 533–53.

—— (1990), *Sex, Money and Morality: Prostitution and Tourism in South East Asia*, London: Zed Books.

Vagg, Jon (1991), 'Vice', in Harald Traver and Jon Vagg (eds.), *Crime and Justice in Hong Kong*, Hong Kong: Oxford University Press.

van Gulik, Robert (1961), *Sexual Life In Ancient China*, Leiden: E. J. Brill.

Yang Memorial Social Service Centre (1982), *A Report Summary on Fishball Stall Study*, Hong Kong: Yang Memorial Social Service Centre.

# 10 The Women's Movement at the Crossroads

*Tsang Gar-yin*

Before discussing the women's movement in Hong Kong, one may ask the question, is there indeed a women's movement to speak of? The answer to that question clearly depends on one's understanding of the meaning of 'women's movement' and similarly, 'feminism'. According to one recent account, the women's movement in Hong Kong should try to understand the root cause of patriarchy (meaning a system of male dominance), and fight it on a personal and structural level (Ho, 1990). Ho uses this definition to classify all women's groups across the spectrum. However, labels like 'conservative' and 'radical' are always controversial; they can be oversimplistic and at times deceptive.[1] As the following account will show, the women's movement in Hong Kong is simply too young to invite an authoritative balance sheet.

With this in mind, a somewhat looser definition of 'women's movement' will be used in this chapter. It will signify the activities of groups, made up largely of women, which are concerned with the disadvantaged position of women in society, and who wish to bring about a significant improvement in the situation of women. The objective is to describe the diversity in methods, concerns, and targets, and to analyse the action of women's groups in Hong Kong as they have evolved over the years. The purpose is to shed light on some of the difficulties as well as highlight the achievements of the women's movement. Any evaluation is offered in a spirit of exploration and tentative proposition.

## The Development of a Women's Movement

The formation of women's concern groups and, more recently, a more self-conscious women's movement in Hong Kong mirrored some of the major stages of the feminist movement in the West. It started from a similar revulsion against glaring maltreatment of women, moved onto a confident liberal outlook criticizing gender inequalities in public and private lives, then to a more fundamental, structural approach to gender subordination and its transformation. It was very like the Western version of feminist history, spanning the suffrage movement to second-wave liberal feminism with the intervention of radical and socialist feminism following (Oakley, 1980; Bouchier, 1983). There are, of course, certain features peculiar to the local situation.

As Benjamin Leung's chapter on women and social change shows, the colonial system, and the space for political and social reform have only recently faced the prospect of change. Also, there has not been a strong labour movement or civil rights movement (the two features that contributed to the strength of feminism in the United Kingdom and United States) during most of the post-war years. Together they explain why the women's movement has made little headway in terms of policy, ideology, and organizational strength. The pressing political questions of the transition of Hong Kong to Chinese rule in 1997 also seem to have marginalized gender issues. It has always been an uphill battle for feminism. A lack of tangible advances and overall momentum often leads to attack by observers, who are not fully aware of the considerations and constraints involved. All the more need now to highlight some of the significant achievements made by people committed to bringing a better future for women (and men) in Hong Kong.

The history of the women's movement in Hong Kong can be roughly divided into three stages. The first stage ran from the immediate post-war years up to the mid-1970s. It was a time when women's concerns were voiced by prominent, committed individuals rather than from a solid organizational base. The Hong Kong Council of Women (HKCW) was formed in 1947. Its platform contained a wide range of concerns, but the general aim was to eradicate all forms of discrimination against women, in law, economic activities, and social status. Issues like separate taxation and equal pay for women were voiced as early as the 1950s. However, the issues that caught the eye and generated most effort were the glaring ones — the perpetuation of concubinage, and the gross disparity between women's and men's pay even in the same job. The former was seen as a legacy of Chinese tradition, the latter a manifestation of the kinds of injustice pervasive within the colonial system. Both were blatant and indefensible, obviously at odds with a thriving modern city taking pride in its championing of new outlooks and morals. One prominent pioneer of the women's movement, Ellen Li, declared in a Legislative Council meeting in 1967 with tremendous eloquence and an unmistakable sense of righteousness, that 500,000 women in Hong Kong were very unhappy, because of the glaring injustice perpetuated by an inert government (AAF, 1992: 3).

Her argument finally won the day. At their height, campaigns against such blatant gender injustice garnered a wide range of support: 140 social groups participated in the anti-concubinage lobby, and the fight for equal pay also saw a solid coalition formed with a healthy number of labour unions. However, despite the hard work of the deeply respected pioneers, it is fair to say that in the aftermath of the campaigns, no sense of a women's movement developed. No permanent organizational base and no long-term strategy for social transformation emerged. Once the obvious problems of concubinage and glaringly unequal pay were dealt with, the women's groups lost impetus by and large, as signified by the relatively stagnant nature of the HKCW between the mid-1960s and early 1970s — senior members had to take a back seat as the numbers of new members rose only slowly.[2]

## Putting the Women's Movement on the Map

The second stage came in 1975 and lasted for around ten years. The HKCW had continued to provide the only important umbrella for women's concerns up to the beginning of that period. The year 1975 saw a range of activities celebrating the International Women's Year. Several members of the International Feminist League subsequently joined the HKCW. They were mostly expatriate women, bringing fresh energy and a new and revitalized set of concerns to local women's groups. A major influence was undoubtedly the emergence of the second wave of feminism in the West in the 1960s, after a period of relative dormancy following the achievement of voting rights for women. It had its beginnings in a re-examination of the diffused but unmistakable frustration of the life of the average American housewife; and extended subsequently into a wholesale questioning of the social, political, economic, cultural, and personal aspects of social life. The timing and context of its emergence also meant that it shared many of the concerns and tactics of the civil rights, anti-war, and New Left movements of the time (Ryan, 1992: 40–1).

The HKCW started a series of activities and campaigns that broadened the concern beyond pay discrimination and legal marital status. There was a heavy slant towards a civil rights emphasis, and women's individual rights and autonomy were seen to be severely violated in many areas of life. The agenda began to shift from a concern with narrow and explicit issues to other broad-ranging and hidden problems. Hence the HKCW campaigned vigorously on paid maternity leave as a recognition of women's rights and contribution (1979). More interestingly it also put its weight behind the long-running 'War on Rape' and 'Against Wife Abuse' campaigns. At the same time, a new focus on consciousness raising was evident. Rapport groups were developed, and there was also emphasis on promoting women's concerns by gaining access to the mass media, and holding public seminars (for example, in 1976 a series of public seminars on law, violence, media, health, and education were held).

Later still, the HKCW elaborated a more grassroots orientation by setting up the Women's Centre and Harmony House, providing refuge for battered wives, and a women's resource centre, setting up hot-lines and counselling services and developing programmes for individual empowerment. The model of second-wave feminism was clearly the impetus behind such new activities. The social climate of the 1970s, with the emergence of a new generation born and bred in Hong Kong, and a more forward-looking orientation displayed by the government of the time, also contributed to that revitalization.[3] The proliferation of such a wide range of activities, organizational forms, and influx of women enthusiastic to change the way things were, can retrospectively be seen as the genuine beginning of a women's movement in Hong Kong. Such flowering of activities put the women's movement on the map. It also led to debates, acts of clarification, and a resultant divergence of opinions and strategies.

However, there were no acts of line-drawing that proclaimed

the coming of a new era. There were vague but unmistakable rumblings, a sense of dissension embodied in the new generation of women having a deep concern for the plight of one-half of the population. The contribution of the HKCW of the time to the women's cause was, by all accounts, substantial. Yet that did not prevent the establishment of a number of women's groups in the 1980s that slowly charted a different course. Many of the founding members of these groups were then in their twenties, with their natural habitat in the thriving student and community movements of the time. By temperament and experience, they were more inclined to embrace social critique and demand radical transformation of society (Cheung, 1992). They were weary of the fact that the relevant movements as they existed never addressed gender issues. The apparently 'more important' questions of poverty, employment inequality, and housing took centre-stage. They did not identify completely with the strategies and principles of the HKCW at that time.

There were three major areas of dissension. First, many of the activities of the HKCW targeted the victim role of women — women being raped or abused — and how to provide remedial measures to help the victims. The notion of individual empowerment smacked of a tendency to zoom in on the more psychological level, neglecting the structural pressure that most women face in their daily lives — rape, violence, and discrimination not as deeds perpetuated by individuals, but a systematic outcome of the ways gender relations were organized in society. Portraying women as victims of personal misdeeds may gain a wider appeal, but if the underlying issue of male power is ignored, then the solution can only be *ad hoc* and remedial.

Second, and relatedly, the modest, non-confrontational approach championed by certain sections of the HKCW was deemed to be only a partial approach to changing women's plight. For example, in reflecting on the success of the 'War on Rape' campaign, Fanny Cheung stated that a community approach, stressing the interest to the community as a whole, would be more effective in gaining popular appeal than a confrontational approach emphasizing the systematic domination of men over women in society (AAF, 1992: 19). That strategy might gain wider acceptance among government officials and the public, but whether limiting the role of women's organizations, and indeed the women's movement, to such issues and methods could really bring lasting gains for women, was doubtful.

In addition to these strategic and analytic problems, the third area of dissension was one that addressed the practical inability of the HKCW to speak the language of the grassroots population. This line of critique is represented by Ho's evaluation of the Council's 'War on Rape' campaign:

> In the process of campaigning in local communities on the issue of rape, the inherent weakness of the HKCW was exposed. The Council's active membership was largely made up of middle-class, expatriate women who enjoyed some forms of social privilege in colonial Hong Kong. Ignorant of the socio-economic cultural dynamics of the local community, many of the Council's proposals on the prevention of rape were found to be impractical, especially in the low-cost housing areas where rapes happened most often (Ho, 1990: 187).

## Confronting Patriarchy

One major feature of the third stage of the women's movement in Hong Kong was the proliferation of new groups, sharing, however vaguely, the above points of dissension. The concern now was to go local and to reach out to the grassroots. The aim to build a women's movement more consciously radical emerged in ensuing campaigns and activities.[4] For example, the Hong Kong Women's Christian Council, formed in 1988, has been working hard within Christian circles to promote the necessity and possibility of women's theology, aiming to rethink the role and situation of women within religious bodies and society at large. It has also actively participated in a wide range of campaigns for women's rights, often in association with grassroots women's organizations. In recent years, it has been vocal on the issue of democratization and the need to develop a strong grassroots social movement in Hong Kong (AAF, 1991).

Another new group prominent in recent years is the Hong Kong Women Workers Association. Formed by a combination of female workers, social workers, and labour organizers, the Association has a more specific focus on the situation of women workers, especially their experience of marginalization and exploitation at the lower end of the employment hierarchy. In the past few years, it has done intensive work among part-time female workers, outworkers, and women who are thrown into major difficulties by the relocation and restructuring of manufacturing industries in Hong Kong. It combines research, promotion, campaigns, and demonstration activities to fight for the rights of working women, while also developing learning courses to equip and develop women workers (AAF, 1991).

Displaying a similar trend of localization and grassroots organization is the Women's Centre, previously a subsidiary organization of the HKCW. Since the late 1980s, the Women's Centre has further developed its role in the community by enhancing its resource centre, counselling activities, and also by joining in coalitions of women's groups campaigning on a wide range of issues (AAF, 1991).

The new emphasis of the third stage can also be seen in a comprehensive manner in the work of the Association for the Advancement of Feminism (AAF).[5] Formed in 1984, several of the founding members of the AAF espoused a socialist feminist perspective, stressing the necessity to unravel the full, complicated dynamics of capitalist patriarchy as a precondition for bringing genuine emancipation for women.[6] The official platform of the AAF itself did not explicitly advance such a view, but the concern has consistently been to go one step beyond seeing women simply as victims and also against a makeshift approach to improving the status of women. It proposes a comprehensive critique and reappraisal of the existing system of gender relations in society. Women as sex objects in pornographic literature are seen as intimately connected with their subservient position in the labour market. This subservience is further reinforced by legal and welfare measures that systematically treat women as dependents and men as breadwinners in the family (AAF, 1990; 1993).[7] As the subordination of women is seen as emanating from a system with tightly connected parts, the women's movement needs to further expand its scope of concern, uncovering mechanisms of female subordination in all major areas of life. It also needs to aim for fundamental changes by developing resources, mobilizing women and campaigning for major policy change (Ho, 1990).

As discussed above, a significant feature of the 1980s was the establishment of several women's groups broadly sharing the above orientation. Most of them, however, developed specific fields of concern; for example, the Hong Kong Women Workers Association concentrated on improving the employment and working conditions of working-class women in particular, focusing on the systemic pressure generated by capitalism and the effects of patriarchy on women. The AAF, among the earliest of this new crop of feminist bodies, had a wide range of engagements, even though lack of resources and other problems retarded its achievements. Below are some of the activities that give an indication of the current, major concerns of women's groups.

## Grassroots Consciousness Raising

During the 1980s the AAF was persistent in trying to reach women at the grassroots level directly by organizing multiple series of courses in various public housing estates. Parts of the courses, such as lectures and activities on women's rights in Hong Kong, were designed to tie in with women's daily immediate interests; there were also courses introducing women to an analysis of gender-role systems, sexism and the media, and the women's movement in China. Large scale mobile exhibitions and street dramas were also attempted. The emphasis has in recent years shifted to liaison with the so-called change agents in the local community; for example, the AAF initiated the setting up of a working group on women under the Hong Kong Council of Social Service in 1986, and a joint forum for women organizers in 1987. It is envisaged that social workers and other community workers may be in a strong position to spread the platform and concerns of the women's movement. This is also augmented by direct campaign action involving women's groups at the grassroots level.

## Campaigns and Lobbying

These have been the prominent forms of action taken by the new feminist groups in the past ten years. Campaigns have been mounted on child care (1990) involving a coalition of approximately twenty women's groups, demanding that the government increase subvented nursery places and reform its underlying approach to child care, to see it as a necessary and valuable contribution to society. In the past few years, there were also campaigns from coalitions of women's groups on women's equal employment rights, separate taxation, sexual abuse, and women voters. These were put forward simultaneously in an effort to lobby politicians, especially the elected Legislative Council members after the 1991 elections. The campaigns were couched not in terms of one-off material remedies of specific difficulties, but rather as part of a grand attempt to understand and change the structural obstacles to gender equality and women's development.

## Resource Development

One feature of women's current plight is a general lack of access to resources, including documents and analysis that can illuminate their contribution and sacrifice. The Women's Centre under the HKCW has been collecting and making available important documents and resources for women since its inception in 1986. The work is augmented by the Women's Resource Centre of the AAF, which in addition to providing library resources, is also keen on producing various kinds of packages and publications for documentation and educational function. For example, it has recently produced videos on child care, battered women, the situation of women in Hong Kong, pamphlets on legal aspects of child abuse and wife abuse, an educational manual on women's rights for local women's groups, and various publications presenting the research work of the policy study section.

## Co-operation of Different Organizations

As already mentioned, several feminist groups sprang up in the 1980s aiming to provide persistent challenges to the status quo in specific areas of women's lives. The limitations of each working on its own are well recognized. Hence there are many instances in which the groups have banded together as coalitions advancing a unified platform and exerting concerted pressure on policy-makers and arousing public attention. For example, in the campaign to extend the United

Nations Convention on the Elimination of All Forms of Discrimination Against Women (CEDAW) in December 1992, more than ten women's groups joined hands, issued a common declaration and persistently lobbied Legislative Council members. That coalition was itself an extension of an earlier one promoting the education of women voters for the 1991 direct elections. In early 1993, the groups were seeking to establish a permanent forum for the exchange of views, and planning to devise a common long-term strategy for improving the situation of women in Hong Kong.

## Celebrating Pluralism

Writing as one deeply involved in the women's movement, the author cannot but experience a rather ambivalent feeling when trying to compose a balance sheet of the gains and losses. In comparison with the gains of feminist movements in the West, our achievements are quite modest. However, this account of the movement has been written largely in a spirit of cautious optimism. It has tried to chart some of the developments of the women's movement in Hong Kong. Whether in terms of scope of concern, number of sympathizers and committed organizers, in the depth of the underlying analysis of women's subordination, and in the range of education and campaign activities attempted, the women's movement in Hong Kong has indeed made some important advances.

Such advances are first manifested in the fact that women's concerns have been recognized as a legitimate and even urgent issue by the major political groups and members of the Legislative Council. During the first direct election held for the Legislative Council in 1991, in response to the campaigning effort of women's groups, the major political groups adopted in their political agenda demands outlined in a joint Women's Platform. In the past two years, the campaigns to set up a Commission on Women and to extend the United Nations CEDAW, two demands high on women's groups priority list, won support from the Legislative Council.

Whilst women's groups are fully aware of the limitations of such potentially token recognition, some also feel that the eventual extension of CEDAW can provide the platform for a new and more tangible round of debate on measures to eradicate women's subordination. The future debate on the principles and means for bringing about gender equality is set to provide a new impetus for involving women in the process of changing their own lives.

The women's movement has also made its presence felt at the ideological level. The advertising industry has to pay serious attention to the constant critique by women's groups and possibly reorient their presentation strategies. The media in general have been picking up stories on gender inequality, some of them taking for granted that a feminist voice has to be sought and presented in many of the controversial issues of the day. Political groups, as discussed above, are also more willing to seek and accept the analysis offered by the women's groups on issues relating to employment, social security and families. Academia is also opening fast to feminist thinking and research, attested to by the quantity of publications on Hong Kong women and the range of women's issues in the curriculum. All this has occurred as a result of the active work done by people within the women's movement.

Finally, all the above would be largely meaningless if there are not more women gaining a new level of consciousness and trying to look at their lives in a new light. For many community and social workers, services catering to women have fast become a necessity, as real problems generated by women's contradictory social roles become pressure points in the local community. More women are recognizing these contradictory demands too, by complaining out loud to social surveyors, by joining the proliferating women's groups at the local level, and by participating in campaigns that once appeared too 'political' for them.

However, despite such undoubted and important gains, problems and difficulties still abound. Trying to introduce legislation on equal pay and anti-discrimination at work has been very difficult. Likewise, little headway has been made on improving the status of and provisions for female carers of all types. The double standard of sexuality continues to saturate everyday media output, and women's groups are mostly struggling on a shoestring. As Cheung, and Wan and

Wan (1994) argue, many of the gains in policies related to women's interests were achieved because of the recognition paid to other, apparently more important social groups; for example, separate taxation for women was granted because pressure from the middle class as a group was seen to be so urgent as to require concessions on the government's part. The above observations naturally raise questions for the future of the women's movement.

The causes for the 'underachievement' of the women's movement in Hong Kong are complex. Three areas are worthy of attention. First, the lack of a tradition and an organized basis of social resistance in Hong Kong similar to those of the labour movement in Britain, and the civil rights movement in the USA is one major handicap that only time and accumulated experience of social reform can redress. Secondly, the colonial and non-interventionist nature of the Hong Kong state has not been congenial to fundamental changes from above. Hence the opening up of the political system in recent years may provide a good chance for certain grassroots activists to penetrate into the policy-making arena and generate a new climate of discussion and monitoring of policies that may produce far-reaching consequences for women.

Thirdly, and some would say most significantly, the absence of a united platform among women's groups has retarded the advances of the movement. The fissure in strategic thinking is well captured by several recent articles discussing the issue. On one side is the view of Ho that the women's movement lacks a grand view of what is at stake in the fight against female subordination, and hence what it wants to achieve in that process (Ho, 1990). Ho is adamant that the future strength of the women's movement lies significantly in whether it can present a coherent, common voice that grasps the structural basis of women's current subordination. She argues that the women's movement needs to continue to engage in campaigns and other forms of social action, but all the while with an explicit view to challenging the cornerstone of the patriarchal system. For instance, women's groups have to make it clear that fighting for more subvented child-care places is not a short-term pain relief measure for unfortunate women, but a long-term strategy to bring about equality of opportunity for women and to re-evaluate the worth of caring work in society.[8] To put women's concerns on the agenda would mean ceasing to see women as victims of personal misdeeds, or the plight of most women as the legacy of traditional culture. What is needed is a structural outlook, a feminist principle to unite the hitherto *ad hoc* coalition of women's forces (Ho, 1990: 194–5).

In opposition to this view is the one that sees the primary problem of the movement as the lack of a genuine grassroots orientation. The AAF has been criticized for lacking a coherent strategy and persistent commitment in organizing women at the grassroots level (Cheung, 1992). Partly as a result of a shortage of resources and humanpower, the AAF has been slowly shifting away from its early involvement with the grassroots, to liaising with women organizers, lobbying politicians and officials, and advocating the women's cause at the ideological and policy-research level. That strategic shift may spell the dominance of a top-down, élitist approach, sacrificing what some people would regard as the most significant contribution that the women's movement can make to social transformation (Lui, 1993). Lui argues that the primary aim of the movement should be the mobilization of women at the bottom of the heap and the releasing of their potential for self and social transformation. Consciousness raising for the average woman has, in fact, been a most important part of the feminist movement over the last few decades. It is hence not surprising to see some sections of the movement refusing to play the game of political lobbying or partake in state-policy wrangles. Instead, they want to focus on developing and equipping women who bear the brunt of patriarchal oppression in their everyday life.

There is no doubt that such dissension in strategic thinking has fragmented the movement, and dampened some of its achievements. However, the debate on strategy will go on, because Hong Kong society at large is experiencing unprecedented and uncharted possibilities of social change. The questions on the potential and limitations of a state-led approach for feminist change, and on the principles behind strategies for equality and re-evaluation of women's unique quality and contribution to social life, are as yet unresolved issues in feminist movements in the West (Pateman, 1992). Similar debates will doubtless proliferate in the local context in years to come.

It is not possible to pronounce a 'correct' verdict on the above debate in feminist strategies. Rather, it is a sign of vitality that such dissenting views are aired with the kind of passion and rigour displayed. The pluralization of forms of organization and platforms in the current stage of the movement is something to be celebrated.

## Notes

1. See Ryan (1992) for a similar cautionary tone in writing the history of second-wave feminism in the West. Other accounts in Hong Kong (e.g. Yau, Au, and Cheung, 1992) use the term 'women's concern groups' to characterize the relevant activities and organizations. However, I feel there are good reasons to retain the term 'women's movement', not least because many of the more prominent women's groups to have emerged in the last decade see themselves explicitly as engaging in such a movement. The term also draws out the significant influence that women's movements elsewhere, especially in the West, have on the groups in Hong Kong.
2. See AAF, (1992), p. 26.
3. See this book's Chapter 1 on women and social change for a more detailed discussion of the socio-economic and political changes in Hong Kong since the 1970s.
4. For detailed descriptions of some of these newly formed women's groups, see Ho (1990); Cheung (1992); and AAF (1991).
5. The work of the AAF is discussed in detail here not necessarily because it is the most important or successful in furthering women's interests. However, I do feel the Association's attempts, achievements, as well as failures, capture rather characteristically the concerns and difficulties of the women's movement at the current stage. The author's deep involvement in the AAF obviously informs the analysis too.
6. See this book's introductory chapter for a brief discussion of the major feminist perspectives. The socialist feminist perspective is not discussed, but it shares some similarities with the Marxist feminist perspective. It also provides an account of the relationship between capitalism and patriarchy in the Hong Kong context.
7. For an expanded discussion of such legal and welfare measures, see this book's Chapter 7 on women and crime. Women's subordinate status within the family is analysed in detail in Chapter 3 on women and the family.

8. The argument here concerning child care as an obstacle to women's emancipation concurs with Leung's in his chapter on women and social change in this book.

## References

*Annual Reports 1985 to 1992*, Hong Kong: Association for the Advancement of Feminism.
—— (1985), *Report on Women's Participation in Public Affairs*, Hong Kong: Association for the Advancement of Feminism.
—— (1990), *Women and Welfare Policy in Hong Kong*, Hong Kong: Association for the Advancement of Feminism.
—— (1991), *Feminist Organisations in Hong Kong, Fact Sheet Series, No. 1*, Hong Kong: Association for the Advancement of Feminism.
—— (1992), *The Other Half of the Sky: Women's Movement in Hong Kong Since the Post-War Years*, Hong Kong: Association for the Advancement of Feminism.
Association for the Advancement of Feminism (1993), *The Hong Kong Women's File*, Hong Kong: Association for the Advancement of Feminism [in Chinese]
Bouchier, D. (1983), *The Feminist Challenge*, London: Macmillan.
Chan, S. H. (1987), 'The State of the Women's Movement in Hong Kong', *Women's Centre's News*, October, Hong Kong: Women's Centre.
Cheung, F. M. (1989), 'The Women's Centre: A Community Approach to Feminism in Hong Kong,' *American Journal of Community Psychology*, 17(1): 99–107.
Cheung, C. W. (1992), 'Women's Movement: the Hong Kong Experience' Unpublished speech presented on January 30 at the Monthly Dinner Talk of the Hong Kong Chinese University Office of International Studies Programme.
Cheung, F. M., Wan, S. P. and Wan, O. C. (1994), 'The underdeveloped political potential of women in Hong Kong', in Barbara Nelson and Najma Chowdhury (eds.), *Women and Politics Worldwide*, New Haven: Yale University Press.
Ho, C. K. A. (1990), 'Opportunities and Challenges: The Role of Feminists for Social Change in Hong Kong' in L. Albrecht and R. M. Brewer (eds.), *Bridges of Power — Women's Multicultural Alliances*, Philadelphia: New Society Publishers, pp. 182–98.
Hong Kong Council of Women (1980 to 1992), *Annual Reports*, Hong Kong: Hong Kong Council of Women.
Hong Kong Council of Women (1987), *The Hong Kong Council of Women — 1947–1987, 40th Anniversary*, Hong Kong: Hong Kong Council of Women.

Hong Kong Women's Christian Council (1989 to 1992), *Annual Reports*, Hong Kong: Hong Kong Women's Christian Council.

Hung, S. L. (1991), 'Women's Movement', in N. W. Kwok and A. M. Y. Wong (eds.), *Christian Witnesses in Hong Kong*, Hong Kong: Hong Kong Christian Institute, pp. 25–35.

Khor, D. (1985), 'Alienated Allies — Fetters of Feminism', *Hong Kong, Psychological Society Bulletin*, 14: 47–58.

Leung, L. C. (1990), 'Yesterday, Today and Tomorrow — Advancement of Women and Women's Movement', in *Annual Report 1988–1989*, Hong Kong: Association for the Advancement of Feminism.

Lui, Y. (1993), 'Reflection on the Women's Movement in Hong Kong' in *People's Resistance, No. 3*.

Oakley, A. (1980), *Subject Women*, Glasgow: Fontana.

Pateman, C. (1992), 'The Patriarchal Welfare State', in L. McDowell and R. Pringle (eds.), *Defining Women*, Cambridge: Polity Press, in association with Open University Press, pp. 223–45.

Ryan, B. (1992), *Feminism and the Women's Movement*, London: Routledge.

Yau, B. L. L., K. C. Au, and F. M. Cheung (1992), *Women's Concern Groups in Hong Kong, Occasional Paper No.15*, Hong Kong: Hong Kong Institute of Asia-Pacific Studies, The Chinese University of Hong Kong.

# Index

ADMINISTRATIVE SERVICES: women in, 140, 141
Adultery: double standards, 171
AIDS, 250, 255
Anti-concubinage lobby, 278
Anti-discrimination laws: absence of, 167
Anti-sex discrimination act, 113
Arts subjects, 111; feminine image, 112
Association for the Advancement of Feminism (AAF), 76, 78, 86, 153, 283, 288; perspectives of, 282; Women's Resource Centre, 284
Au Kit-chun, 114
Ayanian, J.Z. and Epstein, A.M., 231

BAKER, H.D.R., 174
Bangladesh, 237
Basic Law, 151, 185
Battered spouses, 205, 279
Bill of Rights, 10, 151, 187; debate on, 189
Birth control, 218, 220
Britain: and China, 171; labour movement in, 287
British: administrators and customary law, 185; and Chinese custom, 184; Empire, 167; law 170; rule, 168; view of Chinese, 22
Brothels, 250, 255

CALBOURNE, M.J., 217
Cancer: among women, 225; dietary factors as contributor to, 227; epidemiological studies, 225; lifestyle as contributor to, 225

Capitalism 2, 5, 283; in Hong Kong, 7
Care and Protection Order, 198
Care and protection system, 203–4
Career women, 35, 91, 92
Carlen, P., 195, 199
Cashmore, E.E., 34, 35, 91, 92
Certificate of Education Examination, 109; gender ratios for 1976–92, 110
Chan Po-king, 29, 32, 40
Chan, T.S., 232
Chan, W.T., 205, 207
Cheung, Fanny, 280
Child-rearing: burden of, 51
Children: custody of, 171
China: 156, 253; civil war in, 24; first government brothel in, 250; open-door policy, 25
Chinese: culture and women, 5; customary law, 179, 183, 186, customary rights, 176, customs, 169, 185, 188; double standards, 250, family, 78; leadership, 156; mothers and female babies, 236, patriarchal, 78; tradition, 180; traditional culture 83; traditional medicine, 218
Chinese University of Hong Kong: a survey of sexual behaviour and gender differences in, 124
Chow, A.M., 197, 201
Chun, A., 186, 187
Civic education, 125
Civil and Miscellaneous Lists, 141
Clans: of New Territories, 174
Cohen, Erik, 269

Colonial: administration, 179, 180, 185; authorities, 180; government, 22, 134, 167; policy towards Chinese law and custom, 181; regime, 88, 141
Colonialism, 167
Commercial sex, 15; and the police, 253; arithmetic of, 254; explanations for existence of, 244; in China and Hong Kong, 251
Commercial sex industry: and triads, 253; as a career, 246; attracting factors, 246; client's requirements, 264–5; customers of, 262; double standards, 250; in Hong Kong, 15; most vulnerable women of, 254; organization of, 245, 249; precipitating factors, 246; reasons for entry into, 246, 249, 257–8
Commercial sex workers, 244; at Shamshuipo, 255; attitude towards, 251–2; background of, 258; control over, 259; debts, 259; from overseas, 254–5; lifestyles, 258–60; perceptions on future, 267; relationship with clients, 262–3; strata of, 255; study in New Jersey, 264–5
Commercial sex worker's attitudes, 251; towards foreign prostitutes, 261; towards themselves and their jobs, 260–1
Concubines, 6, 23, 170, 179, 250
Confucianism, 189, 206; legacy, 154; virtue, 206
Conjugal: power, 80; support, 76
Convention on the Elimination of All Forms of Discrimination Against Women (CEDAW), 10, 13, 19, 133, 134, 150, 155, 285, 286; and China, 155
Correctional Services, 201; Department, 204
Crime victims, 205–9, legal definition of, 205; social process definition of, 205
Criminal justice system, 194, 203
Cruelty to children, 194
Cultural: imperialism, 188, 189; transmission, 101
Curriculum, 109–14; genderization of, 16, 103
Custom and culture, 186
Customary: land trusts, 184; law, 175; law rights, 182; marriage, 170

DELINQUENCY, 206; AS A symptom, 201; explanations for, 200; reactions of authority to, 200
Democratization, 148, 158
Deviance: attitude towards, 210
Differential association theory, 200
Discrimination: in the workplace, 189
District: Administrative Scheme, 5; Board, 25, 179; Court, 182
District Officer, 180, 186; in New Territories, 175
Division of labour, 54, 93; domestic, 68; sexual, 3
Divorce, 171, *see also* Hong Kong: divorces in
Domestic: helpers, 91, *see also* Filipina; ideals, 93; ideology, 85; violence, 170
Downes, D. and Rock, P., 95

EDUCATION: AND CAREER prospects, 108; and disparity, 33, 57, 58; and gender, 101; and gender inequalities, 12; and occupation, 59; and social inequality, 101; and social placement, 101; and women's health, 240; as form of cultural transmission, 109; by sex and conjugal status, 64; gender issues in, 127; gender segregation, 102–3; in practice, 109; women in, 16

Elections: direct, 157; voters participation in, 145–6

Élites: Chinese, 6, 14, 25, 169, 185, 188; and British, 245; and expatriate, 172; male, 169, 187; of Hong Kong and China, 187

Employers: and women, 8

Employment Ordinance, 86

Equal Opportunities: Act, 113; Bill, 10; Commission, 11; for Women and Men, 9

Equal Pay: fight for, 278; for Equal Work, 10; laws, 189

Executive and Legislative Council: appointment of women, 156

Executive Council, 26; women members in, 139

FACTORY WORK: NATURE OF, 248

Family: and working women, 8; centripetal, 38, 39, 41; change, 15; decision making, 81

Family Planning Association, 120, 126, 220, 238; *Adolescent Sexuality Study*, 122; Education and Youthwork Sub-Committee, 121; survey on adult sexuality, 250

Fecundity, 5, 219

Female: and social controls, 209; candidates, 157; chastity, 126; contamination, 123; cultural image, 124; household heads, 79; household responsibilities, 79; inheritance, 174; juvenile delinquency, 193, 209, 210; life expectancy, 220, 222; mortality in Hong Kong, 225, 223; offenders, 195, 196, 197–9, 201, 206; power, 80; professions, 157

Female cancer incidence rates: Hong Kong, 1974–88, 226

Feminism, 277; advancement of, 159; in the West, 91, 278, 288; Marxist, 5; second-wave, 277–9; socialist, 282

Feminist: groups, 153, 284; movement, 276; studies, *see* women's studies; theories, 2, 19

Fertility rate, 27, 51, 218–9

Filipina, 9, 169

Fishball stalls, 253

GARCIA, ARTHUR, 184

Gender: bias in arts and science subjects, 113; differences in gainful employment, 48; discrimination, 8; disparity in occupational groupings, 56–7; division of labour, 52; income gap, 66, 61; inequality, 2, 4, 5, 74, 84,

127, 277; socialization, 5; stereotypes, 83, 126; subordination, 277
Gender role: and sexuality, 120; theory, 82; traditional, 152; values, 52
Gender-role acceptance, 120–3; among secondary students, 121
Gender-role socialization, 91; and women's subordination, 82; frame work, 83; stereotypes, 63; theory, 75
Gender segregation: 101, 103; at secondary school level, 113; in fields of study, 103, 109
Girls: bad, 250; menstruation, 122; over-socialization of, 195
Government, 13, 133; and gender discrimination, 18
Grindrod, B., 208

HALL, C., 85
Hareven, T., 85
Health care: and gender disparity, 239
Health Service, 218, 228; history, 88; owned industrial firms, 7; tasks, 94
Health status: of Hong Kong women, 237; gender discrimination in, 17
Heath, A., 63, 65
Heung Yee Kuk, 138, 172, 177, 186, 187, 188; as advisory body, 181
Heyzer, Noeleen, 245
High Court, 182
Ho, C.K.A., 281, 287
Ho, S.C., 26
Hobsbawn, E. and Ranger, T., 185

Hoigard, Cecilie and Finstad, Liv, 249
Hong Kong: as a colony, 22; as an economic success, 8, 189; before 1950s, 22; brothels in, 250; colonial rule in, 6; crime rates in, 196; divorces in, 39; factories, 247; franchise in, 158; from mid-1970s, 25; gender inequalities in, 81; in 1950s, 24; industrial restructuring in, 37; industrialization and social change, 33; laws on the books, 167; manufacturing sector, 247; political issues in, 12; since 1982, 25; since Second World War, 11; territory of, 173; transition of rule, 277; victim assistance in, 205, 207; working daughters of, 89
Hong Kong Bill of Rights, 177
Hong Kong Council of Social Service, 283
Hong Kong Council of Women (HKCW), 277, 278, 279, 280, 281, 284; history of, 277; on paid maternity leave, 279
Hong Kong Education Department, 125; and Education and Manpower Branch, 117
Hong Kong factories: relocation of, 247
Hong Kong government, 182; social policy, 40
Hong Kong law, 168, 177; and women's rights, 170; gender bias in, 203
Hong Kong Women's Christian Council, 281

*Hong Kong Women's File*, 56, 60
Hong Kong Women Workers Association, 281, 283
Hong Kong Young Women's Christian Association, 79
Honig, Emily, 87–8
Housewives, 93, 279
Human Rights and Equal Opportunities Commission, 11
Hyam, Ronald, 251

INCOME DIFFERENTIAL: between sexes, 31–2, 59–63
Industrialization, 28, 76, 84; and family change, 75, 76; and gender equality, 38; and patriarchy, 38; and women, 40, 86; impact of, 27; in women's studies, 84 nature of, 95
Inequality: among occupations, 62–3
Infants: care of, 232; health of, 215
Infant mortality, 215, 217, 218, 219, 236, 237, 238
Infanticide, 4
Inheritance system in New Territories, 6, 167–70, 182–4
Interest groups, 135, 158
International Covenant on Civil and Political Rights, Article 26, 177
Intestates Estates Ordinance, 179

JASCHOK, MARIA, 23
Joint Declaration on the Future of Hong Kong, 13, 187
Jones, C., 176

LABOUR FORCE PARTICIPATION rate, 28, 49, 50

*Laissez-faire* policy, 25, 41, 170, *see also* Capitalism
Lau, Chun-kwok, 108
Lau, S.K. and Wan, P.S., 79
Law Reforms Commission, 183
Laws of Hong Kong, 167–89
Lee, M.K., 47
Lee, M.S.Y., 193, 203
Lee, T.Y., 196, 200
Legal reforms, 170, 181
Legislative Council, 10, 133, 159, 172, 252, 278; female representation, 139; in 1991, 26; members, 284, 285; restructuring in 1985, 25
Legislators and the feminist cause, 155
Lethbridge, Henry, 246
Levin, David, 60, 247
Li, Ellen Shu-pui, 139, 278
Lockwood, D., 189
Loh, Christine Kung-wai, 177, 188
Lugard, Frederick, 180
Lui Tai Lok, 90
Lui, H.W. and Suen, W., 56, 61–2
Lui, Y., 288
Luis, B.P.K. and Chan Kwok Leung, 250
Luk Hung-kay, 111
Lung cancer: among Hong Kong Chinese women, 225

MAK, GRACE, 31
Male dominance, 2
Manufacturing sector: gender inequality in, 37; wage differential, 37
Marital status and work opportunities, 63
Market: competition, 85; mechanisms, 10; guiding value of, 76

Marriage and retreat from labour market, 29
Marriage Reform Ordinance, 179
Married men, 64–5
Married women: 64–5; study of, 36; working, 50
Martin, J. and Roberts, C., 59
Marxism, 68
Mass media, 82
Maternal and child mortality in Hong Kong, 17
Maternal and infant health: Hong Kong (1955–90), 216
Maternal mortality: Hong Kong, 222
Media and women, 124
Medical and Health Department, 223
Miners, Norman, 251
Mitchell, Robert, 39
Mortality: cardiovascular, 228, 239; from heart and cerebrovascular diseases, 227; from infectious diseases, 223; gender differences in, 17, 222–3
Mother and paid employment, 27, 39
*Mui tsai*, 6, 23, 184
Murray, Alison, 252

NELSON, G.H., 186
New Orientalism, 171
New Territories, 167, 168, 172, 173, 178, 180, 181, 183, 184, 187, 188; customary law, 181; (Exemption) Bill, 177; Inheritance Law, 14, 173, 186; Land (Amendment) Ordinance, 183; Land (Exemption) Ordinance, 177; Ordinance, 174, 175, 176, 177, 180, 182, 183

Ng, C.H., 35, 36, 38, 39, 75, 77, 78

OAKLEY, ANN, 93
Occupational distribution, 57; by age groups, 52–3; by sex, 54, 55
Occupational group: by gender distribution, 55–6; by sexual and conjugal status, 64–5
Occupational ratio: by sex, 12
Ocko, J., 186
Offenders: as victims, 208; female, 203; gender breakdown of, 194; studies on, 196
Orwell, George, 70
Ou Hang-yue, 103
Outwork, 29, 90; participation of married woman in, 29

PATMAN, CAROLE, 70
Patriarchal: custom, 170; domination, 107; system, 69; values, 7, 172
Patriarchy, 3, 276; in Hong Kong, 5
*Pen Ts'ao Gan Mu*, 219
Policy of non-intervention, 179
Political decision making: women's representation in, 156
Political equality: women's quest for, 159
Political office: female candidates, 145, 158
Political participation, 135, 136; and familial obligations, 153; of women, 150, 151, 154; passivity of women, 157
Political parties: female leadership, 148; participation by gender, 148

Political system in Hong Kong: councillors by gender, 138
Polity: role of women in, 147
Polygyny, 1
Pong Suet-ling, 51
Pre-colonial Hong Kong: status of women in, 171
Pre-delinquency, 193–4, 200, 203, 207; in girls, 209
Pre-marital sex, 250
Pressure groups, 154
Probate and Administration Ordinance, 179, 183
Prostitution: and law in Hong Kong, 253; legal regulation of, 171; part-time, 208
Public opinion: expression of, 150; in Chinese newspapers, 151; in English language newspapers, 150

RAPE: THREAT OF, 188
Rape victim: attitude towards, 207
Ratio of: earnings between men and women, 61; female to male employees, 32; income for selected occupations, 62; male to female illegal immigrants, 201–2; male to female wages, 38; wages in western societies, 62
Red light area, 254
Refugees, 24
Regional Council: women in, 138
*Report of an Inter-Departmental Working Group on Sex Discrimination*, 13, 189
*Report on the Working Mothers in Family Functioning*, 29
Representative government, 26
Rural committees: women in, 172
Rural District Boards: women in, 138

SALAFF, JANET W., 35, 36, 38, 59, 89
Sankar, Andrea, 23
School: authority structure of, 115; gender segregation in, 112; genderization of subjects, 114; traditional gender patterns in, 17
Science subjects: masculine image, 112
Scott, Ian, 25
Selby, S., 176, 182, 183, 184
Service: employment in, 38; occupations, 53; sector, 38, 248
Sex discrimination, 92; Bill, 11
Sex education, 124–6; gender attributes in, 127; materials, 127
Sex industry: amount of profit, 252; position of female workers, 245
Sex-role stereotypes, 153
Sex: right to choose to sell, 249
Sexism, 2
Sexist ideology, 2, 40, 193
Sexual act: socio-cultural context of, 126
Sexual behaviour: double standard of, 171; standards, 15, 250
Sexual crime, 123
Sexual discrimination, 159; at work, 155; in payment, 33
Sexual equality, 133; commentaries on, 151; in China, 155–6
Sexual exploitation, 126
Sexual harassment, 123, 126
Sexual mores, 193
Sexual needs: men and women, 250
Sexuality: as commodity, 124; double standard of, 286
Shamshuipo, 15, 244, 255

*Shan Hai Ching*, 219
Shop lifting, 14, 194
Shue Yan College, 79
Singapore, 232, 236
Singh, Mantosh, 231
Single women, 64; discrimination of, 66
Single-parent families, 199
Sino-British Joint Declaration 1984, 25, 134
Sino-British relations, 181, 187
Small-house policy, 178
Smith, A.D., 78
Smith, Wesley, P., 186
Social Darwinism, 113
Social deviance: views on, 206
Social equality: and change of sovereignty, 134; determinant of, 134
Social Indicators Survey, 79, 81, 92
Social welfare, 38; services 37, 138
Social Welfare Department, 39, 201; custodial facilities, 203, 204; correctional homes, 202–3
Socialism, 70
Society: patriarchal nature of, 209
*South China Morning Post*, 150, 152, 172, 184
South-East Asia, 251; women in, 8
Stacey, J., 87
State: intervention, 168; hegemony of, 187; policies, 86
Status of women, 139; and legislative changes, 170; *see also*, women
Statutory and non-statutory bodies and councillors, 141
Street sisters: pragmatism of, 258
Streetwalkers, 255; and charges, 256; and customers, 256–7; and family relationships, 265–6; and health, 257; and triads, 256; and use of condoms, 257; case studies, 257–68
Suicide rates: gender differences, 232
Sutherland, E. and Cressey, D., 200
Symons, Catherine Joyce, 139

TEACHER TRAINING: feminization of, 107
Teachers: age and gender profile (1991) of, 115; and gender segregation, 111
Text books: as channel of gender socialization, 114; roles and images depicted in, 114
Topley, M., 87
Tourism: and commercial sex, 251
Traditional Chinese households: women in, 86
Triad, 246, 254; affiliate, 197, 198; societies, 245
Tsang Wing-kwong, 108

UNITED KINGDOM, 193; *see also* Britain
United Nations, 24, Committee on Economic, Social and Cultural Rights, 178; CEDAW *see* Convention on the Elimination of All Forms of Discrimination Against Women
Universities and colleges: gender ratio, 117
US troops: sexual needs, 251

VAGG, JON, 252, 253
Vertical segregation, 59, 60

Victimization, 207; of women, 205–9
Victorian colonial policy, 180
Victorian society: legal status of women in, 171
Victorian values, 180
Violence: against spouses, 205; against victims, 231; self-inflicted, 232
Violent crimes, 194
Vocational Training Centre, 106
Vocational Training Council, 60, 247; enrolment by gender in 1993, 248

WALDRON, I., 237
Wanchai, 251
Wang Shu-nu, 250
War on Rape, 279, 280; evaluation of, 281
Watson, Rubie, 23
Welfare protectionism, 193
Welfare services, 40
Well-Woman Clinic, 239
White Paper: Further Development of Representative Government in Hong Kong (1984), 157; on Representative Government (1988), 157
White-collar crimes, 195
WHO: health statistics, 236
Wife, 23; abuse, 279; battering, 240
Women: and career development, 35; and chastity, 69; and crime, 193; and decision-making, 36; and family change, 81; and family studies, 83; and health care, 17; and paid work, 51; and social change, 12; and work, 28; as offenders, 14; as primary school teachers, 17; as sex objects, 282; as victims, 18, 194, 269, 280, 282, 205, 240; at grassroots, 283; at home, 8; before industrialization, 87; child-bearing role, 28; contradictory roles, 85; derision, 69; discrimination against, 277; dual demands on, 8; economic contribution of, 87; economic inertia, 16; empowerment, 18, 280, 70, 238; expatriate, 278; exploitation of, 7; family and work, 70; fear of deportation, 254; freedom from unreal loyalties, 69; from low income families, 35, 36, 39; from peasant families, 87; from Thailand and the Philippines, 251; import of, 254; in cash-earning occupation, 87; in civil service, 139; in farm work, 87; in high-status occupations, 66; in judiciary, 139, 141; in-labour force participation, 26; in media, 86; in political campaigning, 154; in political participation, 152; in politics, 13, 152, 159; in pressure groups, 13; in prison, 210; in the professional world, 69; in the world of work, 8; in traditional Chinese society, 4; legal prohibition on inheritance, 172; life expectancy, 17; major causes of death, 17; mean age of marriage, 29; mobility, 109; of imperial

China, 87; outside employment, 30; post-menopausal, 239; poverty, 69; pre-menopausal, 228; social image, 28; status of, 81, 282; subjugation of, 2; subordination of, 7, 12; survey findings, 95; treatment of, 41; voting rights for, 278; voting, 154; work profile, 49
Women's Centre, 282, 284
Women's Commission, 155
Women's economic participation: reason for, 90
Women's groups: 18, 152, 154, 170, 276, 285; and government, 10; and Green Paper, 9; and political parties, 148; as critics, 151; development of, 147; in Hong Kong, 147
Women's liberation, 30, 39, 40; impediments to, 41
Women's movement, 276, 282; 283, 285; at ideological level, 286; debate on strategies, 287–9; first stage, 277–8; history of, 277; second stage, 278–81; third stage, 281
Women's political participation, 158–9
Women's rights, 13, 158, 160; in Chinese culture, 170; *see also* Women's groups
Women's status, 40; future of, 134; *see also* women
Women's studies, 77, 78, 90, 112; in Hong Kong, 1, 3, 23; in the West 87, 81;
Wong Fai Ming, 75, 76, 77, 80
Woolf, Virginia, 69
Workforce: participation of women in, 26
Working-class women, 81, 87, 246, 283; and patriarchy, 41
*Working Daughters of Hong Kong*, 35, 36, 90
Working women: and child care, 9; paid work, 66–7; public reaction to, 47; status of, 33; subjugation of, 38; unpaid work, 66–7; upper and middle-class, 34; with University education, 57
Wu, Anna, 10

Yang, C.K., 76
Yaumatei social hygiene clinic, 257